CLIFFS

Advanced Placement
English Literature
and Composition
Examination

PREPARATION GUIDE

by
Allan Casson

Series Editor
Jerry Bobrow

INCORPORATED
LINCOLN, NEBRASKA   68501

Charlotte Mew: "The Farmer's Bride" from *Collected Poems and Prose,* © Copyright 1981. Reprinted by permission of Carcanet Press Limited.

Wilfred Owen: "S. I. W." from *Collected Poems of Wilfred Owen,* © Copyright 1963 by Chatto and Windus, Ltd. Reprinted by permission of New Directions Publishing Corporation.

Claude McKay: "Flame Heart" from *Selected Poems of Claude McKay,* Harcourt, Brace, Jovanovich. Reprinted by permission of the Archives of Claude McKay.

George Orwell: "Some Thoughts on the Common Toad" from *Collected Essays, Journals and Letters of George Orwell,* IV © Copyright 1968 by Sonia Brownell Orwell. Reprinted by permission of Harcourt, Brace, Jovanovich, Incorporated.

ISBN 0-8220-2305-9

FIRST EDITION

CONTENTS

PART III: THREE FULL-LENGTH PRACTICE TESTS

PREFACE

This book is about the AP literature exam, not about literature. Unlike other books with a similar title, it makes no attempt to teach you how to read a novel or to analyze a play. The Advanced Placement exam in literature is a test of what you've learned in four years of high school and, in particular, in your AP class in your junior or senior year. No book can replace this experience. This one simply gives you more accurate information about the exam and how to prepare for it than any other now available.

Part I: Introduction

FORMAT OF A RECENT
AP LITERATURE AND COMPOSITION EXAM

Section I	Multiple-Choice	53–57 Questions
60 minutes (one hour)	passage from Shakespeare	14 questions
	passage from Victorian prose	16 questions
	passage from modern novel	13 questions
	poem by modern poet	12 questions

Section II	Essay	3 Questions
120 minutes (two hours)	Emily Dickinson poem for analysis (45 minutes)	
	prose passage from Boswell for analysis (35 minutes)	
	open question on two contrasting places in a novel or play (40 minutes)	

The multiple-choice section counts 45% of the grade and the essays 55%.

GENERAL FORMAT AND GRADING OF THE AP LITERATURE AND COMPOSITION EXAM

Contents of the Exam

The Advanced Placement literature exam has two parts, a multiple-choice section and an essay, or free-response, section. The one-hour multiple-choice part counts for 45%, while the two-hour essay section determines 55% of the final grade.

The multiple-choice section of the exam is based on four selections from literature in English written from the sixteenth century to the present. Two passages are prose selections and two are poetry. They represent three or four different periods and include the work of a female or a minority writer. A characteristic selection would include a short poem by a metaphysical poet of the early seventeenth century (say, Herbert), a prose passage from an eighteenth-century writer like Swift, a prose selection from a Victorian novelist (say, Charlotte Brontë), and a poem by a twentieth-century American poet (say, Gwendolyn Brooks). There are between fifty and sixty questions in the one-hour exam, normally fifteen or sixteen questions on each of two of the passages and twelve or thirteen on the other two.

The free-response section consists of three essay questions with two hours of writing. Though there is no absolute guarantee that the three essays will be alike every year, the form of the exam for the last fifteen years has been one essay on a passage of poetry, one essay on a passage of prose (on rare occasions, a complete short story), and one essay on a topic allowing the student to choose an appropriate novel or play (and sometimes a poem or work of autobiography). Students usually spend forty minutes on each of the essays.

How the Exam Is Written and Graded

The AP literature and language exams are written by a committee of eight English teachers—four men and four women—four teachers of Advanced Placement classes in public and private high schools and four teachers of English in colleges and universities. The committee is geographically and ethnically representative, and since most of the members serve for only three years, its member-

4

ship is constantly changing. Working with testing professionals from Educational Testing Service, the committee selects the passages upon which the essay and multiple-choice questions are based and composes the questions for the free-response section of the exam. All of these questions are pretested in college literature or writing classes before they can be selected for use on an AP examination.

The examinations are read in a seven-day period in early June. In 1992, more than 450 readers from throughout the United States and Canada read more than 115,000 AP literature exams. Slightly more than half of the readers are college teachers, and about forty-five percent are high school and preparatory school AP teachers. Each reader reads only one question throughout the reading, so each exam has a minimum of three different readers. Since many essays are used as samples and many more are read twice (by a reader and by one of sixty or so table leaders who check the readers' scoring), many essays have more than three readers.

Each student essay is scored on a scale from zero to nine. The standards for the grading are determined before the reading begins by a study of the essays students have written in May. The grading standards do not anticipate the students' performance, but are based on a wide sampling of actual tests. Using sample papers to represent each digit on the scale, readers are trained to grade one of the three essays. The result of the reading is three scores of zero to nine, or a total score of zero to twenty-seven.

The scores on the multiple-choice section and on the essay section are combined to make up a scale from zero to 150.

With the current weighting of 55% for the essay section, the total score of zero to twenty-seven is converted to a scale of zero to 82.5. The number of right answers on the multiple-choice section is converted to a scale of zero to 67.5, or 45% of the total scale. The chief reader then determines where the scale will be divided to determine the final scores of one, two, three, four, and five that are reported to the colleges and the students. The cutoff points are not predetermined nor are they chosen to guarantee a certain percentage of scores at any level. The results differ from year to year as do the percentage of scores in the one, two, three, four, and five categories.

ANSWERS TO YOUR QUESTIONS ABOUT THE AP LITERATURE AND COMPOSITION EXAM

Preparation for the Exam

When should I study this book?

Browse through it early in the year before you take the AP exam, and read it carefully six weeks or so before the May exam. Don't spend too much time studying this book, especially time that could be spent reading or rereading poetry, fiction, or drama.

What College Board publications do you recommend?

Teachers of an AP literature course will certainly want to have the most recent *AP Course Description in English* (the Acorn book), the *Teacher's Guide to AP Courses in English Literature and Composition,* and the latest *AP English: Free Response Scoring Guide and Sample Student Answers.* They will probably want to own all or some of the complete exams that have been released.

The *Student Guide to the AP English Courses and Examinations* includes nothing that is not already available in the *Course Description* and *Free Response Scoring Guide* booklets, though it does cover the most recent exam each year.

There are additional publications like these on the Language and Composition examination. A list of publications and prices can be obtained from the Advanced Placement Program, P.O. Box 6670, Princeton, New Jersey, 08541-6670. Allow four to six weeks for delivery.

If I'm preparing to take the literature exam, would it help me to consult the old language exams?

Perhaps. The multiple-choice section of the language exam has questions on four prose passages similar to the two prose passages on the literature exam. And the essay questions include a prose passage for analysis that is similar to the prose analysis question on the literature exam. The passages on the literature exam are more likely to come from fiction or criticism, but the language exam may use prose written by scientists, historians, or sociologists.

7

If shortly before the exam I have time to review only one book, how do I decide which one?

Review the book you like best. If you're really short of time, review one or two plays instead of a long novel. The open question usually allows you to choose either a play or a novel, and because plays are so much shorter, it's easier to have command of the details of a play than a novel. Be sure to have more than one work ready, since you can't be sure your favorite will suit the question on the exam.

What should I study on the night before the exam?

Ask your AP teacher. He or she knows what you need better than I do. But don't stay up late. The exam is really testing all your years of English study, so if you need to study on the night before the exam, you're in trouble. You will probably perform better on the exam if you relax the night before. Watch television, and above all, get a good night's sleep. If you're so compulsive that you feel you must study, look over the definitions of some technical terms, and browse through the novels and plays you may use to refresh your memory of the names.

Multiple-Choice Questions

Where can I get old multiple-choice exams to practice with?

You can order the complete literature exams that have been released from the College Board at the address given earlier. The annually published *AP Course Description in English* (the Acorn book) has a few sample multiple-choice sets.

Does it make sense that the multiple-choice exam, which takes only one hour, should count for 45% of the grade, while the essay exam, which takes two hours, counts only 55%?

No. But the grading of the multiple-choice section is more reliable, and it discriminates more widely than the essay section. There are now only three essay scores, and they do not spread out nearly as well as the multiple-choice scores. Statisticians argue that the 45% weighting of the multiple-choice scores makes the exam more reliable. That is, a student retaking the exam would be more likely to receive the same final score with a 45% weight for the multiple-choice than with 40% or 33%. If the essay answers were read by two readers, the reliance on the multiple-choice score could be decreased.

When should I guess on the multiple-choice section?

Answer as many of the questions as you can. Avoid losing points by mismanaging your time and spending too long on one passage or one question. Don't be afraid to guess if you can eliminate at least two of the five choices. You get no credit for an unanswered question and lose a quarter of a point for each wrong answer. But if you have reduced the options to three instead of five, your chances are one in three, while your loss, if you choose incorrectly, is one-fourth.

When a question seems hopeless, don't waste time on it. Leave it out and go on, taking care to skip the unanswered question's space on the answer sheet. If you are unsure of an answer, mark out the answers you know are wrong in the question booklet:

$$(A)$$
$$?(B)$$
$$(C)$$
$$?(D)$$
$$(E)$$

The question marks indicate possible answers. If you go on and come back to the question later, you will not waste time considering wrong answers you have already eliminated.

What if I don't finish all the multiple-choice questions?

Many students don't finish all the multiple-choice questions and still receive high scores on the whole exam. If you don't finish, don't worry about it. Go on and do a good job on the essays. You can afford to miss some points on the multiple-choice section if you write three good essays. If you find that you have no time left, don't fill in answers for all remaining questions on your answer sheet. Chances are four to one against your getting the right answer, and each wrong answer costs a minus .25. Leaving the answer blank is zero.

Are there any trick questions in the multiple-choice section?

No. If you read the passage carefully, you should be able to answer the question.

Is it advisable to do the multiple-choice sets in the order they appear on the exam?

Do them in whatever order makes it easiest for you. If you find the passage that comes first very hard, go on and come back to it when you've finished the other parts. Remember, your score is determined by the number of correct answers, so you don't want to spend too much time on one section if it will prevent you from doing the other parts. Many students don't answer all of the multiple-choice questions, but you want to answer as many as possible in the hour allowed.

What if a multiple-choice question seems too easy?

Be glad it's too easy rather than too hard. Don't assume that because a multiple-choice question seems obvious there must be some trick. In every set of multiple-choice questions, there are a few very easy questions and a few very hard ones. Don't throw away a chance to get easy points by trying to second-guess the exam. If the question asks for the name of the hero of *Hamlet* and the choices are Lear, Romeo, Othello, Macbeth, and Hamlet, take Hamlet. The first question of a multiple-choice set is often an easy one.

What if I've had five answers in a row of (C) in the multiple-choice section, and I'm pretty sure the sixth is (C), but (B) is possible? Which do I choose?

Choose (C). You've probably made a mistake in the five (C) choices in a row. *Don't* play games with letter patterns in the multiple-choice section of the exam. Choose the answer that you think is right regardless of the answer to the question before it.

Exactly what scores do I get for a wrong answer, a right answer, and no answer on the multiple-choice section?

A right answer is one point, an omitted answer is zero, and a wrong answer is minus .25. The total score is converted to equal 45% of 150, or 67.5 points, if you get all the multiple-choice questions right. If there were fifty-five questions and you got forty-five right, eight wrong, and omitted two, your score would be forty-five minus two, or forty-three (or 52.7 out of a possible 67.5—see the explanation of converting raw score to scaled score on page 25).

How many multiple-choice questions do I have to get right to get a final grade of three on the exam?

It depends on your essay scores and on how well all the other students taking the exam perform.

Your final score is on a scale of 150, with a possible 82.5 points on the free-response (essay) sections and a possible 67.5 points on the multiple-choice section. A student who gets nines on all three of the essays and answers all the multiple-choice questions correctly would score 150. But the number of points required for the final scores of one through five is determined anew each year.

In the 1987 exam, when the multiple-choice section counted 40% rather than 45% and the multiple-choice exam had sixty-one questions, a student who got fives, that is the middle score on the scale of nine, on all three essays would have needed a raw score (number of correct answers minus .25 for each wrong answer) of nineteen to thirty-six on the multiple-choice section to get a final score of three. On the same exam, a student with fives on all three essays and a raw score of thirty-seven to fifty on multiple-choice would have gotten a final score of four.

Free-Response, or Essay, Questions

On the essay section of the exam, which question is the most important?

All three count one-third. Though you've probably spent much more time in your AP class preparing for the open question than for the others, the open question counts no more than the poetry or the prose analysis questions.

Since the multiple-choice section is all close reading of poems and prose, the exam has six passages for close reading but only one question about a novel or play of your choice. Since the multiple-choice section counts for 45% of your grade and the two passages in the essay section count for two-thirds of the other 55%, the open question determines only 18.3% of the final score.

How should I begin my essay? Should I paraphrase or repeat the question?

Begin your essay in whatever way makes it easiest for you to write. If you simply cannot begin on your own without rephrasing the question, then do so. Your reader will not consciously hold it against you, but keep in mind that your reader is reading hundreds of essays that also begin with the same unnecessary restatement of a question he or she already knows by heart and that you've wasted a small amount of time. If you can, get to the point right away.

For example, assume a question on a prose passage asks you to "discuss Dickens's attitude to Pip and Joe and the stylistic devices he uses to convey his attitude." If you begin your essay—and thousands will—"Dickens in this passage conveys his attitude to Pip and Joe by using devices of style. This essay will discuss his attitude and also the devices of style he uses to convey it," all you have accomplished is to have bored the reader briefly. A better start is something like "In this passage, Dickens regards Pip with a combination of sympathy and disapproval," or whatever the attitude is.

If you are one of those writers to whom writing a first sentence is like setting a first toe in the ocean on the coast of Maine, then use the question to get you started. Better still, begin by addressing the first task in your first sentence.

Should I outline before I write my essay?

If you write better essays by writing an outline first, then do so. If not, not. The outline won't be graded or counted in any way. Do whatever makes it easier for you to write well-organized, specific, and relevant essays.

Should I write a five-paragraph essay?

If by a five-paragraph essay you mean an essay in which the first paragraph is introductory and says what you're going to do in paragraphs two, three, and four, and the fifth recapitulates what you've done, write a three-paragraph essay and forget about the introduction and conclusion. Use the time you save to give more support to your argument or to develop other topics. Readers don't count paragraphs, and there is no advantage or disadvantage in writing five paragraphs as opposed to three or seven. You should write in well-developed paragraphs. Let their number be determined by what you have to say in answer to the questions.

How long should an essay be?

Long enough to answer all the parts of the question specifically and fully. There is no extra credit given to a very long essay, especially if it is repetitious or off the subject. A *very* short essay (one paragraph of only a few sentences) will fall into the scoring guide's "unacceptably brief" category and receive a very low score. If you've said all you have to say about a question, don't try to pad out your answer. Go on to the next question. A student with average sized handwriting usually writes one and a half or two pages in the pink booklets, but many write more and many write less. Your reader will not count your words and will not thank you if you write an extra page repeating what you've said already.

How important is spelling and punctuation?

Not very, unless yours is dreadful. The readers are not looking for spelling and punctuation errors, but if there are so many or if they are so flagrant that they interfere with a fluent reading, you will lose some points.

How important is correct grammar?

The readers realize that you are writing rapidly, and they are tolerant of a lapse here and there. But if your writing suggests inadequate control over English prose, you may be penalized. On the literature exam, essays that are "poorly written" can score no higher than a three, but "poorly written" means much more than an occasional split infinitive, agreement error, or dangling participle.

How important is handwriting or neatness?

I'd like to say not at all. Readers certainly try to avoid being influenced one way or the other by good or bad handwriting, but there may be an unconscious hostility to a paper that is very difficult to read. So make your writing as legible as you can.

In the essay part of the exam, do I have to use a pen?

Your proctor will instruct you to write your essays with a pen, but every year some exams are written in pencil by students without pens or whose pens break down in midexam. A reader will certainly not penalize an exam written in pencil, but like bad handwriting, pencil is harder to read. Why make it more difficult for your reader if you don't have to?

What are the most important qualities of a good AP essay?

1. That it answers all the parts of the question fully and accurately.
2. That it is supported with specific evidence.
3. That it is well written.

Should I use a title for my essay answers?

Suit yourself. It almost certainly will not improve your grade. I don't recall ever reading one that I thought was good, but I do remember many inappropriate ones.

Will the readers of my essays reward creativity?

The readers are looking for accurate and thorough answers to the questions on the exam. If you can combine "creativity" with answering the question well, so much the better. But no amount of ingenuity will take the place of a response to the tasks set by the exam. If you write a brilliant poem that fails to answer the question, you will get a low score. If you write a straightforward essay that answers the question, you will get a high score. Remember that the direction on most questions is "write an essay" or "in a well-organized essay, discuss."

Do the examiners want detail in the essays?

If by detail you mean specific evidence from the passages on the exam or from the novel or play of your choice, yes. But they don't want long passages quoted from memory or detailed plot summaries. Remember that your readers have a copy of the passage in front of them and that they have already read the novel or play you're writing about.

Should I quote from the poem or the prose passage on the exam in my essay?

It depends. You must deal with the passages specifically, and quotation is the best way to do so. There is no point, however, in copying out five lines of poetry when you could say "in lines 1–5" and let your reader do the work. But if you're seeking to prove a point about, say, the diction of a passage and there are single words throughout the passage that support your case, you should say something like "the optimistic tone is supported by words and phrases such as 'happy' (line 2), 'cheerful' (line 3), 'ecstatic' (line 7), and 'out of his gourd' (line 11)." Be specific, but don't waste time. Readers have copies of the passage in front of them and will look at a line if students direct them to it.

What if I don't finish an essay on the free-response section?

Readers are told again and again to reward students for what they do well. If you have left out only a few sentences of conclusion but have answered the question, it will probably not affect your score at all. And if you have written three-fourths of an essay on the topic, you will certainly get credit for all you have done. A blank page earns no points at all, so if you find yourself with only a few moments, jot down as much as you can of what you were going to write, even if it's only in fragments. It may get one or two points, and any score is better than zero.

Divide your time evenly, or nearly evenly, among the three essays. They all count one-third, regardless of how much or how little you write on each.

What suggestions about style would you make?

1. Avoid clichés. Nine out of ten AP exams written about the imagery of a passage will describe it as "vivid," regardless of how bland it may be. If the question suggests a proverb to you, resist the temptation to quote it because fifty thousand other students will have thought of the same proverb and used it in their first paragraph.

2. Write naturally.

In discussing the poem, should I write about the sound effects?

If the question calls for a discussion of the sound (prosody, metrics of the poem), you must answer the question. But if the question does not ask about this aspect, beware of overdoing it. Too many papers waste time finding "l's" that suggest sunsets or "s's" that denote deceit, death, and broccoli. Even more papers count alliterations and exultantly discover five "f's" in lines one and two of the poem without noticing that their own sentence has six.

Should I write about the punctuation of a poem or a prose passage?

Only if it is *very* unusual or *remarkably* important and you can say something meaningful about it. Every passage on the exam will be punctuated, and the punctuation will almost never be worth discussing. Most students who waste time writing about the punctuation do so because they can't think of anything else to write about.

Is it likely that the essay exam will not include a prose passage, a poem, and an open essay question?

No. Any change from this pattern would be a very slight variation, such as using a question on two poems or two prose passages or using a short story. If the form of the exam is going to change, the AP publications will say so in advance.

What is a "rubric," or scoring guide?

The scoring guide ("rubric") is the one-page outline of scores that readers of the free-response section of the exam use to score the papers. Each of the three essays is scored on a scale of zero to nine. The readers are trained using sample papers and a scoring guide that describes the characteristics of each of the scores. Like the questions, the scoring guides follow familiar patterns.

They begin with general instructions to the reader that include judging the paper as a whole, rewarding students for what they do well, and scoring very poorly written essays no higher than a three.

Assume you wished to write a scoring guide for questions on a passage from Shakespeare on justice and mercy which calls for an analysis of the author's attitudes and how the choice of details, imagery, and diction convey his attitudes. A scoring guide would probably look like this:

9–8 These responses are well written and discuss clearly and accurately the attitudes toward *both* justice and mercy. Using specific and appropriate references to the text, they analyze the choice of details, imagery, and diction of the passage. The student writing may not be errorless, but it will demonstrate a mature command of effective prose.

7–6 These essays also discuss the attitudes of the passage toward both justice and mercy, but they may do so less fully or less convincingly than the essays in the 9–8 range. They deal with the choice of details, imagery, or diction, but less well than the very best papers. These essays are written clearly and effectively, though they may be less mature than papers in the 9–8 range.

5 These essays attempt to deal with the author's attitudes toward justice and mercy and his use of detail, imagery, and diction, but they do so merely adequately. The attitudes they discuss will be simple or obvious ones, and the remarks on detail, imagery, and diction may be lacking in specificity or depth. These essays often summarize rather than analyze the passage. The writing is, as a rule, less clear and well organized than that of the upper-half essays, and the thinking is often simplistic.

4–3 These lower-half essays often fail to understand parts of the passage and/or fail to answer part or parts of the question. They may define Shakespeare's attitudes vaguely or inaccurately. Their handling of detail, imagery, and diction may be perfunctory or unclear. The writing may demonstrate weak compositional skills. These essays often contain errors in reading and writing and are rarely supported by evidence from the passage.

2–1 These essays are weaker than the papers in the 4–3 range. They have serious errors in the reading of the passage and often omit the second half of the question altogether. Some papers are unacceptably short. The writing is poor, lacking clarity, organization, or supporting evidence.

  0 A blank paper or an essay that makes no attempt to deal with the question receives no credit. This score must be reconfirmed by a table leader.

Open Questions

On the open question, is it better to write on a book on the list of suggested works or to choose one that is not on the list?

Every year some students pay no attention to the line in the instructions that says, "You may write your essay on one of the following novels or plays *OR on another of comparable quality."* You should choose the work that best fits the question and that you know best. Whether or not you choose a work on the list will not affect your grade. If the work you choose is not widely known, it will be read only by someone who knows the book. No reader has read all the works that are used on the open question, and a reader finding an essay on a work he or she does not know simply passes it on to another reader who is familiar with it. The important thing is to choose an appropriate work or an appropriate character within that work.

In answering the open essay question, can I write about works in translation?

Yes. Many students use works by classical authors as well as those by more modern European, African, Asian, and South American authors. The list of suggested works on the exam frequently includes those of Achebe, Aeschylus, Camus, Cervantes, Chekhov, Dostoevski, Euripides, Homer, Ibsen, Sophocles, Tolstoi, and Voltaire, to name only some. Use the work that best fits the question.

On the open question, what if I don't know any of the books on the list of suggested works?

Reread the question very carefully and think about the books you do know to see if one of them is appropriate. You don't have to use a book from the list, but the work you use must fit the question.

On the open question, is it better to use an older author than a modern one?

Use the author that you know best that best fits the question. The time period doesn't matter.

In answering the open question, how can I tell whether or not the book I want to use is of "comparable quality" or "similar literary merit"?

If you are in doubt about any of the works you might use on the exam, consult with your AP teacher *before* you take the exam. The works used on the exam should be ones that would be likely to be read in an introductory college literature class. The readers are not stuffy about the use of contemporary writers, but if you write about what is clearly light weight (Danielle Steel, the *Gone with the Wind* sequel), or a popular mystery story (Agatha Christie), or an ephemeral mass-market bestseller, you will not get a good score. Marginal works like those of Ayn Rand or many works of science fiction might get by, but your reader cannot help noticing your choice of a book of dubious merit; unless you know no other suitable works, you should choose something else.

If I write a really good essay using one of the books on the list but on a topic of my own rather than the question on the exam, what score will I get?

A *really low* one.

On the open question, is it better to write on a long or difficult work (like Moby Dick*) than a shorter or easier work (like* Ethan Frome*)?*

The important thing is to answer the question. You don't get extra credit for using a hard book, and you lose no credit for choosing a shorter work. You can't use a short story if the question calls for a novel, but if you don't answer the question and write about *Ulysses* or *War and Peace,* you will get a much lower score than if you do answer the question and write about *The Secret Sharer* or *The Catcher in the Rye.*

On the open question, can I write on two works when the question asks for one?

You can, but you shouldn't. The exam will be read and scored on the basis of one of the two works you write about, whichever is the better of the two. But you will probably have written only half as much as the other exams that followed directions and wrote on only one. You can, of course, refer to other works if doing so improves your essay, but focus on one work unless the question specifically calls for a comparison.

Can I write on a novel or play that has been made into a film if I've read the book and seen the movie?

Yes, but be careful. Most of the classic (and many not-so-classic) novels have been made into films. Be sure what you say in your essay comes from your reading, not from the movie. The old Greer Garson movie of *Pride and Prejudice* changes the gorgon Lady Catherine into an ally who willingly brings Darcy and Elizabeth together, and the Hollywood *Wuthering Heights* ends at the halfway point in the novel. Olivier's and Mel Gibson's *Hamlet* leave out about one-third of the play. Be sure what you're remembering is what you've read, not what you've seen.

What if I can't remember a character's name?

Do the best you can. You can sometimes use a phrase like "Hamlet's uncle" (if you forget Claudius), or you can explain that you've forgotten and substitute an X. If you make it clear, the reader will give you the benefit of the doubt. There have been quite good essays written about Hamlet in which he was (inadvertently) called Macbeth. The readers are aware that the essays must be written quickly and are tolerant of slips of the pen. I don't recommend inventing names. The effect can be unintentionally comic, as in "I can't remember Othello's wife's name, so I'll call her Darlene."

Do you have any further suggestions about answering the open essay question?

Be sure to understand whether or not the exam is asking about the author, the reader, or the characters in the work. There are, obviously, differences between our perception of Gatsby and Nick's, Daisy's, or Fitzgerald's. Ask yourself whether or not the question calls for a discussion of technique—that is, what the *author* does for specific purposes—or for a discussion of a character as if that character were alive. In *Lord of the Flies,* Piggy doesn't know that he is a symbol, but Golding and the reader do. And in *Hamlet,* Shakespeare and the reader use Horatio in ways that Hamlet doesn't know about. Don't confuse art and life. Remember that a play or a novel is a play or a novel, and though Horatio is necessary to Fortinbras to tell him what has happened or necessary to Shakespeare to say some things he wants to have said at the end of the play, *we* don't need him to tell us what has happened because we've just seen or read the whole play. Fortinbras, Horatio, and Hamlet, like Murphy Brown, are fictional characters, and educated people should recognize the difference between art's imitation of life and the real thing.

How many books should I prepare for the open question on the exam?

There's no single answer. The more, the better, so long as you know them well. Be sure to cover several periods and several genres. I'd recommend that you know one Shakespearean tragedy and at least two twentieth-century plays. And I'd recommend a minimum of at least one nineteenth-century and two twentieth-century novels. More would be better. Think about reviewing some of the works you read in tenth or eleventh grade. Choose works you like. Review the works carefully. A few years ago, a large number of students wrote on *Romeo and Juliet* on the open question on child-parent conflicts. But very few remembered the play well, probably because they had read it two or three years before and had not reviewed it.

The Exam as a Whole

Is the exam equally difficult each year or are there years when it is easier or harder?

Although the Development Committee that writes the exam tries to maintain the same level of difficulty, no two exams can be equally difficult or exactly alike. Each year one of the three essay questions turns out to be harder than the other two questions, but there is no pattern from year to year. The question on poetry was the most challenging when the poem was Sylvia Plath's "Sow" or Emily Dickinson's "The last night that she lived." But the prose questions had lower scores when the passage was from Conrad's *Typhoon* and from Joan Didion's "Self-Respect." The point is that exams are graded by comparison with all the other exams taken that year, so if your exam seems harder to you than other exams you've seen, it probably will also seem harder to the 120,000 other students also taking the exam and against whom your score will be measured. That *any* exam is always hardest in the year *I* take it is a sad fact of human life. Fortunately, with the AP exam, the grading is not on an absolute standard, but by comparison of all of the test-takers.

One of the four sections of multiple-choice questions on each exam is repeated from an earlier examination, but this is the only exact measure of the performance of one year's AP students against that of another year, and the scores in a previous year have no effect on the final grades of this year's exams.

Are the passages on the exam taken from any set time period?

The multiple-choice and the essay questions are based on passages of literature written in English from the sixteenth century to the present. Passages are in modern English, that is, the English written from 1575 to the present. The exam has never used Middle English (the language of Chaucer) or Old English (the language of *Beowulf*).

To do well on the exam, do I have to understand metrics?

Chances are you can get by without knowing anything at all about metrics if you can read and write well. It has been a number of years since an essay question specifically asked for comments on the sound of a poem. In the multiple-choice section, you can expect two questions, at most, about metrics and maybe only one. Obviously, the more technical knowledge you have about prose and poetry, the better off you are, if you use this learning with care. Essays on poetry are far more likely to say too much about metrics than too little.

In fact, prosody (the art of versification) is not hard to master, and if you know the terms defined beginning on page 139, you should have no trouble with metrical questions in the multiple-choice section.

Other Questions

What is the difference between the AP literature and the AP language exams?

The literature exam tests a student's ability to read and write about literature in English. It includes questions about poetry, drama, fiction, and nonfiction prose; the exam has one hour of multiple-choice questions and two hours of essay questions.

The language exam tests a student's ability to read and write about English prose and to write expository, analytical, and argumentative essays. Though a passage from a work of fiction could appear on the exam, the emphasis of the question or questions on the passage will be on language, style, and rhetoric. The exam has three forty-minute essays (two hours) and four sets of multiple-choice questions (one hour).

Can I take both the language and the literature exams in the same year?

Yes. The exams are now given at different times, so students can take both exams in the same year if they wish to do so. Before this change in scheduling, many students took the language exam in their junior year and the literature exam in their senior year.

How can I tell what college credit I'll get for my AP scores?

Look in the catalogs of the colleges you're interested in. Unfortunately, many college catalogs are vague about exactly what subject and unit credit each AP score will earn. With two English exams (literature and language) to add to the confusion, it's wise to get a statement from the admissions office. Write or call the admissions office and ask for an explicit statement of the policy on AP credit.

The *Advanced Placement Course Description* booklet names the colleges that give some credit for AP exams, but since the list gives no specific information and makes no distinction between the language and the literature exam, it is not very useful.

Will it affect my score if I check the box to refuse to allow my exam to be used as a sample for research?

No. Nor will it affect your score if you check the "yes" box. The people who select samples consult these boxes to be sure no exams are used that have not been released by the students, but the readers of the exams never notice or care about what box you check.

Can I find out my scores on the multiple-choice section and what I got on each essay?

No. The only score reported to you is the final grade of one to five, the score that is reported to the colleges.

Will the college know my scores on the parts of the exam?

No. All the colleges receive is the single score. Colleges may request the essay exam, but they will not be told what scores each essay received.

Can I take the exam without having taken an AP course?

Yes. Some schools have no designated AP English classes, and their students still do very well. And some students may do well without taking any course in an AP subject (speakers of a foreign language, for example, are likely not to need a course in their native tongue). Though the English language AP exam is designed for students who have taken an AP English language class, students who have had only an AP literature class will often do well on the test.

How long does it take to receive the results of my AP exam?

The exams taken in May are read early in June, and the results are sent to the schools in July, usually just after the fourth, that is, about eight weeks after the exam is written.

How do I convert my scores on a sample test to the one-through-five scores that are sent to the colleges?

The total score on the exam is 150. Since the essay and multiple-choice parts are weighted 55% to 45%, there are 82.5 points for the essays and 67.5 for the multiple-choice questions. Since the three essays are graded on a nine-point scale (plus zero), each point on your essay raw score would be multiplied by 3.055. Three nines would total twenty-seven times 3.055, which would total 82.5. If there are fifty-five multiple-choice questions, each point in the raw score would be multiplied by 1.227 to equal 67.5. Remember that the raw score in the multiple-choice section is determined by the number of correct answers less one-quarter point for each wrong answer. A test with thirty right, twenty wrong, and five omitted would have a raw score of thirty minus five, or twenty-five. This raw score converts to a total of 30.675 (25 × 1.227).

The total number of points required for a final score of five, four, or three is different each year, but a very reasonable assumption is 100–150 for a score of five, 86–99 for a score of four, and 67–85 for a score of three. The following chart will give you an idea of the scores you need on the essay and the multiple-choice sections to receive final scores of three, four, or five. It assumes that there are fifty-five multiple-choice questions and three essay questions graded from zero to nine.

If a student received fives on all three essays, in order to receive a final score of three, he or she would need a raw score (the number correct less one-quarter times the number wrong) of at least eighteen on the multiple-choice section; to receive a final score of four, the same student would need a raw score of at least thirty-four on the multiple-choice section; and to receive a five, that student would need a raw score of at least forty-six on that section.

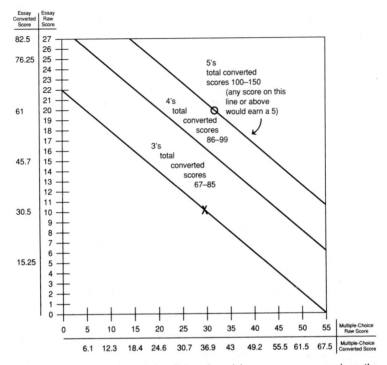

The angled lines on the graph tell you the minimum score you need on the multiple-choice and essay sections to earn a final score of 3, 4, or 5. For example, the point marked by a circle on the top line equals 61 converted points on the essay and 39 converted points on the multiple-choice section for a total of 100, the minimum score for a 5. The point marked by an x on the bottom line equals 30.5 converted points on the essay and 36.9 converted points on the multiple-choice section for a total of 67, the minimum score for a 3.

Part II: Analysis of Exam Areas

THE AP LITERATURE EXAM SECTION I
MULTIPLE-CHOICE QUESTIONS

INTRODUCTION

The multiple-choice section of the exam contains between fifty and sixty questions on four different passages. One passage has at least fifteen questions and is reused on a future exam. Two of the passages are prose; two are poetry. Though the poems are usually complete works, the prose passages are likely to be taken from longer works such as novels or works of nonfiction.

The four passages represent different periods of British and American literature. It is likely that one is chosen from the sixteenth or the early seventeenth century and one from the Restoration or eighteenth century, unless these periods are represented by passages on the essay section of the test. The two other sections are from nineteenth- and twentieth-century writers. The exam as a whole is likely to include several works by female and by minority writers.

You may, by extraordinary good luck, find a passage on the exam that you've studied in your English class, but the odds are heavily against it. The passages chosen for the exam are almost always those that have not found their way into textbooks and anthologies. Though your AP class should study shorter poems of poets like Shakespeare and Donne, and though a sonnet by one or the other may someday appear on the exam, it will not be one of the popular favorites like "My mistress' eyes are nothing like the sun" or "Death, be not proud." The passages are often by writers you are familiar with, but the text is not one you are likely to recognize. To be prepared for the multiple-choice section, you must be able to sight-read a reasonably complex poem or passage of prose written in English within the last five centuries. If your studies are limited to a narrow period—the twentieth century, say—you will be at a serious disadvantage on the multiple-choice section of the exam.

The passages chosen for the exam are not easy. They must be complex enough to generate fifteen or so multiple-choice questions that discriminate among the hundred thousand or more students taking the exam. If the passages are too hard or too easy, they won't work.

To answer the multiple-choice questions, you don't need any special historical or philosophical knowledge. The passages are self-contained and self-explanatory. If a particularly difficult word occurs that is crucial to the understanding of the passage, it is explained in a footnote. But the exam expects you to be familiar with the common terms of literary analysis and to have some familiarity with classical mythology and the more popular parts of the Old and New Testaments. Since so much of British and American literature of the earlier periods is religious, it is quite possible that a religious poem by a writer like George Herbert or Edward Taylor or Anne Bradstreet might be on the exam. But the examiners are eager to make sure that no one is given any special advantage, and if a religious text is used, it should be just as accessible to a nonbeliever as to an evangelical and to a modern Moslem or a Jew as to a Christian. The questions will always be on literary, not doctrinal, issues.

Be glad if you have a teacher who insists on spending weeks on seventeenth- or eighteenth-century works when you would rather be talking about Vonnegut or Stoppard. Unless you're comfortable with the unfamiliar vocabulary, syntax, and conventions of the literature written before our own, you'll have trouble with the multiple-choice section of the exam and possibly with two-thirds of the essay section as well.

Though it will be helpful if you practice multiple-choice exams before you take the exam in May, your first task is to learn to analyze a poem and a prose passage. To practice your skills, you'll find the best exams are those published by the Advanced Placement Program of the College Board. The multiple-choice sections of the some past literature exams are available and can be ordered. Though several commercially published AP study guides contain sample multiple-choice exams, their questions and choice of texts are often not sufficiently like those on the real exams to make them very useful. (The exams in *this* book, it goes without saying, are an exception to this rule.)

There is no quick and easy way to master the analysis of literature. If there were, you wouldn't need to spend four years in high-school English classes and English teachers would be selling real estate or practicing law or out of a job. The Advanced Placement literature exam is testing all that you've learned about reading and writing English in junior and senior high school. But you *can* develop a method for approaching the literary texts you'll be asked to read on the AP exam.

ANALYZING POEMS

Some students have trouble with sight-reading poetry because they don't know where to start. They see the word "death" in the first line and "tomb" in the third and jump to the conclusion that this poem (which, in fact, is a sentimental lover's pitch to a woman who has turned him down) must be about mortality and spend the next ten minutes trying to make the poem fit these gloomy expectations.

To avoid premature conclusions, and to prepare yourself for the kind of question the multiple-choice section asks, try going through each poem asking the following questions in something like this order.

1. What is the dramatic situation?

That is, who is the speaker? Or who are the speakers? Is the speaker a male or female? Where is he or she? When does this poem take place? What are the circumstances?

Sometimes you'll be able to answer all of these questions: The speaker is a male psychopath living in a remote cottage, probably in Renaissance Italy, who has strangled his mistress and is sitting with her head propped upon his shoulder. (Browning's "Porphyria's Lover"). Sometimes you'll be able to answer only a few and sometimes only vaguely: The speaker is unnamed and unplaced and is speaking to an indeterminate audience. No matter. Already you've begun to understand the poem.

2. What is the structure of the poem?

That is, what are the parts of the poem and how are they related to each other? What gives the poem its coherence? What are the structural divisions of the poem?

In analyzing the structure, your best aid is the punctuation. Look first for the complete sentences indicated by periods, semicolons, question marks, or exclamation points. Then ask how the poem gets from the first sentence to the second and from the second to the third. Are there repetitions such as parallel syntax or the use of one simile in each sentence? Answer these questions in accordance with the sense of the poem, not by where a line ends or a rhyme falls. Don't assume that all sonnets will break into an 8–6 or a 4–4–4–2 pattern, but be able to recognize these patterns if they are used.

Think about the logic of the poem. Does it, say, ask questions, then answer them? Or develop an argument? Or use a series of analogies to prove a point? Understanding the structure isn't just a matter of mechanics. It will help you to understand the meaning of the poem as a whole and to perceive some of the art, the formal skills that the poet has used.

3. What is the theme of the poem?

You should now be able to see the point of the poem. Sometimes a poem simply says "I love you"; sometimes the theme or the meaning is much more complex. If possible, define what the poem says and why. A love poem usually praises the loved one in the hope that the speaker's love will be returned. But many poems have meanings too complex to be reduced to single sentences. When this is true, a good multiple-choice writer won't ask for a single theme or meaning.

4. Are the grammar and meaning clear?

Make sure you understand the meaning of all the words in the poem, especially words you thought you knew but which don't seem to fit in the context of the poem. Also make sure you understand the grammar of the poem. The word order of poetry is often skewed, and in a poem a direct object may come before the subject and the verb. ("His sounding lyre the poet struck" can mean a poet was hit by a musical instrument, but as a line of poetry, it probably means the poet played his harp.)

5. What are the important images and figures of speech?

What are the important literal sensory objects, the images, such as a field of poppies or a stench of corruption? What are the similes and metaphors of the poem? In each, exactly what is compared to what? Is there a pattern in the images, such as a series of comparisons all using men compared to wild animals? The most difficult challenge of reading poetry is discriminating between the figurative ("I love a rose"—that is, my love is like a rose, beautiful, sweet, fragile) and the literal ("I love a rose"— that is, roses are my favorite flower). Every exam tests a reader's understanding of figurative language many times in both the multiple-choice and essay sections.

6. What are the most important single words used in the poem?

This is another way of asking about *diction*. Some of the most significant words in a poem aren't figurative or images but still determine the effect of the poem. A good reader recognizes which words—usually nouns and verbs, adjectives and adverbs— are the keys to the poem.

7. What is the tone of the poem?

Tone is a slippery word, and almost everyone has trouble with it. It's sometimes used to mean the mood or atmosphere of a work, though purists are offended by this definition. Or it can mean a manner of speaking, a tone of voice, as in "The disappointed coach's tone was sardonic." But its most common use as a term of literary analysis is to denote the inferred attitude of an author. When the author's attitude is different from that of the speaker, as is usually the case in ironic works, the tone of voice of the speaker, which may be calm, businesslike, even gracious, may be very different from the satiric tone of the work, which reflects the author's disapproval of the speaker. Because it is often very hard to define tone in one or two words, questions on tone do not appear frequently on responsibly written multiple-choice exams, but it is a topic you can't afford to ignore because the essay topic may well ask for a discussion of the tone of a poem or a passage of prose.

8. What literary devices does the poem employ?

The list of rhetorical devices that a writer might use is enormous. The terms you should worry about are, above all, metaphor, simile, and personification.

9. What is the prosody of the poem?

You can, in fact, get away with knowing very little about the rhyme, meter, and sound effects of poetry, though versification is not difficult once you're used to the new vocabulary you need and can hear the difference between an accented and an unaccented syllable. The essay question has not asked about sound in a poem for several years now, and the last time a question asked about the "movement of the verse" the answers on that part of the question were so vague as to be of no use in the grading. But it is, of course, always possible that such a task may turn up as part of the essay question. Chances are that of the thirteen to fifteen multiple-choice questions asked on each of the two poems, only one question will ask about the meter or the use of rhyme or the sound effects of a line. So a total of just two of the fifty-five questions may be on metrics.

ANSWERING MULTIPLE-CHOICE POETRY QUESTIONS

Types of Questions

This process of analysis—or whatever your own method may be—should precede your answering the multiple-choice questions. The question writer has already gone through the same process, and the questions that you find on the exam will be very much like the ones you've just asked yourself.

1. Questions on **dramatic situation:**

   Examples:

   Who is speaking?
   Where is she?
   To whom is the poem addressed?
   Who is the speaker in lines 5–8?
   Where does the poem take place?
   At what time of the year does the poem take place?

2. Questions on **structure:**

   Examples:

   How are stanzas 1 and 2 related to stanza 3?
   What word in line 20 refers back to an idea used in lines 5, 10, and 15?
   Which of the following divisions of the poem best represents its structure?

3. Questions on **theme:**

   Examples:

   Which of the following best sums up the meaning of stanza 2?
   With which of the following is the poem centrally concerned?
   The poet rejects the notion of an indifferent universe because . . .

4. Questions on **grammar and meaning of words:**

Examples:

Which of the following best defines the word "glass" as it is used in line 9?

To which of the following does the word "which" in line 7 refer?

The verb "had done" may best be paraphrased as . . .

When answering questions on grammar or meaning, you must look carefully at the context. In questions of meaning, more often than not, the obvious meaning of a word is not the one used in the poem. If it were, there would be no reason to ask you a question about it. The answers to a question about the meaning of the word "glass," for example, might include

(A) a transparent material used in windows
(B) a barometer
(C) a mirror
(D) a telescope
(E) a drinking vessel

Without a context, you would have to call all five answers right. On an exam, a poem with a line like "The glass has fallen since the dawn" might well ask the meaning of "glass" with these five options, and the logical answer would be (B). The next line of the poem would make the correct choice even clearer.

Similarly, grammar questions may exploit double meanings. The verb form "had broken" looks like a past perfect tense: I had broken the glass before I realized it. But a poem might also say "I had broken my heart unless I had seen her once more" in which case "had broken" is not a past perfect indicative verb, but a subjunctive in a conditional sentence. And this sentence could be paraphrased as "If I had not seen her once more, it would have broken my heart."

5. Questions on **images and figurative language:**

   You should expect a large number of these. Because the poems used on the exam must be complex enough to inspire ten to fifteen good multiple-choice questions, it is rare that a poem which does not rely on complex figurative language is chosen.

   Examples:

   To which of the following does the poet compare his love?
   The images in lines 3 and 8 come from what area of science?
   The figure of the rope used in line 7 is used later in the poem in line . . .

6. Questions on **diction:**

   Examples:

   Which of the following words is used to suggest the poet's dislike of winter?
   The poet's use of the word "air" in line 8 is to indicate . . .
   The poet's delight in the garden is suggested by all of the following words EXCEPT . . .

   Notice that some questions use a negative: "all of the following . . . EXCEPT" is the most common phrasing. The exam always calls attention to a question of this sort by using capital letters.

7. Questions on **tone, literary devices, and metrics:**

   Examples:

   The tone of the poem (or stanza) can best be described as . . .
   Which of the following literary techniques is illustrated by the phrase "murmurous hum and buzz of the hive"? (onomatopoeia)
   The meter of the last line in each stanza is . . .

Examples of Poetry Selections, Questions, and Answers

Set 1

The following poem, a sonnet by Keats, is a good example of the level of difficulty of the poetry on the literature exam. The selected poems are usually longer than the sonnet, but shorter poems appear sometimes. Read this poem carefully. Then answer the twelve multiple-choice questions that follow. Choose the *best* answer of the five.

On the Sonnet

> If by dull rhymes our English must be chained,
>   And, like Andromeda, the Sonnet sweet
> Fettered, in spite of pained loveliness,
>   Let us find out, if we must be constrained,
> (5)   Sandals more interwoven and complete
>   To fit the naked foot of poesy;
>   Let us inspect the lyre, and weigh the stress
>   Of every chord, and see what may be gained
>   By ear industrious, and attention meet;
> (10) Misers of sound and syllable, no less
>   Than Midas of his coinage, let us be
>   Jealous of dead leaves in the bay-wreath crown;
>   So, if we may not let the Muse be free,
>   She will be bound with garlands of her own.

1. The "we" ("us") of the poem refers to
    (A) literary critics
    (B) misers
    (C) readers of poetry
    (D) the Muses
    (E) English poets

2. Which of the following best describes the major structural divisions of the poem?
   (A) Lines 1–3; 4–6; 7–9; 10–14
   (B) Lines 1–8; 9–14
   (C) Lines 1–6; 7–9; 10–12; 13–14
   (D) Lines 1–4; 5–8; 9–12; 13–14
   (E) Lines 1–6; 7–14

3. The metaphor used in the first line of the poem compares English to
   (A) carefully guarded treasure
   (B) Andromeda
   (C) a bound creature
   (D) a necklace
   (E) a sonnet

4. In lines 2–3, the poem compares the sonnet to Andromeda because
   I. both are beautiful
   II. neither is free
   III. both are inventions of classical Greece

   (A) III only
   (B) I and II only
   (C) I and III only
   (D) II and III only
   (E) I, II, and III

5. The main verb of the first grammatically complete sentence of the poem is
   (A) "must be" (line 1)
   (B) "be chained" (line 1)
   (C) "Fettered" (line 3)
   (D) "let . . . find" (line 4)
   (E) "must be" (line 4)

6. The phrase "naked foot of poesy" in line 6 is an example of which of the following technical devices?
   (A) Simile
   (B) Personification
   (C) Oxymoron
   (D) Allusion
   (E) Transferred epithet

7. In line 9, the word "meet" is best defined as
   (A) suitable
   (B) concentrated
   (C) unified
   (D) distributed
   (E) introductory

8. The poet alludes to Midas in line 11 to encourage poets to be
   (A) miserly
   (B) generous
   (C) mythical
   (D) magical
   (E) royal

9. In line 12, the phrase "dead leaves" probably refers to
   (A) boring passages in poetry
   (B) the pages of a book of poetry
   (C) worn-out conventions of poetry
   (D) surprising but inappropriate original metaphors
   (E) the closely guarded secrets of style that make great poetry

10. All of the following words denote restraint EXCEPT
    (A) "chained" (line 1)
    (B) "Fettered" (line 3)
    (C) "constrained" (line 4)
    (D) "interwoven" (line 5)
    (E) "bound" (line 14)

11. Which of the following best states the central ideas of the poem?
    (A) Poems must be carefully crafted and decorously adorned.
    (B) Poets must jealously guard the traditional forms of the sonnet.
    (C) Sonnets should be free of all restrictions.
    (D) The constraint of the sonnet form will lead to discipline and creativity.
    (E) Poems in restricted forms should be original and carefully crafted.

12. The poem is written in
    (A) rhymed couplets
    (B) blank verse
    (C) rhymed iambic pentameter
    (D) Shakespearean sonnet form
    (E) rhymed triplets

Answers for Set 1

1. (E) The first question asks you to identify the speaker and his audience. This is one of the poems which tell us nothing about the time period or the location of the speaker. But we do know he is a poet, since the poem is called "On the Sonnet" and deals with his ideas about how the sonnet should be composed. Since he speaks of English as "chained" by the rhymes of poetry (and since he writes in English), we infer that the speaker and his audience are English poets. The correct choice is (E). The next-best choice is (A), but though the poem does include some literary criticism, (E) is the "best" answer. The very existence of this poem tells us the speaker is a poet, and his plural pronoun defines his audience as like himself.

2. (C) The best choice here is (C), dividing the poem at the semicolons (which might have been periods) at the end of lines 6, 9, and 12. Those of you familiar with other sonnets will recognize that this is an unusual poem. Most sonnets break naturally in units of eight and six lines (Italian sonnets especially) or into three four-line units and a closing couplet (the

English, or Shakespearean, sonnet). But it is these restrictions Keats is complaining about. And so his poem falls into units of six, three, three, and two lines. And it pays no attention to the abba, abba, cdcdcd rhyme scheme of the Italian sonnet or to the abab, cdcd, efef, gg of the Shakespearean sonnet. Notice that you cannot stop at the comma in line 3. The first three lines are a dependent clause, and the sentence is not yet grammatically coherent.

3. (C) The metaphor presents English chained without defining any more clearly whether the language is compared to a human or an animal. The comparison to Andromeda in line 2 is a simile.

4. (B) This is an example of a question where part of your answer comes from reading the poem carefully and part from your general information. Both I and II are clear from the poem, since both Andromeda and the sonnet are said to be "sweet" and to have "loveliness" and both are "Fettered." Though Andromeda is the creation of Greek mythology—she was chained to a rock and rescued by Perseus—the sonnet is not an ancient Greek poetic form.

5. (D) The main verb of the sentence is "let (us) find." The verbs "must be chained" and "Fettered" are part of the dependent clause.

6. (B) There is no "like" or "as," so the figure is a metaphor, not a simile. It is also a personification, in this case, a metaphor in which poetry is represented as possessing human form, having a foot that can wear a sandal. Keats is probably punning here on another meaning of foot, the term to denote the metric unit of a line of verse.

7. (A) As it is used here, "meet" is an adjective meaning "suitable" or "fitting" (compare Hamlet's line "meet it is I set it down" or the phrase "meet and just").

8. (A) This question calls for a literal reading of the line, not an explanation of the figure. Surprisingly, since Midas is usually viewed as a fool or a villain, Keats urges poets to be miserly, like Midas, though not with money but with the sounds and syllables of their poems.

9. (C) Here the question calls for an explanation of the metaphor "dead leaves." The adjective "Jealous" in this sentence does not mean "envious," as it usually does, but "watchful" or "very attentive to." The poet is urging other poets to scrupulously keep "dead leaves" from the bay-leaf crown that is traditionally associated with the poet. The metaphor, in keeping with the advice of the rest of the poem, is probably a reference to poetic practices that are no longer alive or natural like the green leaves of the laurel (bay) wreath. The word "leaves" here might be a play on "leaf" as "page," but the more important meaning is the metaphorical one, and (C) is the best of the five options.

10. (D) The question combines diction and structure. The word "interwoven" in its context refers to the structure of the sandal. Arguably, since an interwoven sandal fits the foot, even this word suggests constraint, but the question calls for the best answer of the five, and constraint is much more clearly the denotation of the other four choices. The reference of the sandals metaphor is probably to the rhyme scheme into which the poem (the foot) must fit. The more interwoven rhyme scheme Keats has in mind is the one he uses here: not the abab, cdcd, efef, gg of the traditional English sonnet where new rhymes appear in each of the following quatrains, but the "interwoven" abc, abd, cabcdede.

11. (E) This is the theme-of-the-poem question. Though Keats might agree with choice (A), this poem doesn't make this point. In all multiple-choice sets, beware of the answer that in itself is true or morally uplifting or an idea that poems often express but which is not the issue in the poem you're dealing with. Good, wrong answers, test writers believe, must sound true even if they are irrelevant. Choice (B) is an idea some poets may hold, but this poem rejects the traditional forms if they have become

"dead leaves." Choice (C) is not an issue here. Keats begins with the condition of English poetry chained by rhymes, and though this suggests some sympathy with the idea of even greater freedom, the poem never advocates giving up all restrictions. Choice (D) is another of those good-sounding wrong answers. It is an idea that many poets, perhaps including Keats, would endorse, but it is not the theme of this sonnet. Choice (E) is the best of the five.

12. (C) This is an example of a question on the metrics of the poem. Choice (C) is right; choices (A), (B), (D), and (E) are all untrue. Given the concern of this poem with the rhyme scheme of the sonnet, one should not be surprised to find a question about the rhyme scheme Keats uses here in a set of questions on the poem.

Set 2

The following poem, a sonnet by Wordsworth, was written twelve years before the Keats poem you've just studied. Read this poem carefully, analyze it quickly, and then answer the multiple-choice questions that follow.

> Nuns fret not at their convent's narrow room;
> And hermits are contented with their cells;
> And students with their pensive citadels;
> Maids at the wheel, the weaver at his loom,
> (5) Sit blithe and happy; bees that soar for bloom,
> High as the highest Peak of Furness-fells,
> Will murmur by the hour in foxglove bells:
> In truth the prison, unto which we doom
> Ourselves, no prison is: and hence for me,
> (10) In sundry moods, 'twas pastime to be bound
> Within the Sonnet's scanty plot of ground;
> Pleased if some souls (for such there needs must be)
> Who have felt the weight of too much liberty,
> Should find brief solace there, as I have found.

1. Which of the following best represents the structural divisions of the poem?
   (A) Lines 1–4; 5–8; 9–12; 13–14
   (B) Lines 1–7; 8–10; 11–13; 14
   (C) Lines 1–7; 8–9½; 9½–14
   (D) Lines 1–8; 9–11; 12–14
   (E) Lines 1–9; 10–13; 14

2. Which of the following best describes the organization of the poem?
   (A) A series of logically developing ideas with a concluding personal application
   (B) A series of examples followed by a generalization and a personal application
   (C) A generalization followed by examples
   (D) A specific assertion followed by examples followed by a contradiction of the initial assertion
   (E) An answer followed by a question that cannot be answered

3. In line 3, the phrase "pensive citadels" can be best paraphrased as
   (A) towers in which students are imprisoned
   (B) castles under siege
   (C) dreary fortresses
   (D) refuges for contemplation
   (E) strongholds that inspire thought

4. The "we" of line 8 could refer to all of the following EXCEPT
   (A) criminals
   (B) poets
   (C) nuns
   (D) hermits
   (E) students

5. In line 8, "prison" is parallel to all of the following EXCEPT
   (A) "narrow room" (line 1)
   (B) "pensive citadels" (line 3)
   (C) "Peak of Furness-fells" (line 6)
   (D) "foxglove bells" (line 7)
   (E) "scanty plot of ground" (line 11)

6. Lines 8–9 ("In truth the prison unto which we doom/ Ourselves no prison is") is an example of
   (A) hyperbole
   (B) personification
   (C) alliteration
   (D) simile
   (E) paradox

7. In line 10, the assertion "'twas pastime" is parallel to all of the following phrases EXCEPT
   (A) "fret not" (line 1)
   (B) "are contented" (line 2)
   (C) "Sit blithe" (line 5)
   (D) "Will murmur" (line 7)
   (E) "we doom" (line 8)

8. The figure of speech in line 11 ("Within the Sonnet's scanty plot of ground") is
   (A) a simile comparing the writing of poetry to a field
   (B) a simile comparing the poet and a farmer
   (C) a metaphor comparing the sonnet and a small piece of land
   (D) a metaphor comparing the pleasures of writing poetry and the pleasures of gardening
   (E) an apostrophe

9. In line 14, "there" refers to
   (A) the sonnet (line 11)
   (B) the soul (line 12)
   (C) pleasure (line 12)
   (D) weight (line 13)
   (E) liberty (line 13)

10. Which of the following phrases from the poem best sums up its central idea?
    (A) "hermits are contented with their cells" (line 2)
    (B) "Maids at the wheel . . ./ Sit blithe and happy" (lines 4–5)
    (C) "the prison, unto which we doom/ Ourselves, no prison is" (lines 8–9)
    (D) "such there needs must be" (line 12)
    (E) "Who have felt the weight of too much liberty" (line 13)

11. From the poem, the reader may infer all of the following about the speaker EXCEPT that he
    (A) feels deep compassion for nuns
    (B) sometimes finds liberty onerous
    (C) respects literary traditions
    (D) finds conventional verse forms congenial to his talent
    (E) has written a number of sonnets

12. The rhyme scheme of this poem is especially appropriate because
    I. lines 1–8 employ the traditional abba, abba of the Italian sonnet
    II. it is restricted to only four rhymes in the fourteen lines
    III. it makes judicious use of slant rhymes

    (A) III only
    (B) I and II only
    (C) I and III only
    (D) II and III only
    (E) I, II, and III

Answers for Set 2

1. (and 2) Line 8 and half of line 9 state the thesis of the poem: that a self-chosen restriction is not a restriction at all. The first seven lines of the poem give six different examples of self-chosen restrictions: the nuns in their convent, the hermits in their cells, the students withdrawn to contemplation, the maids at their spinning wheels, the weaver at the loom, and finally the bee which seeks nectar in the narrow confines of the foxglove

blossom. Lines 9½, 10, and 11 apply the idea of self-elected restrictions to the poet's choosing to write in the difficult and limiting sonnet form. Lines 12–14 express the poet's satisfaction in others' finding the same pleasure in his sonnets.

The structure then is that described in (C) on question 1, and the organization is explained by (B) in question 2. Notice that one of the divisions of the poem falls in the middle rather than at the end of a line. Though the rhyme scheme of abba, abba suggests an eight-line unit to begin the poem, the real unit is seven lines.

3. (D) A citadel is a tower, a fortress, a refuge. The adjective "pensive" means thoughtful, meditative. Since a citadel cannot think, the phrase is surprising. The device the poet uses here is a *transferred epithet,* the shift of a word or phrase from the noun it would logically modify to another. Shakespeare writes of a sailor high on the "giddy mast" of a ship in a storm. It is, of course, the sailor, not the mast, who is "giddy." It is the students here who are "pensive," but the adjective is transferred to modify the place where they meditate.

4. (A) The exception is the criminals. A criminal in prison has not chosen prison voluntarily, while, according to the poem, the nun, poet, hermit, and students have chosen the restrictions of the convent, the sonnet, the cell, or the citadel.

5. (C) The prison is parallel to other self-chosen forms of restriction such as the narrow room, citadels, bells (or flowers) of the foxglove, and the scanty plot of the sonnet. In line 6, the reference to bees flying as high as the mountain peak is to demonstrate the freedom the bees might enjoy contrasted with the narrow space inside the foxglove flower which they choose instead. Choice (C) is the opposite of prison, not a parallel.

6. (E) This is a paradox, an apparently self-contradictory statement. To say a prison is not a prison is paradoxical. Another term for this figure is oxymoron.

7. (E) The phrase is the expression of the speaker's pleasure in restriction. The phrases parallel to this are "fret not," "are contented," "Sit blithe" and "Will murmur," all of which are used to express satisfaction with elected restraints. The exception, and right answer, is "we doom."

8. (C) This is a metaphor (a simile would use "like" or "as") comparing the sonnet and a small plot of land. Apostrophe is direct address to a person or thing.

9. (A) The "there" refers to the sonnet, where the poet has found and, he hopes, the reader will find some pleasure.

10. (C) This option, using the prison metaphor, explicitly states the theme of the sonnet.

11. (A) There is no reason to feel compassion for the nuns, whose confinement is self-chosen. That he has "felt the weight of too much liberty" supports (B). That he finds pleasure in the restrictions of the sonnet suggests his respect for tradition and for conventional restrictive forms.

12. (B) Among a number of possible rhyme schemes for the sonnet, the poet has chosen one of the most restrictive, in keeping with the thesis of the poem that a chosen restraint is not restraining. The first eight lines have only two rhymes (as in the Italian sonnet), and only two more rhymes are used in lines 9–14. A slant rhyme is an off-rhyme, a rhyme that is incomplete. If "bells" were rhymed with "calls" or "ills," both rhymes would be slant rhymes. This poem, predictably, does not take advantage of this license.

ANALYZING PROSE

Though the analysis of a prose passage is like the analysis of a poem in many ways, there are important differences quite apart from the absence of meter. The prose selections are normally longer than the poems, running from 450 to 850 words. Like the poetry, they represent writing in English in the sixteenth, seventeenth, eighteenth, nineteenth, and twentieth centuries. Some of the prose is more difficult because of differences between style in the earlier periods and that of our time. Some passages are on unfamiliar subjects. Excerpts come from a variety of both fictional and nonfictional sources: novels, short stories, history, philosophical writing, sermons, journals, letters, essays, biography, autobiography, or literary criticism, and the list could go on.

One approach to sight-reading prose is to deal first with the issues of genre (the kind of work, such as novel or essay) and content, then, of structure, and finally, of style.

1. genre

From what kind of a work is the selection taken? Is it fiction or nonfiction?

If you're dealing with a work of fiction, chances are you'll have to think about the character or characters in the passage, while a work of nonfiction probably focuses on an issue, on an idea, or on the narrator, him or herself.

2. narrator

Whether the passage is from a work of fiction or of nonfiction, you must be aware of who is speaking and what his or her attitudes are toward the characters or the subject of the passage. If you can, identify who is speaking, where and when, why, and to whom. You will often be unable to answer all of these questions, but answer as many of them as you can.

3. subject

Then ascertain what the purpose of the passage is. Is it to present an argument or to introduce a character? To cajole, or entertain, or stir to action? If you can define an author's purpose clearly, most of the questions on the interpretation of meaning will fall neatly into place.

4. structure

The normal unit of prose is the paragraph, and the passages on the AP exam run from a single long paragraph (the prose writers of the seventeenth century sometimes wrote paragraphs that seem as long as chapters to modern readers) to ten shorter paragraphs. As with a poem, try to see how each part advances the progress of the whole. How are the paragraphs related to each other and to the passage as a whole?

5. style

The style of prose is determined by diction, imagery, figurative language, and syntax—all matters you deal with in the analysis of poetry. In addition, the analysis of prose is certain to raise questions about the rhetoric of a passage, that is, its use of words to persuade or influence a reader. There is, of course, a rhetoric in poetry, but the questions about rhetoric are more likely to be asked about prose passages.

ANSWERING MULTIPLE-CHOICE PROSE QUESTIONS

Types of Questions

Most of the multiple-choice questions on the prose passage take the following forms:

1. Questions on **situation and content:** on the passage as a whole; on a single paragraph; on a single sentence.

   Examples:

   The main subject of the passage is . . .
   The primary distinction made in the first paragraph is between . . .
   According to lines 3–7, which of the following is the chief . . .
   In the third paragraph, the author is chiefly concerned with . . .

2. Questions on **meaning of words or phrases:**

   Examples:

   As it is used in line 2, the word x can be best understood to mean . . .
   In line 7, the word x employs all of the following meanings EXCEPT . . .
   The phrase xyz is best understood to mean . . .

3. Questions on **grammar:**

   Examples:

   In the opening clause, the word "which" refers to . . .
   In line 12, the antecedent of "it" is . . .
   The subject of the long sentence that makes up the third paragraph is . . .

4. Questions on **diction:**

   Examples:

   The speaker's choice of verbs in the paragraph is to stress the . . .
   The speaker's anger is suggested by all of the following EXCEPT . . .

5. Questions on **figurative language:**

Examples:

The comparison in lines 1–3 compares . . .
The analogy of the second paragraph compares . . .
The phrase xyz is best read as a metaphor relating to . . .
The purpose of the astronomy metaphor in line 9 is to . . .

6. Questions on **structure:**

Examples:

The transitions from the first to the second and the second to the third paragraph are dependent upon . . .
The last paragraph of the passage is related to the first chiefly by . . .

7. Questions on **literary techniques:**

Examples:

In the third paragraph, the description of the cat on roller skates is an example of . . .
All of the following phrases are paradoxes EXCEPT . . .
The phrase "silent scream" is an example of . . .

8. Questions on **rhetoric:**

Examples:

The rhetorical purpose of lines 1–6 is to . . .
The argument of the passage can be best described as progressing from . . .
Which of the following best describes the function of the last sentence?
The effect of shifting from the past to the present tense in the third paragraph is . . .
The happiness of the speaker is conveyed primarily by the use of . . .

9. Questions on **tone:**

Examples:

The tone of the passage may be described as . . .
In discussing x in the second paragraph, the speaker adopts a
tone of . . .

Examples of Prose Selections, Questions, and Answers

Set 1

The following passage is taken from George Eliot's novel *Adam
Bede* (1859). Though the passage comes from a work of fiction, it
could just as well have appeared as a short essay. To read it, you do
not need to know anything about the rest of the novel. The passage
was used in the essay section of an AP exam. Read it very carefully.
It is not so easy or straightforward as it may at first appear to be.
Then answer the multiple-choice questions which follow.

> Leisure is gone—gone where the spinning-wheels are
> gone, and the pack-horses, and the slow waggons, and the
> pedlars, who brought bargains to the door on sunny after-
> noons. Ingenious philosophers tell you, perhaps, that the
> (5) great work of the steam-engine is to create leisure for
> mankind. Do not believe them: it only creates a vacuum for
> eager thought to rush in. Even idleness is eager now—eager
> for amusement: prone to excursion-trains, art-museums,
> periodical literature, and exciting novels: prone even to
> (10) scientific theorising, and cursory peeps through micro-
> scopes. Old Leisure was quite a different personage: he only
> read one newspaper, innocent of leaders, and was free from
> that periodicity of sensations which we call post-time. He
> was a contemplative, rather stout gentleman, of excellent
> (15) digestion—of quiet perceptions, undiseased by hypothesis:
> happy in his inablilty to know the causes of things, prefer-
> ring the things themselves. He lived chiefly in the country,
> among pleasant seats and homesteads, and was fond of
> sauntering by the fruit-tree wall, and scenting the apricots

(20) when they were warmed by the morning sunshine, or of sheltering himself under the orchard boughs at noon, when the summer pears were falling. He knew nothing of weekday services, and thought none the worse of the Sunday sermon if it allowed him to sleep from the text to the blessing—

(25) liking the afternoon service best, because the prayers were the shortest, and not ashamed to say so; for he had an easy, jolly conscience, broad-backed like himself, and able to carry a great deal of beer or port-wine,—not being made squeamish by doubts and qualms and lofty aspirations. Life

(30) was not a task to him, but a sinecure: he fingered the guineas in his pocket, and ate his dinners, and slept the sleep of the irresponsible; for had he not kept up his charter by going to church on the Sunday afternoons?

Fine old Leisure! Do not be severe upon him, and judge

(35) him by our modern standard: he never went to Exeter Hall, or heard a popular preacher, or read *Tracts for the Times* or *Sartor Resartus.* *

*Exeter Hall was a London building used for lectures and meetings, especially of a religious nature. *Tracts for the Times* and *Sartor Resartus* are important Victorian religious and philosophical books.

1. The phrases "Even idleness is eager now—eager for amusement" (lines 7–8) exemplify which of the following devices?

    I. Metaphor
    II. Personification
    III. Paradox

    (A) III only
    (B) I and II only
    (C) I and III only
    (D) II and III only
    (E) I, II, and III

2. According to the passage, all of the following are the activities
   of the present EXCEPT
   (A) restoring antiques
   (B) railway excursions
   (C) reading fiction
   (D) amateur biology
   (E) attending lectures

3. The phrase "innocent of leaders" (line 12) can be best said to
   mean
   (A) guiltless of ambition
   (B) free of editorials
   (C) ignorant of competition
   (D) pure as a commander
   (E) blameless of power

4. Old Leisure had not been "made squeamish by doubts and
   qualms and lofty aspirations" (lines 28–29) because
   (A) he has no reason to feel guilty
   (B) his honesty protects him against doubt
   (C) he never thinks about doubt or aspiration
   (D) he has fulfilled his charter by attending church
   (E) they are inventions of the modern age

5. The word "sinecure" in line 30 can be best defined as
   (A) a well-rewarded but undemanding position
   (B) a paid vacation
   (C) a hard-won and deserved triumph
   (D) an irresponsible indulgence in pleasure
   (E) an assuming of responsibility for the well-being of others

6. The point of view in the question "had he not kept up his charter by going to church on the Sunday afternoons?" (lines 32–33) is that of

    I. old Leisure
   II. new or modern leisure
  III. the narrator of the passage

  (A) I only
  (B) II only
  (C) III only
  (D) I and III only
  (E) II and III only

7. In lines 26–27, the phrase "he had an easy, jolly conscience, broad-backed like himself" employs
  (A) only one simile
  (B) only one metaphor
  (C) one metaphor and one simile
  (D) two metaphors and one simile
  (E) two similes

8. The social position of old Leisure is suggested by all of the following words EXCEPT
  (A) "gentleman" (line 14)
  (B) "pleasant seats" (line 18)
  (C) "port-wine" (line 28)
  (D) "guineas" (line 30)
  (E) "charter" (line 32)

9. Old Leisure's observance of his religious obligations may be best described as
  (A) hypocritical
  (B) ardent
  (C) grudging
  (D) perfunctory
  (E) skeptical

10. Of the following phrases, all of them work to make a similar point about old Leisure EXCEPT
    (A) "rather stout" (line 14)
    (B) "of excellent digestion" (lines 14–15)
    (C) "undiseased by hypothesis" (line 15)
    (D) "able to carry a great deal of beer" (lines 27–28)
    (E) "ate his dinners" (line 31)

11. Of the following techniques, which is the most important in the presentation of old Leisure?
    (A) Hyperbole
    (B) Simile
    (C) Personification
    (D) Paradox
    (E) Apostrophe

12. Compared to the leisure of modern times, old Leisure is characterized as more
    (A) religious
    (B) cynical
    (C) unthinking
    (D) eager
    (E) carnal

13. The passage implies all of the following contrasts between the leisure of the past and of the present EXCEPT
    (A) rural vs. urban
    (B) science vs. art
    (C) mind vs. body
    (D) complacency vs. aspiration
    (E) belief vs. doubt

14. From the whole passage, the reader can infer that the narrator feels

    I. some nostalgia for the leisure of the past
   II. an awareness of the complacency of the present
  III. a concern for the anti-intellectual self-interest of the past

  (A) I only
  (B) II only
  (C) I and II only
  (D) I and III only
  (E) I, II, and III

15. The tone of the passage is best described as
  (A) gently satirical
  (B) harshly sarcastic
  (C) mawkishly sentimental
  (D) coolly objective
  (E) cheerfully optimistic

Answers for Set 1

The instructions tell you that the passage is from a novel but that it might have come from an essay. What is striking about the passage is the characterization of the idea of old Leisure. George Eliot personifies the leisure of the past and devotes most of the passage to describing this fictitious character. In the course of the passage, the speaker or narrator reveals her views about the leisure of her own era and about old Leisure, and she cautions her contemporaries not to be too quick to pronounce the up-to-date to be superior.

1. (E) The first question asks you to identify the technical devices in "even idleness is eager." All three terms apply. "Idleness" is personified (and personification is a form of metaphor in which an abstract quality is compared to a person), and an eager idleness is a paradox, an apparent contradiction, since eager and idle seem to be opposites.

2. (A) The passage lists all of the activities except restoring antiques as leisure activities of the mid-Victorian world.

3. (B) This question is an example of a vocabulary word where the obvious modern meaning is not relevant. A "leader" is a newspaper editorial. The word is still used by journalists, but it is more common now in England than in the United States. The context of the phrase, introduced by "newspaper," as well as what we are told of old Leisure's lack of interest in almost anything requiring some thought could suggest the right answer even if you had never heard of a "leader" as a "newspaper editorial."

4. (C) Doubts, qualms, and lofty aspirations do not bother old Leisure because he never thinks about such serious or disturbing things. He is, we have been told, glad to be ignorant of causes and unconcerned with theories. This phrase is one of several which suggest that the narrator is not wholly on old Leisure's side. Can she really endorse an approach to life that avoids doubts and aspirations?

5. (A) A "sinecure" is a position that is well paid but that requires very little work. Unlike the Victorians, celebrated for their earnest approach to life, old Leisure is in the happy position to regard life as a free ride.

6. (A) Old Leisure, thoughtless as he is, would see no irony in the question and assume the answer is yes. But the narrator is not quite so sure. Though she tweaks old Leisure gently by putting this question in his mouth, it's hard for a modern reader to believe that the author thinks a snooze in church is an adequate fulfillment of religious duties.

7. (D) The figurative language here is complex. To begin with, we have the basic metaphor of the passage in which the abstraction, old Leisure, is compared to a person (metaphor one) with the phrase "he had an easy, jolly conscience." But this conscience is also personified as "jolly" and "broad-backed" (metaphor two) and in being stout is said to be "like himself" (a

simile). So the phrase has a simile and two metaphors, both personifications.

8. (E) One of the subtle touches in George Eliot's portrait of old Leisure is her clearly placing him in the moneyed class. He is not a farmer who plants crops or gets up early, though he no doubt owns agricultural lands that others work for his profit. He is a "gentleman" (often in British parlance a man of good birth and social position whose wealth is inherited—Mr. Bennet in *Pride and Prejudice,* as Elizabeth proudly tells Darcy, is a "gentleman"). He drinks port, lives among pleasant seats, and fingers his guineas. His guineas, notice, not his pennies or shillings. A guinea was a gold coin equal to a year's wages of a serving girl in nineteenth-century England. Only the word "charter" here does not suggest old Leisure's social position.

9. (D) A case could be made for "grudging," but given the fact that he does go to church on Sunday, sleeps comfortably, and is satisfied with his performance, "perfunctory" is a better choice.

10. (C) Another of the pleasures of the passage is the suggestion that old Leisure eats a lot and is, perhaps, a bit overweight— certainly "stout" and "broad-backed." Though his digestion may be relevant to old Leisure's girth, the phrase "undiseased by hypothesis" is only a metaphor revealing his anti-intellectuality.

11. (C) The chief technique is personification.

12. (C) Old Leisure is presented as more unthinking. Modern leisure may think too much; old Leisure avoids thought at all costs.

13. (B) The passage does not use the art-science contrast. In fact, modern leisure is said to be interested in both art museums and microscopes, while old Leisure would be indifferent to both.

14. (E) All three of these ideas are implied. The author sees the charm as well as the limitations of old Leisure and warns against complacency in the last paragraph.

15. (A) The best choice here is (A), though it is not the whole story. Sometimes you have to select an imperfect answer because the other four are inferior or outrightly wrong. Here, (B), (C), (D), and (E) are all clearly worse than (A).

Set 2

The following passage, from Joseph Conrad's short novel *Typhoon*, was used on the essay section of the 1989 literature exam, but it could have been used for multiple-choice questions. Read the passage carefully and choose the best answer of the five options in the multiple-choice questions following the passage.

> Captain MacWhirr, of the steamer Nan-Shan, had a physiognomy that, in the order of material appearances, was the exact counterpart of his mind: it presented no marked characteristics of firmness or stupidity; it had no pro-
> (5) nounced characteristics whatever; it was simply ordinary, irresponsive, and unruffled. . . .
> Having just enough imagination to carry him through each successive day, and no more, he was tranquilly sure of himself; and from the very same cause he was not in the
> (10) least conceited. It is your imaginative superior who is touchy, overbearing, and difficult to please; but every ship Captain MacWhirr commanded was the floating abode of harmony and peace. It was, in truth, as impossible for him to take a flight of fancy as it would be for a watchmaker to put
> (15) together a chronometer with nothing except a two-pound hammer and a whipsaw in the way of tools. Yet the uninteresting lives of men so entirely given to the actuality of the bare existence have their mysterious side. It was impossible in Captain MacWhirr's case, for instance, to
> (20) understand what under heaven could have induced that perfectly satisfactory son of a petty grocer in Belfast to run away to sea. And yet he had done that very thing at the age of fifteen. It was enough, when you thought it over, to give you the idea of an immense, potent, and invisible hand

(25) thrust into the ant-heap of the earth, laying hold of shoulders, knocking heads together, and setting the unconscious faces of the multitude towards inconceivable goals and in undreamt-of directions.

His father never really forgave him for this undutiful
(30) stupidity. "We could have got on without him," he used to say later on, "but there's the business. And he an only son, too!" His mother wept very much after his disappearance. As it had never occurred to him to leave word behind, he was mourned over for dead till, after eight months, his first
(35) letter arrived from Talcahuano. It was short, and contained the statement: "We had very fine weather on our passage out." But evidently, in the writer's mind, the only important intelligence was to the effect that his captain had, on the very day of writing, entered him regularly on the ship's
(40) articles as Ordinary Seaman. "Because I can do the work," he explained. The mother again wept copiously, while the remark, "Tom's an ass," expressed the emotions of the father. He was a corpulent man, with a gift for sly chaffing, which to the end of his life he exercised in his intercourse
(45) with his son, a little pityingly, as if upon a half-witted person.

MacWhirr's visits to his home were necessarily rare, and in the course of years he dispatched other letters to his parents, informing them of his successive promotions and of his movements upon the vast earth. In these missives could
(50) be found sentences like this: "The heat here is very great." Or: "On Christmas day at 4 p.m. we fell in with some icebergs." The old people ultimately became acquainted with a good many names of ships, and with the names of the skippers who commanded them—with the names of Scots
(55) and English shipowners—with the names of seas, oceans, straits, promontories—with outlandish names of lumber-ports, of rice-ports, of cotton-ports—with the names of islands—with the name of their son's young woman. She was called Lucy. It did not suggest itself to him to mention
(60) whether he thought the name pretty. And then they died.

1. The word "physiognomy" in line 2 can be best defined as
   (A) temperament
   (B) personality
   (C) face
   (D) manner of behaving
   (E) pragmatism

2. The point of the simile in lines 13–16 ("It was, in truth . . . way of tools") is to illustrate
   (A) a difficulty
   (B) an impossibility
   (C) a subtlety
   (D) a technicality
   (E) an unlikeness

3. The passage represents the young MacWhirr's decision to go to sea as
   (A) youthful rebelliousness
   (B) a search for adventure
   (C) personal ambition
   (D) romantic escapism
   (E) an unexplainable action

4. In line 29, the word "undutiful" may be best defined as
   (A) unusual
   (B) extreme
   (C) unexpected
   (D) disobedient
   (E) uncharged

5. The phrase "undutiful stupidity" in lines 29–30 reflects the point of view of which of the following?

    I. The narrator of the passage
   II. MacWhirr's father
  III. MacWhirr's mother

(A) I only
(B) II only
(C) I and II only
(D) II and III only
(E) I, II, and III

6. Of the following phrases, which has the effect of reducing our feelings of sympathy for MacWhirr's parents?

    I. "but there's the business. And he an only son, too!" (lines 31–32)
   II. "His mother wept very much after his disappearance." (line 32)
  III. "Tom's an ass," (line 42)

(A) II only
(B) I and II only
(C) I and III only
(D) II and III only
(E) I, II, and III

7. MacWhirr does not comment on the prettiness of the name Lucy in his letters to his parents because
(A) he wants them to know only the external events of his life
(B) he does not think they care enough about him to be interested
(C) he has not thought about it himself
(D) such a comment would be effeminate
(E) such a comment would suggest that her face was not pretty

8. The word "names" is repeated six times in the last paragraph to
   (A) contrast with the single repetition of the singular "name"
   (B) suggest the slow passage of time at sea
   (C) expose the unnatural absence of feeling in Captain Mac-Whirr
   (D) emphasize Captain MacWhirr's commitment to actuality
   (E) enhance the poetic quality of the prose

9. In the last sentence of the passage, the antecedent of "they" is probably
   (A) the old people
   (B) skippers
   (C) Scots ship owners
   (D) English ship owners
   (E) Captain MacWhirr and Lucy

10. MacWhirr's prose style is best characterized as
    (A) episodic
    (B) baroque
    (C) metaphorical
    (D) ironic
    (E) factual

11. The narrator's prose style differs from that of Captain Mac-Whirr in its use of

    I. figurative language
    II. irony
    III. generalization

    (A) III only
    (B) I and II only
    (C) I and III only
    (D) II and III only
    (E) I, II, and III

12. To which of the following does the passage attribute Mac-
Whirr's success as a commanding officer?

I. His attention to detail
II. His lack of imagination
III. His ability to do the work

(A) II only
(B) III only
(C) I and III only
(D) II and III only
(E) I, II, and III

13. All of the following words accurately describe Captain Mac-
Whirr EXCEPT
(A) fanciful
(B) ordinary
(C) cool
(D) serious
(E) confident

Answers for Set 2

The Conrad passage is centrally concerned with the character of
Captain MacWhirr, and it also includes brief comments on and
dialogue of his parents. The passage establishes what is to be the
key to Captain MacWhirr and to the action of the story. MacWhirr
is so completely lacking in imaginative ability that he cannot
imagine the power and the peril of a typhoon. And so when others
are paralyzed by fear, MacWhirr keeps his head and steers his ship
through the storm.

1. (C) "Physiognomy" is a long word for face. Notice that this
paragraph does not call MacWhirr firm or stupid or their
opposites. It says his face, like his mind, had "<u>no</u> pronounced
characteristics."

2. (B) The point of the simile is to show impossibility: "as impossible for him . . . as"). Don't be surprised if you find some multiple-choice questions that strike you as very easy, and don't assume that because a question seems easy there must be a trick and the right answer must be the unexpected choice. Each set of questions contains a few very hard questions and a few very easy questions. No set is all of one or the other.

3. (E) The narrator admits that MacWhirr's decision is unexplainable: "impossible . . . to understand" and wholly "mysterious."

4. (D) The word "undutiful" means lacking in a sense of duty, disobedient, disrespectful.

5. (B) Remember that, in the first paragraph, the narrator doesn't charge MacWhirr with stupidity. MacWhirr's mother doesn't say enough for us to know her opinion, but the idea is certainly one the father would endorse.

6. (C) The first of the father's remarks is not that of a dutiful parent, as it suggests that the business is more important than the loss of the company of the child. The third remark is even clearer. The mother's tears—at least on the first occasion—don't reduce our sympathy. And why did MacWhirr go off without telling his parents he was leaving? Why didn't he spare them all their needless worry? The answer, we infer, is that it never occurred to young Tom MacWhirr that his parents would worry. Such an idea requires some ability to imagine what others will feel, and MacWhirr, as we know, has no imagination at all.

7. (C) Again the key to MacWhirr's actions is his inability to imagine, to think in terms other than the starkly factual. It would not occur to him to comment on the prettiness of a name because he would never think about whether a name was pretty or not.

8. (D) To MacWhirr, a name is a name and no more, and the repeated use of the word in the last paragraph drives home the notion of MacWhirr's life "entirely given to the actuality of the bare existence." The purpose of a name, to MacWhirr, is to denote a reality.

9. (A) It is grammatically possible to refer the pronoun to "Lucy" and to "he," which are, in fact, closer to the "they." But the logic of the passage as a whole, the focus from the beginning on MacWhirr, should suggest that there is more to follow and that MacWhirr will be more fully described.

10. (E) MacWhirr's style is, of course, factual: "The heat here is very great."

11. (E) Fortunately, the narrator writes a more sophisticated prose than does MacWhirr, employing all three of these devices, which MacWhirr would not understand.

12. (A) According to the second paragraph, MacWhirr's lack of imagination makes for harmony on the ship. MacWhirr may possess the other qualities, but the passage attributes his success to II.

13. (A) Again, it is MacWhirr's lack of imagination, his inability to be fanciful, that answers the question.

THE AP LITERATURE EXAM SECTION II
ESSAY QUESTIONS

THE PROSE PASSAGE

Answer all the parts of the question on the exam.

This section would say the most important thing it has to say if it simply repeated that sentence for five pages. And, unfortunately, there would still be students who paid no attention.

If the question asks you to discuss the narrator's attitude toward cars, toys, and pigs and the literary devices he uses to convey this attitude, the directions on the scoring guide for the top scores will read like this: "These essays accurately discuss the narrator's attitude toward cars, toys, and pigs. They deal fully and specifically with the literary devices (such as diction, figurative language, and irony) used in the passage." And if the question should ask you to write an essay without ever using the letter "z" (it won't), the first line of the scoring guides describing the best papers would begin, "These well-written essays completely avoid the letter z." Which is to say, **answer all the parts of the question. Don't write your own question,** regardless of how much more interesting it may be than the dull one on the exam. If a question calls for a play or a novel, write about a play or a novel. One play or one novel, not two plays or one play and one novel. Not one short story or one essay. If the question calls for tone, diction, and syntax (and it will), write about tone, diction, and syntax.

In preparing for the exam, you should practice reading AP questions as if your life depended upon it. Your life doesn't, but your grade does. Go over in class with your teacher and fellow test takers as many of the old AP exam questions as you can stand. You don't have to write essays on all the old questions, but you should use them to train yourself to answer *all* the parts of the question.

Don't be in a hurry to begin writing. A well-thought-out, well-organized, and specific essay of three paragraphs will score higher than a disorganized and repetitive essay two or three times as long. You must answer all of the question, and since the essay questions usually have three or four tasks, a very short answer—say, a single paragraph—is not likely to be adequate. But papers earning the highest scores are often distinguished by their economy as well as by their insights. Remember that your readers are spending all day reading essays on a single topic. They don't need to be told what the question asks, and frankly, they don't care if Shakespeare is your favorite writer or that your life has been transfigured by your reading of *A Tale of Two Cities*. What they do want to see is whether or not you understand the question, understand the passage, and can write an essay demonstrating this mastery. You don't need to write an introductory paragraph outlining what you will do in your next three paragraphs. And you shouldn't write a final paragraph repeating what you've just said. Assume you have a reader smart enough to understand it the first time. If you answer the question the exam has put, you don't need a cute title, a dramatic opening, or a snazzy close.

Questions often ask you to identify an "attitude," a "state of mind," or a "tone." A common mistake is the assumption that the answer requires only one word, that there is only one attitude, one state of mind, or one tone. More often than not, the best answer is the one that sees complexity or a change. The good student sees that, though an author endorses a character or a position, he or she may do so with reservations. And though a character may feel relief or elation at the beginning of a passage, the second or third paragraph may present a change, a new feeling of disillusion or disappointment, for example. Don't assume that the singular or plural ("attitude" may really mean "attitudes," and "state of mind" might more clearly be called "states of mind") makes it perfectly clear. Chances are, if the answer is too simple, you're missing something. On the essay exams, if an answer is obvious, everyone will get it right, and the readers will be unable to discriminate among the papers. Don't let this warning lead you to be too inventive, to see too much, to see what isn't there. But read carefully, and with the knowledge that a poem or a passage which simply says "Mothers are good" or "'Murder is not nice" is an unlikely prompt for one hundred and twenty-five thousand essays.

Determining the Task on Essay Questions

Practice reading AP questions before you begin to practice writing answers. None of the following questions has appeared on the AP exam, but they closely mimic the real ones. Practice for the exam by studying them and determining exactly what it is the question asks you to do. Formulate your answers to each of the questions before reading the commentary that follows. There are three mock-prose questions.

1. The following passage is the opening of a novel. Read it carefully. Then write an essay in which you analyze how the speaker conveys her attitude to the marriage of Mr. and Mrs. Smith, paying special attention to the diction, figurative language, and tone.

2. The author of the following letter questions the traditional distinctions between comedy and tragedy. Read the passage carefully. Then write a cohesive essay in which you discuss his agreement and disagreement with the definitions of other writers and the literary devices he employs to justify his definitions of the two dramatic forms.

3. The passage that follows presents the conversation of a man and woman looking back on forty years of their marriage. Write an essay in which you discuss the differences between the husband's and the wife's attitude toward marriage and the family. Explain how the author uses the resources of language to make a reader more sympathetic to the wife's point of view than to the husband's.

Comments on the Prose Question Tasks

1. This looks like a straightforward question, but notice that it asks "how" not "what." Your first job is to figure out what the speaker's attitude to the marriage is. Then, you must think about how she conveys this attitude. The question, then, is chiefly about means—more about style than content. Those stylistic techniques that you must talk about are the three listed in the

question: diction, figurative language (metaphor and simile, especially), and tone. All of them probably relate to characterizations of Mr. and Mrs. Smith or to specific assertions about the nature of their marriage.

2. Without the passage, it's impossible to say how many other writers are mentioned, but you do know that the question expects you to talk about more than one. And you must talk about the writer's agreement and disagreement with at least two of the other writers' definitions. And you must also talk about at least two devices he uses (diction is usually one, and imagery or figurative language is often the easiest second choice), being sure to refer to his definitions of both comedy and tragedy.

This question is probably asking more than the real test would ask, but the point here is to be sure you understand all the things the question requires you to do. Mercifully, you don't have to write real essays on these three questions.

3. You should have highlighted or underlined "husband's," "wife's," "attitude to marriage," and "family." You have four tasks already. A fifth or fifth and sixth task would be an analysis of the "resources of language" (another test phrase for "style," "devices," or "techniques") that work to favor the wife and/or to disfavor the husband. Here, too, you have a choice among topics like diction, images, syntax, contrast, irony, and others.

Almost every prose passage question begins with the injunction "Read the following passage carefully." Obey this order. All your care in understanding what the question asks you to do is useless if you don't read the passage well enough to give convincing answers.

EXAMPLES OF PROSE PASSAGES AND STUDENT ESSAYS

Prose Passage 1

The following George Eliot passage, which you've already read in the multiple-choice section, originally appeared as the subject for an essay on the AP exam of 1987.

Leisure is gone—gone where the spinning-wheels are gone, and the pack-horses, and the slow waggons, and the pedlars, who brought bargains to the door on sunny after-noons. Ingenious philosophers tell you, perhaps, that the

(5) great work of the steam-engine is to create leisure for mankind. Do not believe them: it only creates a vacuum for eager thought to rush in. Even idleness is eager now—eager for amusement: prone to excursion-trains, art-museums, periodical literature, and exciting novels: prone even to

(10) scientific theorising, and cursory peeps through micro-scopes. Old Leisure was quite a different personage: He only read one newspaper, innocent of leaders, and was free from that periodicity of sensations which we call post-time. He was a contemplative, rather stout gentleman, of excel-

(15) lent digestion,—of quiet perceptions, undiseased by hypoth-esis: happy in his inability to know the causes of things, preferring the things themselves. He lived chiefly in the country, among pleasant seats and homesteads, and was fond of sauntering by the fruit-tree wall, and scenting the

(20) apricots when they were warmed by the morning sunshine, or of sheltering himself under the orchard boughs at noon, when the summer pears were falling. He knew nothing of weekday services, and thought none the worse of the Sunday sermon if it allowed him to sleep from the text to the

(25) blessing—liking the afternoon service best, because the prayers were the shortest, and not ashamed to say so; for he had an easy, jolly conscience, broad-backed like himself, and able to carry a great deal of beer or port-wine,—not being made squeamish by doubts and qualms and lofty

(30) aspirations. Life was not a task to him, but a sinecure: he
      fingered the guineas in his pocket, and ate his dinners, and
      slept the sleep of the irresponsible; for had he not kept up
      his charter by going to church on the Sunday afternoons?
            Fine old Leisure! Do not be severe upon him, and judge
(35) him by our modern standard: he never went to Exeter Hall,
      or heard a popular preacher, or read *Tracts for the Times* or
      Sartor Resartus.

Comments on Prose Passage 1

Students were asked to discuss the attitudes of the speaker to
both the leisure of the present and the leisure of the past. They were
also required to discuss the style used to present both the past and
the present. There are, then, four tasks: defining the attitudes of the
past and of the present and discussing the style the passage uses to
present "old Leisure" and contemporary leisure.

If you take the time to enumerate the required tasks of the
question with care, you'll usually find that the question offers you an
organizing scheme for your essay. This scheme may be mechanical,
but it's foolproof; it's safe. If you can invent a more interesting and
original way to organize your paper without losing sight of all the
required tasks, do so. If not, take the secure road. Here, you can
begin with a well-developed and specific paragraph on what George
Eliot thinks about the leisure of her day; your second paragraph can
discuss (at even greater length, since the passage is chiefly about
"old Leisure") the leisure of the past. The third paragraph could
deal with the stylistic devices used to describe modern leisure—for
example, diction (words like "eager," repeated three times, or
"rush," or the "cursory peeps" which undercut any claim to genuine
intellectuality)—and the contrast of these words suggesting haste
with the diction of old Leisure, suggesting a more quiet and more
slowly paced time ("slow waggons" vs. "trains"; "sauntering,"
"sheltering").

The fourth paragraph could go on to the other devices of style
used to describe old Leisure. You would probably want to talk
about personification, by which George Eliot transforms the abstract idea of leisure into a pudgy country gentleman, bored by
sermons, theories, science, or debates but appreciative of summer
pears, beer, and port. If you are especially perceptive, you would

talk about the irony of the passage, the reservations George Eliot suggests about both leisures despite her apparent preference for the old over the new. As you know now from answering the multiple-choice questions on the passage, the stylistic devices could also include other figures of speech, other personifications. You could allude to the use of allusion (the proverbial "slept the sleep of the irresponsible"). All of these aren't necessary. Papers that understand George Eliot's approval of and reservations about both leisures and discuss only her use of contrast and personification would get top scores.

The four papers that follow were written by high school seniors near the end of their AP course. The essays were part of a full-length practice exam, and the students spent thirty-five minutes on this question.

Student Essay 1

George Eliot presents "old leisure" in a more relaxed way than on leisure in society of her own time through the uses of tone, syntax, and imagery.

Eliots views on old leisure are way more relaxed than on leisure in the society of her own time and this is clearly shown in the tone. Eliot writes about old leisure in a lazy tone where all the time is leisure to the people who "slept the sleep of the irresponsible." The tone on the leisure of her times is much more serious trying to imply that there was no leisure. Her opposing views of leisure are directly shown in her tone.

The syntax used tells us alot about her attitude toward leisure. The syntax on old leisure are long and redundant showing us that old leisure had too much leisure time. Her attitude is saying that it was much easier then than in her time. She has a negative attitude toward old leisure and it clearly shows in the writing she spends three fourths of the passage on old leisure putting it down.

Imagery is used by personification of the ideas. She exaggerated how much leisure time there was in old leisure. Trying to prove a point but she has stepped over the line, gone too far.

Eliots devices used to help her convey the message were tone, syntax, and imagery but she mainly just stated that old leisure was too relaxed and that people of that time just sat on their butts. Her views are clearly shown and overly exaggerated.

Student Essay 2

In this selection, George Eliot reminisces about "Old Leisure"— "Old Leisure" that was killed with the introduction of the Industrial and Scientific Revolution (represented by the steam engine), "Old Leisure" that incorporated spinning wheels, pack horses, and slow wagons. She describes her longing for this Old Leisure through personification, contrast, diction, and gentle sarcasm.

George Eliot describes leisure as being a man—a chubby, rather laid back man. In doing this, she is representing all the people and their habits of that era into this one man. By contrasting this gentle man to the impersonal feeling of the "new leisure," George Eliot inclines the reader toward the "Old Leisure." Whereas the New Leisure is very rushed and mechanical ("prone to excursion-trains, art museums . . . scientific theorising . . ."), "Mr. Old Leisure" was relaxed, reading only one newspaper. George Eliot describes old leisure as innocent and free of leaders; had no sensational periodicals to read and fill his mind with, no corrupted politicians to listen to. He was contemplative on his own, uncontaminated by other people's ideas and theories, as new Leisure is. He was simple, not bothering to discover the mechanism of everything around him, but content with simply enjoying his surroundings. He loved nature rather than being caught up in the man made things. Here, Eliot describes nature with both temperature, scent, and view, drawing the reader into the aura of the surroundings. Old Leisure smelled the apricots, sat in the shade of orchard boughs, watched the summer pears fall. Old Leisure was carefree; he did not have to worry about goals, about being judged, or of "making the best use of his time." Instead, he could relax at home, and sleep irresponsibly. By glamourizing Old Leisure, Eliot put the New Leisure into a bad light, deeming the rush for learning and developing unnecessary and secondary to complete relaxation and enjoyment. By personifying Old Leisure as a stout gentleman, Eliot conjures an image of a jolly old man, one who is perfectly content and happy. Finally, Eliot ends the comparison by gently mocking new Leisure, requesting forgiveness for Old leisure for not going to Exeter Hall, hearing a popular preacher, or reading Tracts for the Times. In doing this, she takes one final poke at the ridiculousness of the activities New Leisure found so fulfilling.

Response to Student Essays 1 and 2

These two essays are examples of a weak answer (the first) and a good response to the question. With a below-average performance on the multiple-choice questions, a student who wrote three essays of the quality of the first paper would probably get a reported exam score of two. Assuming a good performance on the multiple-choice section, a student who wrote three essays of the quality of the second would get a final score of five, and this essay would probably get a seven on the nine-point scale used for evaluating the three essays.

Though essay 1 is a poor essay, it is, surprisingly, one of the very few that saw that the passage expresses reservations about "old Leisure.' It overstates the case and fails to see that new leisure is also criticized. Its real deficiency is in the handling of the stylistic devices. Though the first paragraph promises an account of tone, syntax, and imagery, the three paragraphs on these topics are all inadequate. The student's writing problems compound the problems in the paragraph on tone. Though the student approaches a real and important difference between the old ("lazy") and the new ("more serious"), the essay is not really sure what tone is, and it misses the nostalgic, tolerant, affectionate, and sensuous tone that is used to describe the leisure of the past.

The bad writing interferes with the paragraph on syntax. The student probably meant to say that the *sentences* on old leisure are long, not the syntax. The rest of the paragraph talks about attitude rather than syntax, and what it says is inaccurate.

The fourth paragraph uses the word "personification" but doesn't make clear whether or not the student understands exactly how the device is used. The whole essay fails to use enough specific evidence from the passage.

The final paragraph says nothing new. The slang phrase "just sat on their butts," incidentally, has nothing to do with the low scoring of the essay, and slang is a device that good writers may use. The trouble here is that the student is not a good writer and has not answered the question on the exam clearly or coherently.

You should notice that it wouldn't take much to turn this paper into a first-rate essay. Of course, the quality of the writing would have to be improved, and the evaluation of George Eliot's attitudes would have to be expanded. This done, a paragraph on tone that contrasted the lazy quiet of the old with the frantic activity of the new, followed by a paragraph on syntax that saw how short sentences like "Do not believe them" and "Even idleness is eager now" contrast with the more langorous and much longer sentences associated with old Leisure, followed by an accurate account of how the passage uses personification would make a fine response to the question.

Essay 2 is, as far as it goes, excellent. Its reading of the passage, though incomplete, is sensible, and its specific and well-supported discussions of diction, contrast, and personification are very good. There can be no doubt that this student knows just what these terms mean and how these techniques are used in George Eliot's prose. The essay does not deal with the implied criticism of old Leisure, but many papers on this topic scored well without seeing the most subtle aspect of the passage. Readers reward student essays for what they do well. They don't expect perfection on an essay that a student must plan and write in only forty minutes.

Student Essay 3

In this passage, Eliot presents a conception of leisure in which he begins by comparing the absence of leisure to the absence of the Old West. The author has a very pessimistic view towards today's leisure, or what people consider to be leisurable. The present form of leisure is only discussed in the first eleven lines of this passage, and the good, old leisure is discussed in the rest.

In describing "Old Leisure," the author of this passage describes the typical man who enjoys this leisure. The author obviously believes that "ignorance is bliss" by the way that he optimistically describes the man's actions and blinded knowledge.

In describing the leisure of the present time, at the beginning of the passage, the language is very straightforward and it is very obvious that the author does not believe that it is true leisure. The old leisure is not described as straightforward, but it is more in-depth and descriptive.

In the last sentence of the passage, the author defends old leisure from those who believe that somehow a steam-engine is leisurable.

Student Essay 4

George Eliot longs for a time long gone. She laments the replacement of "old Leisure" by the leisure of her own society. Eliot feels that it has lost feeling, lost personality. She feels that leisure has become a representation of the masses rather that the individualistic whims of the few.

Eliot refers to "Old Leisure" as being "innocent" and "free . . . of sensations." She presents him as "contemplative" and perceptive, yet simple. He is a man "undiseased by hypothesis, happy in his inability to know . . . things." She admires this view of "Old Leisure" and sees it as a symbol of individual freedom. She sees him "living . . . in the country." He is a man who saunters rather than walks, who scents the apricots rather than smells them. "Old Leisure" has "an easy, jolly conscience," characteristic of the free and independent.

Eliot despises the new leisure. It is a symbol of rush, hustle and bustle, impersonality. She immediately relates it to "the steam engine" which serves "mankind," not individual men. She sees the leisure of her time as a tool of idleness and primitive amusement, referring to "excursion-trains," "exciting novels" and "cursory peeps through microscopes."

Eliot conveys her views by personifying "Old Leisure." She presents him as the respectful, humble gentleman that every girl wants to bring home to the parents. She uses exalting phrases, giving her gentleman a special grandeur and reverence. She states that he is "rather stout" and "of excellent digestion." She has created the perfect man: one who is free of problems from "doubts and qualms and lofty aspirations."

Eliot also makes a statement by her omission of new leisure as a person. She feels that new leisure is impersonal and unfeeling, therefore undeserving of a personality. She describes it very briefly, condensing her phrases in the exact same way that new leisure has condensed the individual wants of mankind.

Eliot leaves the reader with no doubt about her feelings for old and new Leisure. Her love for the former and hatred of the latter are convincingly presented. The contrast between her perfect gentleman and the non-person plainly reveals her heart.

Response to Student Essays 3 and 4

This pair of essays also illustrates the lower and the upper half of the grading scale. The surprising reference in the first sentence of essay 3 to the Old West arises, I suppose, from the student's association of spinning wheels and slow wagons (covered, I suspect) with the American past. Be sure to look carefully at the context and the details of the passage. The old Leisure here must have been some time before the 1830's. Another lesson is to beware of thinking that everything is about the United States. The details of this passage such as "guineas" or "Exeter Hall" place it in England.

The essay does suggest an awareness of a preference for the old Leisure but does not explain clearly or with support from the passage George Eliot's attitude. It is even weaker on technique. A phrase like "the language is very straightforward" or "in-depth" and an adjective like "descriptive" are useless. In fact, the language is not at all straightforward, and any adjective can be called "descriptive." You must be ready to talk about specific stylistic devices, even when the question does not enumerate specific ones.

Essay 4 does a decent job on the question without reaching the level of essay 2. The second paragraph illustrates the use of diction, and the fourth handles personification, but the case for old Leisure ("the perfect man") and the case against the new leisure ("despises") are both overstated. The essay would probably get a six score on the nine-point scale, an upper half paper but not an upper quarter.

Prose Passage 2

Let's look at one more example of a question on a prose passage. This passage on the escaped slave Frederick Douglass's response to his arrival in the North appeared on the English language AP exam, but it could just as easily have been used on the literature exam.

The wretchedness of slavery, and the blessedness of freedom, were perpetually before me. It was life and death with me. But I remained firm, and according to my solution, on the third day of September, 1838, I left my chains, and
(5) succeeded in reaching New York without the slightest interruption of any kind. How I did so—what means I adopted,—what direction I travelled, and by what mode of conveyance,—I must leave unexplained, for the reasons before mentioned.
(10) I have been frequently asked how I felt when I found myself in a free State. I have never been able to answer the question with any satisfaction to myself. It was a moment of the highest excitement I ever experienced. I suppose I felt as one may imagine the unarmed mariner to feel when he is
(15) rescued by a friendly man-of-war from the pursuit of a pirate. In writing to a dear friend, immediately after my arrival at New York, I said I felt like one who had escaped a den of hungry lions. This state of mind, however, very soon subsided; and I was again seized with a feeling of great
(20) insecurity and loneliness. I was yet liable to be taken back, and subjected to all the tortures of slavery. This in itself was enough to damp the ardor of my enthusiasm. But the loneliness overcame me. There I was in the midst of thousands, and yet a perfect stranger; without home and
(25) without friends, in the midst of thousands of my own brethren—children of a common Father, and yet I dared not to unfold to any one of them my sad condition. I was afraid to speak to any one for fear of speaking to the wrong one, and thereby falling into the hands of money-loving
(30) kidnappers, whose business it was to lie in wait for the panting fugitive, as the ferocious beasts of the forest lie in wait for their prey. The motto which I adopted when I started from slavery was this—"Trust no man!" I saw in every white man an enemy and in almost every colored man

(35) cause for distrust. It was a most painful situation; and, to
understand it, one must needs experience it, or imagine
himself in similar circumstances. Let him be a fugitive slave
in a strange land—a land given up to be the hunting-ground
for slave-holders—whose inhabitants are legalized kidnap-
(40) pers—where he is every moment subjected to the terrible
liability of being seized upon by his fellow-men, as the
hideous crocodile seizes upon his prey!—I say, let him place
himself in my situation—without home or friends—without
money or credit—wanting shelter, and no one to give
(45) it—wanting bread, and no money to buy it,—and at the
same time let him feel that he is pursued by merciless
men-hunters, and in total darkness as to what to do, where
to go, or where to stay,—perfectly helpless both as to the
means of defense and means of escape,—in the midst of
(50) plenty, yet suffering the terrible gnawings of hunger,—in the
midst of houses, yet having no home,—among fellow-men,
yet feeling as if in the midst of wild beasts, whose greediness
to swallow up the trembling and half-famished fugitive is
only equalled by that with which the monsters of the deep
(55) swallow up the helpless fish upon which they subsist,—I say,
let him be placed in this most trying situation,—the situation in which I was placed,—then and not till then, will he
fully appreciate the hardships of, and know how to sympathize with, the toil-worn and whip-scarred slave.

—Frederick Douglass—

Comments on Prose Passage 2

Students were asked to discuss Douglass's response to finding
himself in a free state. They were also required to write about the
language, especially the figurative language and the syntax, of the
passage that reveals Douglass's feelings.

An essay that defines Douglass's states of mind (excitement,
relief, joy at first but followed by fear, insecurity, loneliness,
suspicion) and talks only about the figures of speech and the syntax
would fulfill the requirements of the question. Though the techniques for discussion are specified here (figures of speech and
syntax), the literature exam has shown no preference for the specific

or the nonspecific requirement. Often, an exam with a prose and poetry question that call for a discussion of style specifies the devices on one question and allows students to choose their own on the other.

The figures of speech in the passage are easy to identify, since most of them are similes rather than metaphors. They include the following:

1. Douglass feels like the unarmed sailor rescued from pirates.
2. Douglass feels like a man who has escaped a lion's den.
3. Kidnappers are like ferocious beasts waiting to capture their prey (the fugitive slave).
4. The fugitive slave may be seized like the prey of a crocodile.
5. Douglass feels as if he were surrounded by wild beasts.
6. The enemies are as greedy as monsters of the deep devouring helpless fish (the fugitive slaves).

The principle of organization here is clear at once; five of the six similes liken the slave-holders or their allies to savage beasts and the fugitive slave to the sought-after victim of their powerful jaws.

Many students, expecting a slave's prose style to be simple and direct, were taken by surprise by Douglass's ornate syntax. Regardless of the evidence on the page, a number of students praised Douglass's prose as "simple and sincere." It may be sincere, but simple it isn't. It has far more in common with the writing of Dr. Johnson, or Winston Churchill, or Martin Luther King, Jr., than with the naive colloquialism of Sojourner Truth.

In discussing the syntax of the passage, the essays could deal with the interplay of long and short sentences or the array of specific contrasts ("wretchedness of slavery," "blessedness of freedom"; "life and death"; "plenty . . . hunger"; "houses . . . no home") or the series of parallel phrases and clauses ("in the midst of" repeated five times in the second paragraph or "let him" repeated four times). Let anyone who imagines this prose to be artless read aloud the blockbuster last sentence, two hundred and twenty-five words long.

Student Essay 1

In the old days of slavery, there were many slaves who rebelled and obtained their freedom. Once free, the ex-slaves were thrust into a terrifying, new environment. Such was the case with Fredrick Douglass.

In his essay, Fredrick Douglass uses a large vocabulary to create a concise essay. This is unusual for a black in the 1800's. Douglass' education despite his difficult background shows his determination to become free. Douglass uses many metaphor and figures of speech to show the reader his strong feeling toward the people in his new "free" environment. Phrases such as "Den of hungry lion," "ferocious beasts . . . lie in wait for their prey," and "legalized kidnappers" show his hatred and distrust of whites. Douglas came out of the evil of slavery into a world of poverty and hardship. The fact that he survived with no home, no money, no food, and no friends shows the reader his adaptability and courage.

"Trust no man!" This was the phrase that Douglas lived by for many years. He could not trust the whites. If he were to tell his sorrowful story to a slave-hunter, he would be subject to a "legalized" kidnapping, and all his pains and sacrifices would have been for nothing. This mistrust and hatred of whites lead to a mistrust of blacks, who could have been in league with the whites in exchange for money. Douglas lived a life filled with paranoia, always fearing that he would be sent back to be a slave once again. Douglas was not relieved of this terrifying way of life until the outbreak of the civil war, and the passing of the 16th Amendment to the Constitution, which forever abolished slavery.

Fredrick Douglas set a great example for generations of blacks, but he himself led a painful, tortured life.

Student Essay 2

What is more freedom? . . . To be enslaved on a Master's land as property toiling in the sun or to be enslaved in the horrid reality of loneliness and inexperience in a cruel world? Frederick Douglas represents all runaway slaves, the unfortunate souls who struggled all their lives to escape slavery only to find later that freedom was just as bad. Douglas effectively conveys his disturbed state of mind after escaping slavery in this passage by using good syntax and diction and several figures of speech.

Syntax is effectively used throughout the passage. Douglas arranges the sentences in such a way as to impact the reader fully. In many instances, long sentences are followed by terse sentences to achieve a dramatic essence. "This in itself . . . of my enthusiasm" is suddenly followed by "But the loneliness overcame me." Parallelisms in sentence structure are also shown in the passage. "let him be a fugitive slave . . . upon his prey!" The parallelisms show the importance of each point Douglas makes because each point adds to his uneasiness and anger. As he continues explaining why freedom was so wretched, he again uses parallelisms to describe point by point the pain and struggling he dealt with. "—without home or friends—without money or credit—wanting shelter . . ."

The irony Douglas portrays in this passage is obvious. He describes escaping slavery as "escaping a den of hungry lions" and that "it was a moment of the highest excitement." Immediately following these statements, Douglas realizes being free meant living in fear of "money-loving kidnappers," no home, food, or money. He describes this condition as "ferocious beasts of the forest lie in wait for their prey." This figure of speech is much more vivid than his analogy of escaping slavery. Taking this into consideration, we realize that these dire conditions are not exactly ironic because it is so common to any "whip-scarred fugitive slave."

Douglas succeeds in convincing the reader how loneliness surpasses almost all hardships. The diction is well-chosen. The adjectives he chooses causes the reader to sympathize deeply with his pain. ". . . in the midst of plenty, yet suffering the terrible gnawings of hunger." "The motto . . . 'TRUST NO MAN' I saw in every white man an enemy." The hatred in his tone and the frustration is immediately relevant in Douglas's voice.

Douglas uses a final figure of speech ". . . half-famished fugitive is only equalled by that with which the monsters of the deep swallow up the helpless fish upon which they subsist . . ." It is here that Douglas manifests a deep truth to all fugitives . . . the hopelessness of inevitably being devoured by inexperience and prejudice.

As Douglas states in his first paragraph, "I left my chains" when referring to his escape from slavery, he only escaped to new territory still bounded by the wretchedness of reality.

Response to Student Essays 1 and 2

Essay 1 as a generalized response to the Douglass passage is not bad, but as a response to the question it exemplifies a very common and mortal mistake. It simply paraphrases the passage without addressing the tasks the question sets. It sees one of Douglass's states of mind, and it alludes to two similes of the passage, but it is too intent on summarizing the content of the passage to answer the question. On a nine-point scale, this essay would score no higher than a three.

One the other hand, essay 2 is excellent. It isn't without minor flaws, but the nines on a nine-point scale aren't flawless. They are simply the best answers to the question compared to the other essays written in that year. The second paragraph handles several aspects of the syntax with accuracy and precision. The third paragraph defines clearly Douglass's two states of mind, while the third and fifth paragraphs discuss the figures of speech. In addition, the student deals with the irony and the diction of the passage. The student's writing throughout is controlled and effective.

THE POETRY QUESTION

The AP poetry essay and the essay on prose are similar. There's no reason for any student to think he or she can do one but not the other. If you can read the prose passage well, you can read the poem well too. And vice versa.

Of course, there are some differences. The poem has fewer words. It is probably more dense. It probably uses more figurative language. Its rhythm and other effects of sound are probably more important. It's likely to be more private, more interior, more personal than the prose passage.

Determining the Task on Poetry Questions

There is one kind of question about a poem that appears occasionally that is unlikely to be used with a prose passage. The student is asked to discuss how one part of a poem is related to another part. For example, the question may require an explanation of how the first four stanzas of a poem prepare, or do not prepare, the reader for the attitudes expressed in the fifth stanza. Or a student may have to contrast the first half and last half of a poem or relate the images of one section to the images of another section.

But most of the poetry questions resemble the prose questions. There is, in fact, an archetype, a paradigm, a mother of all AP prose and poetry questions. This is it:

Read the following (prose passage or poem) carefully. Then write an essay in which you discuss the *author's* (or the speaker's, or x's, or x's and y's) *attitude(s)* toward a (or a and b) and the *devices* the author uses to convey this (these) view(s).

The question has two parts. The first calls for a reading of meaning, an interpretation of what the passage conveys. The question may ask for the *attitude,* or *views,* or *response,* or *feelings* of the *author,* or the *speaker,* or a *character,* or *two characters* who appear in the poem or the passage.

The second part of the question is about style. It calls for a discussion of *devices,* or *literary devices,* or *techniques,* or *language* or *resources of language,* or *stylistic devices,* or *style.* Half of the time the devices will be unspecified. Half of the time the question will contain a list of two or more. The most commonly specified techniques are diction, imagery, figurative language, choice of details, tone, and syntax. Less often, the list may include the following: organization, devices of sound, allusion, and point of view.

Look for a form of this question. Remember, it may ask for one or more attitudes or states of mind. Be sure to deal with more than one technique. If the question reads, "such as diction, imagery, tone, and syntax," you could safely skip one of the four, but if the question says, "discuss diction, imagery, tone, and syntax," deal with all four.

Before beginning to write your essay on the poem, you should go through the same analytical processes that you used on the poetry in the multiple-choice section of the exam. And you must be sure you've defined clearly all of the parts that must be included in your essay.

Practice defining the tasks by using the three following poetry questions:

1. Both of the following short poems are sonnets spoken by a man to the woman he loves. Write a well-organized essay about their similarities and differences. Deal with both theme and style.

2. Read the following poem carefully, and write an essay in which you discuss how the author's diction and syntax reveal his attitudes toward the city and the country in time of war.

3. Read the following poem carefully. Write a well-organized essay in which you discuss how the imagery of the last three stanzas is related to and different from the imagery of the first three stanzas. Explain how this difference determines the tone and meaning of the poem as a whole.

Comments on the Poetry Question Tasks

1. If you highlight, you should hit the words "similarities," "differences," "theme," and "style." What you have is four tasks: similarities of theme, similarities of style, differences of theme, and differences of style. The question allows you to choose what

devices of style you want to discuss. Good essays talk about several, such as diction, figurative language, and if relevant, another. With questions like this, you can skip the areas where you feel insecure (syntax or metrics, perhaps?), but if you're a whiz with metrics, you could show your knowledge in your section on style.

2. Notice that "attitudes" here is a plural, though even if it were a singular, the question might still require more than one (his attitude to the city and his attitude to the country). And remember, this attitude may be complex (for example, he likes the friendliness of the country but objects to its excessive curiosity). Here you have no choice in stylistic devices; you must write on diction, and you must write on syntax. There are four main tasks then: diction and city, syntax and city, diction and country, and syntax and country. This question is an example of the archetypal AP question.

3. To explain how the images of the first three stanzas are like and unlike those of the last three, you must first understand what the images are (the literal sensory objects as well as the figures of speech such as simile or metaphor that evoke sensations). Then you must determine how the images of the beginning of the poem are (1) like and (2) unlike those of the end. Having done this (with specific examples, of course), you can go on to explain how the differences in imagery determine the (3) tone (which you must define, probably in several words, not just one). Finally, you must define (4) a meaning or several meanings of the poem as a whole (that life is transient, that the imagination consoles us for the loss of loved ones, or some such notions) and relate what you've said about the differences in imagery to this meaning. Fortunately, a question with as many demands as this one wouldn't be used on the exam. A real exam would be more likely to ask only how the imagery of the last three stanzas is related to and different from that of the first three. Or it might ask only how the difference in the images at the beginning and end of the poem determine its tone and meaning.

EXAMPLES OF POETRY SELECTIONS AND STUDENT ESSAYS

Most of the poetry questions on the exam have used complete poems, usually lyrics of fourteen to fifty lines. But a few questions have been based on selections from longer poems such as Pope's "Moral Essays" or Wordsworth's "The Prelude." The poem used in 1990 was an excerpt from Shakespeare's *Henry IV, Part II.* This play was chosen because it's almost never taught in the high schools. The examiners are at pains to select poetry that is like the poetry taught in AP classes but that is not likely to have been used in the classroom.

Poetry Selection 1

How many thousand of my poorest subjects
Are at this hour asleep! O sleep! O gentle sleep!
Nature's soft nurse, how have I frighted thee,
That thou no more wilt weigh my eyelids down,
(5) And steep my senses in forgetfulness?
Why rather, sleep, liest thou in smoky cribs,
Upon uneasy pallets stretching thee,
And hush'd with buzzing night-flies to thy slumber,
Than in the perfum'd chambers of the great,
(10) Under the canopies of costly state,
And lull'd with sound of sweetest melody?
O thou dull god, why liest thou with the vile
In loathsome beds, and leav'st the kingly couch
A watch-case or a common 'larum-bell?
(15) Wilt thou upon the high and giddy mast
Seal up the ship-boy's eyes, and rock his brains
In cradle of the rude imperious surge,
And in the visitation of the winds,
Who take the ruffian billows by the top,

(20) Curling their monstrous heads and hanging them
      With deaf'ning clamour in the slippery clouds,
      That with the hurly death itself awakes?
      Canst thou, O partial sleep, give thy repose
      To the wet sea-boy in an hour so rude,
(25) And in the calmest and most stillest night,
      With all appliances and means to boot,
      Deny it to a King? Then, happy low, lie down!
      Uneasy lies the head that wears a crown.

Comments on Poetry Selection 1

Students were asked to paraphrase the passage and to discuss how the feelings of the king are reflected in his word choice, his images, and his syntax.

Before you look at some exam answers, you can begin to analyze this passage. The speaker is King Henry and the piece is a soliloquy, that is, a speech in which a character voices his or her thoughts while alone (*solus* = alone, and *loqui* = to speak). The first lines of the passage seem to be self-addressed, but in line 2 ("O sleep!"), he speaks directly to a personified sleep and continues to do so for most of the passage. The second half of the next-to-last line (line 27) is addressed to the "happy low," and the final line may also be spoken to these poorest subjects, or like the first line of the speech, it may be self-addressed.

The twenty-eight lines of the speech are composed of opening and closing assertions of one and a half lines and twenty-five lines made up of a series of questions to the sleep that eludes the king. The basic organizing method of the passage is the contrast of the low born, who are able to sleep despite their noisy and uncomfortable surroundings, with the king, sleepless amid trappings that would seem to be the most conducive to sleep. The thesis of the speech is the commonplace that high position brings with it responsibilities and disadvantages (such as sleeplessness) that the humble need not endure.

Much of the notable diction in the passage supports the contrast of the "happy low" and the restless king. The "poorest" subjects must suffer "smoky cribs," "uneasy pallets," "buzzing night-flies," and "loathsome beds," while the king lies in a "perfum'd" chamber, under "canopies of costly state," "lull'd" with sweet melodies. The choice of words to describe sleep is also important, as it reflects the changes of strategy of the king. At first, sleep is "gentle" and "soft," but when flattery doesn't work, the king insults the god as "dull," punning on its meanings of slow or lacking spirit and its meaning of stupid.

A wise student, baffled by the difficult comparison of the kingly couch to a "watch-case," would simply leave it out and deal with the other images in the passage. The critics have not satisfactorily explained the figure (they suggest that the watch-case is a sentry box or that, if the bed is the watch-case, the king would be the workings of a watch, which are constantly in motion). In the reading of this essay, any reasonable interpretation of this phrase was treated tolerantly. The most important comparison is the extended image of the sea-boy in what might well be called an epic metaphor, since the figure moves from the sea-boy able to sleep high on the mast in a tempest at sea to the storm itself with the personifications of the surge, winds, and waves whose hair the winds curl, hurling the waves to the clouds with a tumult to awaken the dead.

As usual, syntax was the major problem for the students answering the question. Since grading is determined by comparing one paper with the others, students who could deal with syntax in even the most perfunctory way got some credit. Good students saw the balance in the use of exclamations, then questions, then exclamations, or the breathless piling up of clauses in the sea-boy lines, or the careful balance of opposites in lines 6–8 ("smoky cribs," "uneasy pallets," "buzzing night-flies") versus lines 9–11 ("perfum'd chambers," "canopies of costly state," "sweetest melody").

An unusual aspect of this question is its calling first for a brief summary of the king's thoughts. This task was assigned to help rather than trip up the exam-takers. Aware of the fact that a poetry question based upon a text written before the nineteenth century had not appeared on the exam for many years, the examiners wanted to make sure that the students had worked through the passage carefully and understood its argument before they began to deal with the more challenging topics of its diction, imagery, and syntax. A careful summary of the content of the passage, it was hoped, would lead the student to an understanding of the king's state of mind.

Predictably, on this point, some students were eager to find a single answer, and they failed to see how the tone of the passage shifts from the quiet, cajoling beginning to the annoyance of the middle section to the excitement of the sea-boy figure to the rueful acceptance of the last lines. The techniques that must be discussed were specified in this question, but many papers failed to deal adequately with syntax. So long as students continue to omit or deal weakly with questions about syntax, questions about syntax will continue to appear on the exam.

Here are some examples of high school seniors' responses to this question.

Student Essay 1

In King Henry's lamenting soliloquy, he pleadingly chastises "partial sleep" for failing to "weigh" his "eyelids down." His desperate desire for sleep is conveyed in Shakespeare's choice of words, imagery and rhythmic construction.

In the passage's diction, the beauty and comforts of sleep are exemplified. It is made so appealing that we can understand the King's sorrow for lack of it. Shakespeare chooses soft, soothing words, like "smoky," "sweetest," "dull," and "rock." They reflect the quiet rest that the King desires.

The images that Shakespeare uses also reflect the desirable tranquility of sleep. He describes the "buzzing night flies" in line 8 and the rocking of the stormy sea in line 16. These are relaxing sounds and sensations that might induce slumber. The King, however, is deprived of such slumber, and his personification of sleep, as he questions it, is conveyed in such images as "seal up the ship-boy's eyes" and "nature's soft nurse." He makes sleep seem like a living thing, and therefore justifies his anger at its evasiveness.

Along with diction and imagery, structure plays an important part in conveying the King's desperation. The passage's rhythmic feel contributes to the lulling effect of sleep. It soothes and relaxes, and once more allows us to see its desirability for King Henry. Such a smooth and rhythmic flow could probably not be accomplished, were the passage not in verse form.

Thus Shakespeare's methods of diction, imagery, and structure all work together to create the soothing effects of sleep, and help us share in the King's anger at its unwillingness to find him.

Student Essay 2

Sleep, like other forces of nature, does not scurry obediently to satisfy the whims of man; it knows no law but that of its own, and the hand that holds the golden spectre is as equal in its eyes as the hand of one who holds a ragged fishing net—unfortunately for men such as King Henry, some have not yet learned the impartiality of sleep's judgement, and Henry's elevated status above his subjects does little to prevent his begrudging of that force of nature.

In the first portion of his soliloquy, the King seems to be imploring (something, I would venture to say, he is not used to in the least—nor does he like it) to the indifferent deity for her favor. The diction here is as close to humble as the proud King can stand—"O sleep! O gentle sleep!" . . . but even in his extremities of homage, Henry still manages to toss in a little reminder of his arrogance: He asked sleep, ". . . how have I frighted thee?" Oh, this is indeed noble of him—so gentle, so considerate, so . . . condescending of him to say such a thing? In asking sleep, "nature's soft nurse," whether he, a king and of royal blood but a mortal man nonetheless, had frightened her away, Henry reveals the pomposity and pride that is, doubtless, unavoidable when one ascends the throne and becomes absolute monarch—another added bonus to the crown is the foolishness that stems from being so powerful (among men!).

He talks of sleep in a way that invokes an image of a mother bending to kiss her child on the cheek; and this flighty and desirable kiss "weigh(s) (the) eyelids down, and steep(s)...senses in forgetfulness." The imagery Henry has drawn makes the state of sleep all the more seductive and wonderful . . . and it is this same imagery that makes his inability to sleep all the more tortuous and excruciating.

Following this subtly hidden invocation of sleep, Henry then proceeds to berate sleep for avoiding him and visiting, in his stead, his lowly subjects in their miserable hovels and parasite-infested dwellings. "Why rather, sleep, liest thou in smoky cribs . . . than in perfumed chambers of the great . . . and lull'd with sound of sweetest melody." ("What is the reason for your visitation upon the wretched peasantry and their stinking "uneasy pallets" when you could be frolicking in my house—perfumed, immaculate, richly adorned and beautiful?") Here then is the most blatant of the King's show of arrogance and annoyance—he's very put off by the fact that sleep chooses to habit the houses of his subjects and skip over his own dwelling: inconceivable!

After more embellishing on the subject (Henry complains about the ship-boy—even the ship-boy can sleep!) the King finally heaves a colossal sigh and bows his head in resignation; he has finally come to the realization that he is, in some ways better off than his subjects, but he also has abilities that weigh him down further than others. He sadly says, "Then, happy low, lie down! Uneasy lies the head that wears the crown." In spite of all his arrogance and presumptuousness we should pity Henry. But he should be glad: throughout the play, we notice three major tones—first, his imploring but vastly disguised pride, then his unveiled arrogance in full glory, then finally, resignation and sadness. Maybe King Henry has been enlightened by the whole wretched affair—after all, he's learned that even kings can be insomniacs.

Response to Student Essays 1 and 2

Essay 1 is not a good essay, but it is useful to illustrate a common mistake. The second paragraph discusses the diction of the passage and quite rightly specifically cites words from the speech ("smoky," "sweetest," "dull," and "rock") that "reflect the quiet rest" that Henry longs for. The references to specific words is estimable, but you must see the words in their context in the passage, not in isolation. Why "smoky" should be "soothing" is hard to understand; the "smoky cribs" here are huts with no ventilation for their fires and not at all something "quiet" or "soothing." As it used in line 12, "dull" means stupid, while the verb "rock" refers not to a baby's cradle but to the motion of the sea-boy, high on the "giddy mast" in a storm. Three of the four words are wholly inappropriate choices. Similarly the "buzzing night-flies" and "rocking" of the ship in the storm are not images of "desirable tranquility" or relaxing sounds that might induce slumber, as anyone who has been kept awake by a pesky mosquito can attest.

It's fine to talk about the rhythm of a poem, but you must do so much more specifically and accurately than the fourth paragraph here. Like Henry's mood, the rhythm of the passage changes. Lines 19–22 describing the sea in a storm cannot be called "lulling." They do not "soothe and relax." This essay does not say nearly enough about the king's state of mind. What it says about diction and imagery is largely untrue, and it never mentions syntax at all.

Essay 2, on the other hand, though it fails to deal with syntax, does a good job on the king's changes of mood. It handles diction well but is thin on the imagery of the passage. It shows that a competent essay can be written without mentioning the terms the question had called for. But this student, who clearly understands the speech, would probably have scored better if he or she had referred to diction, citing the examples used here, and to imagery, citing some other examples, and to syntax. The essay should remind you that you can't deal too exclusively with only one part of the question.

Student Essay 3

Henry is a king. He is a king who cannot sleep. He believes it is his divine right yet sleep will not visit him and he resents it. The protagonist of Shakespeare's Henry IV Part, II, the restless king cannot understand this denial.

King Henry pleads for sleep to come. He coaxes it, gently nudges it, then begs it. He tries to reason with sleep, asking "how have I frighted thee, that thou no more wilt . . . steep my senses in forgetfulness?" The entire speech is a plea to a personified sleep. The King knows that thousands of his subjects have been visited, yet he has not.

Henry feels that royalty is special. He believes that it deserves special privileges. He asked why sleep will not come to "the perfumed chambers of the great"? This haughty old man chastises sleep for granting "the wet sea-boy" repose yet denying "it to a King." He feels outraged by this blatant irreverence.

To convey Henry's feeling of bitterness and jealousy, Shakespeare uses a consistent imagery. The reader is bombarded with pictures of the lowly and destitute in simple fulfillment. These are contrasted to a lonely and restless king unaccustomed to such discomforts.

Henry refers to "smoky cribs," "uneasy pallets," and "buzzing night-flies." He compares these to his "canopies of costly state . . . lull'd with sound of sweetest melody." He derides "the vile in loathsome beds" while praising "the kingly couch."

Shakespeare gives an effective personification to sleep. He creates a spirited nymph who delights in toying with the great king. The king tries to persuade her to help, gently calling out to "Nature's soft nurse." When he is refused, his anger flares and he slanders "O thou dull god, why liest thou with the vile."

Shakespeare also uses a consistent diction in this passage. When Henry describes his subjects his spite and jealousy are evident. He uses hateful and hurtful phrases. He refers to "poorest subjects," "smoky cribs," "uneasy pallets," "buzzing flies" and even the ship's "ruffian billows." When the King refers to his trappings he uses positive and exalting phrases. He praises his "perfumed chambers," "canopies of costly state," and "sweetest melody." He mentions, "the kingly couch" and "the calmest and most stillest night" which exists in his abode.

King Henry is a man who feels high rights have been stolen from him. His bitterness and resentment are convincingly portrayed through the language of his speech.

Response to Student Essay 3

Essay 3 is better than essay 2, though it also has no discussion of syntax. But its answers to the questions about Henry's state of mind, about the diction, and about the imagery are accurate and detailed. In the sixth paragraph, the essay refers to a personification of sleep as "nymph," though this figure does not appear in the passage. It goes on to quote "Nature's soft nurse" and "thou dull god." The unnecessary remarks on the nymph would not affect the scoring of this paper. The rest of the paragraph makes it clear that the student does see the personifications accurately, and the readers of the exams are trained to overlook trivial errors and to reward students for what they do well. The flaw in this essay is its failure to discuss the syntax of the speech, and this omission would probably cost the writer two points on the nine-point grading scale.

Poetry Selection 2

Let's look at another poem, a lyric this time, written by Emily Dickinson. This poem was used on the exam about twenty-five years ago when the format of the exam was different. An essay question on this poem today would read:

> Read the following poem by Emily Dickinson carefully. Then write a well-organized essay in which you briefly summarize its content and discuss how the diction and imagery reveal the speaker's attitude toward religious belief.

I never lost as much but twice,
And that was in the sod;
Twice have I stood a beggar
Before the door of God!

(5) Angels twice descending
Reimbursed my store.
Burglar, banker, father!
I am poor once more!

Comments on Poetry Selection 2

The summary task is appropriate here, because the second line of the first stanza is crucial, but it is not easy to say just what it means. And because the poem is so short, the task doesn't take too much time. The first stanza tells of a loss, equaled only by two such losses in the past. Line 2 is problematic because it is so hard to determine the antecedent of "that." The line probably refers to death and burial as the two earlier losses, and you can infer that the occasion of this poem is the death of a third loved one. The second stanza is a cry for comfort, for reconcilement to the loss as the speaker, through divine aid, had been able to come to terms with the two previous deaths.

The diction and images of the first six lines of the poem present the speaker, who in these lines appears to be speaking to herself (let us assume a female speaker) or to an unspecified audience as a "beggar" at the door of God. The petitions of the beggar have been answered on both of the earlier occasions. The figures here and the diction are financial: "lost" (line 1), "beggar" (line 3), "Reimbursed" (line 6; the literal meaning of the verb is to pay back, and its root is the word for "purse"), and "store" (line 6; a supply, reserve, or stock). The attitude toward religious belief, to this point, is that of the grateful suppliant whose prayers have been answered and whom the angels have comforted. Had the poem ended at line 6, it would be a conventional assertion of the restoring powers of prayers using, as often in the Bible, the language of monetary profit and loss.

The extraordinary line of the poem, a line that it is impossible to imagine written by anyone but Emily Dickinson, is line 7: "Burglar, banker, father!" By calling God a burglar, the speaker reveals her blame of Him for her losses. The Lord giveth, and the Lord taketh away. But if God is a thief, He is also a banker able to lend as well as to call in loans. And finally, in a simple, moving statement of her dependence, the speaker calls Him "father." Only this banker father can restore the pauper of the last line to solvency.

THE OPEN QUESTION

If there can be such a thing as a favorite among exam questions, the third question in the essay section, the open question that allows students to select what work they write about, is certainly the choice among AP students and teachers. Many nationally administered tests on literature depend upon a specifically assigned list of works from which the examination questions will be selected. This is the method most used in Europe, and some of the AP exams in foreign languages also use the "set texts" system. Almost every year someone suggests that the AP literature exam adopt this method and assign four or five works upon which one or more exam questions can be based. The development committee has always resisted this proposal. One of the strengths of the AP literature course is its variety. Many of the best teachers agree to teach AP because it gives them the freedom to choose the works the class will study and allows them to teach works that would not be part of the standard high school curriculum. A list of set texts, the committee fears, would take away this freedom and might lead to too great an emphasis on the exam itself rather than on the skills of reading and writing that the exam in its present form tests.

When the examiners choose an open question for the exam, they are looking for one that will allow the student to select from the widest possible choice of works and at the same time discriminate among the well trained and the unprepared. Some questions work much better than others. The 1990 question, for example, on the conflict of a child and parents allowed students to write about an extremely wide range of works from *Antigone* to the present day. On the other hand, the 1985 question calling for a discussion of a work that produced both "pleasure and disquietude" in the reader resulted in essays that were almost all about twentieth-century works, especially works by the novelists and playwrights of the period after World War II. Similarly, the 1989 question on "distortion" produced interesting essays, but almost all of them were on works by modern authors.

The last thing the examiners want to happen is a student's turning to the open question and realizing that he or she doesn't know any work that suits this question. If this happens, both the student and the exam have failed. You must prepare several works, of several genres, of several periods. But if you've done that, there's no reason in the world for you to worry about finding an exam question that you can't answer. If you're still worried about not knowing appropriate books, read over the list in the section on previous exam questions. If you don't know any of these, your worst fears are justified, but chances are you know half a dozen of them or more. If you're still nervous, read over the summary of previous open questions and think about what work and, when relevant, what character in that work you could use to answer. If after reading these questions and this list of works you still find yourself unable to find a work you know or one that could be used on these questions, your AP class is a very unusual one, and you should speak to your AP teacher about the problem.

One reason that the open question is universally preferred by students and teachers is that it's about a work the student has studied and often about a work the student enjoys and admires. The prose passage and the poem are always going to be something of a surprise, and you can never quite get rid of the fear of misreading. Another reason for the preference of the open question is, I think, the nature of the questions. The questions on passages of prose and poetry are almost always one-half to two-thirds questions about style ("literary devices," "techniques," and so on). But the open essay is much more often solely about content. Students can't be expected to write well about style without an example in front of them, and the open question can't possibly give examples from all the plays and novels that may be chosen. So the questions focus upon characterizations, theme, relations of a part to the whole, and the function of characters, events, or settings. When questions do call for literary techniques, they are likely to ask about the handling of point of view or the angle from which the story is told.

Students writing on the open question are not expected to remember every detail of plot or even every character's name. Still, the difference between a merely competent and an outstanding essay is often specificity. The student who can point to a relevant specific scene or even a specific line of dialogue has an advantage over a student who can't. There's no reason to prepare for the exam by memorizing page after page of plays or novels. Readers will often come upon, say, ten lines of Hamlet's "To be or not to be" quoted in the middle of an essay on the role of the supernatural, and the student will not have improved his or her grade. But there may be a question (the question on pleasure and disquietude, for example) where a specific and informed discussion of a speech would be very impressive.

You must have more than one string to your bow. The student who has spent weeks preparing *Othello* to the exclusion of all other works may be confronted with a question on the novel, on a work written after 1900, or on a comedy. It's much better, I think, to know five works very well than ten works vaguely. The more you know well, the better. Then you can choose among more than one suitable work, the one that fits the question ideally.

Your choice of work, character, or scene within a work is crucial. A brilliant essay on a wholly inappropriate work will not score as high as a pedestrian essay on a work that fits the question. And just because the work you write about is on the recommended list on the exam doesn't end your responsibility. You must than select the best character (Ahab or Starbuck? Heathcliff or Hindley?) or best scene, place, or whatever the question calls for you to write about. A bad choice of work or subject on the open question places an essay at an almost insurmountable disadvantage.

Determining the Task on Open Questions

Even before you select the work you'll write on, you must understand exactly what the question asks you to do. The following questions haven't appeared on the exams, but they will accustom you to the format and demands of the questions that do. Read them carefully and determine what the exact tasks are.

1. In many novels, a child plays an all-important part. Choose a novel of recognized literary merit in which a child is significant and write an essay which explains how the author presents the child's point of view and how the child's values are related to the central themes of the work as a whole. Do not merely summarize the plot.

2. The conflict between an idealistic and a pragmatic, or realistic, response to life is a recurrent theme in literature. Choose a work in which such a conflict is central. Write an essay in which you

analyze the reasons for the conflict and its effect upon one idealistic character and one representative of the realistic attitude.

3. Plays and novels frequently argue the issue of the freedom of the individual will as opposed to the controlling pressures of the environment or public world. Choose a play or novel in which this theme is prominent. Write an essay in which you discuss a character who represents this issue, analyzing the nature of the conflict, its effect upon the character, and the meaning of its resolution at the end of the work.

Comments on the Open Question Tasks

Most of the open questions deal with meaning rather than style. Most of the time, you can choose to write on either a novel or a play but not always. The first thing to be sure about is the kind of work called for. It might be just a play, just a novel, or just a tragedy. Or the question may simply say "work" and leave you free to choose an epic poem or a short story. So far, films and television plays have been forbidden, and there are no signs of this rule's being changed.

1. Right away you should notice that you must choose a novel—*Great Expectations* or *Oliver Twist* but not Joyce's "Araby" or *The Children's Hour*. Task one, how the author presents the child's point of view, may be a technical question that requires comment on subjects like who tells the story (it might be told by the child in the first person or by an adult remembering his or her childhood, as in *Great Expectations* or *Jane Eyre*) or how other characters interact with or comment on the child. It may also mean the author's attitude toward the child's position.

The second half of the sentence calls for a definition of the child's values and a definition of some of the central themes of the book before you can begin to relate the former to the latter. With most books, especially novels of the nineteenth century, the moral values of the uncorrupted child are those of novel. *A High Wind in Jamaica* by Richard Hughes would provide a unique and refreshing response to this question.

2. Here, only a "work" is specified, so you can use a novel, a play, or even a short story or a poem. The important point is that the realist-idealist conflict must be central to the work. The tasks are analyzing the reasons (note the plural) for the conflict and describing its effect on each of the two characters (*both* Antigone and Creon if you choose *Antigone*).

3. On this question, a play or a novel can be used so long as the freedom of the will versus environmental control is a prominent theme (as, for example, in Hardy). The question requires that you choose a character to represent the issue, explain the conflict and its effect upon the character, and interpret the significance of the conflict at the conclusion of the work.

You may have noticed that a number of the open questions ask you to talk about "the meaning'" "a meaning," or "the meanings" of a novel or a play. Since this task is so often a part of the open questions, you should carefully prepare for it in your last-minute studies. To define "the meaning" is a task that will reduce or demean some works. What is the meaning of *Hamlet* or *King Lear*? What is the moral of *Wuthering Heights* or *Pride and Prejudice*? It almost seems that the greater the work of art, the more impossible it becomes to reduce its meaning to a sentence or a paragraph. And conversely, the more simple and sometimes simple-minded works are easy to encapsulate in a single morally uplifting aphorism. Since the question still appears on the exam, you should prepare for it. When you've decided on the novels and plays that you might use on the open question, go over each with a mind to define just what the "meanings" you would write about are. Depending on the nature of the question, you may find that several but not all of the meanings in your list will be relevant in your essay.

EXAMPLES OF AN OPEN QUESTION AND STUDENT ESSAYS

Open Question

One of the open questions from the early 1980s asked for the discussion of a villain in a novel or a play. Students were asked to describe the villainy of the selected character and to relate this evil to meaning in the work. Suggested authors included Melville, Faulkner, Hawthorne, Fitzgerald, Dickens, Austen, Brontë, and Conrad among novelists and such playwrights as Shakespeare, Ibsen, Jonson, and Miller.

Student Essay 1

In the novel "Pride and Prejudice" the author creates Wickham to give us a villain. Wickham provides some action and conflict for an otherwise dull novel about a prim and proper life.

In the book Wickham is portrayed as the villain simply because he steals away one of the Bennet's daughter's for primarily sexual purposes. Whereas the daughter would have otherwise gotten married to a wealthy man in town somewhere, Wickham elopes with her despite his lack of money. Their romps throughout many a motel room reach epic proportions.

Wickham throws on a little spice into an otherwise actionless and rather boring novel. Wickham also serves to shake up the small town community that the Bennet's live in.

Wickham is perhaps not a villain in the true sense of the word in that he does not have harmful intentions towards the daughter it just ends up being that way because of the society they live in.

Wickham spices up the plot and makes the novel less dull as a villain.

Student Essay 2

Mr. Wickham came to town a stranger. Arriving with his best friend Mr. Bingley he was perceived as a nice, respectable young man. Mr. Wickham was a deceptive villian in Pride and Prejudice by Jane Austin. He was vital in three important aspects: to the character development of Elizabeth, to show the blindness of other characters, and to teach the lesson of looking past the outside to the real person inside.

Elizabeth was immediately taken in by Mr. Wickham. He was very charming and he used that to toy with her emotions. Carrying her along on a string, he managed to make her blind to her real feelings toward Mr. Darcy. His interference is vital in her learning. He hurts and betrays her by eloping with her younger sister. This throws her into the open arms of Darcy who she had detested. She begins to see past his seemingly rude behavior to the real loyal Darcy who had loved her all along. It took that hurtful, but neccessary blow from Wickham for her to see what was important to see in people. She learned that what may seem like a person outside may not be very good inside and that's what mattered. She learned how to swallow her prejudice and hold up her pride.

Wickham's character also showed how deceptive people could be. After everything that happened Mr. Bennett said that Wickham would always be his favorite son-in-law. He managed to fool almost everyone with his charming and cool exterior. Wickham serves as a warning that not everyone is as they seem.

This brings us to Wickham's third function. He was not what he seemed and operated strictly for his own bennifit and showed by contrast how someone percieved as the villian could turn out to be good like Mr. Darcy. People need to learn about the real inner person their dealing with before they should completely trust them.

It is because of Wickham that Elizabeth may truely be happy. In a way their flirtations and her being taken in by him could've been a blessing. His desceptions made her see how wrong she had been about people. Now that she saw past the outside mask of Darcy they have a possibility of happy future together with a more open and honest relationship. Wickham taught her what to stay away from and served as a warning.

Response to Student Essays 1 and 2

Both of these essays choose Mr. Wickham in Jane Austen's *Pride and Prejudice* as their villain. The exam question gives no definition of the word but assumes that students know that the word refers to a wicked person, a scoundrel, one who opposes the hero or heroine, or would offer their own definitions. As with all of the open questions, choosing a work and a character in the work that fits the question is the crucial first step, and the choice of Wickham is appropriate. He is, after all, a liar, a fortune-hunter, a seducer, perhaps even a blackmailer, though a charming and good-looking scoundrel.

The wise choice of Wickham is about the only point in the first essay's favor. Anyone who has read Jane Austen will be enchanted by the notion of two characters in her novels on epic "romps throughout many a motel room" a century before the automobile, let alone the motel, has been invented. The analysis of the nature of Wickham's villainy is incompetent, inaccurate, and self-contradictory, since the essay suggests that Wickham is not, after all, a villain. And though some readers may agree with the contention that Wickham's role is to liven up an otherwise dull novel, this is not the kind of answer to the question that will impress readers of the exam. Don't use your essays as a platform from which to express your views on life or literature. To denounce Jane Austen to an audience of English teachers is self-destructive behavior, but the student who imagines that praising Jane Austen's art will earn points is also mistaken. Answer the question on the exam.

Essay 2 does answer the question. It begins with an error, confusing Mr. Wickham with Mr. Darcy, who does arrive with his friend Mr. Bingley. But this is the sort of error that readers are trained to overlook. It's a minor slip of the pen like misspelling Austen or forgetting a name or place, but it doesn't mar the essay in any important way. The rest of the paper makes clear that the student knows exactly who Wickham is and why he can be called a villain.

The essay refers to more than one meaning in the novel that is revealed through Wickham. The essay does answer both parts of the question, but it also has mechanical weaknesses and a misguided third paragraph. The student takes Mr. Bennet, the ironist of the novel, seriously when he calls the villainous Wickham his favorite son-in-law. This is a different kind of error from the confusion of Wickham and Darcy in the the first paragraph of the essay, since it reveals a misunderstanding of a character, not just a lapse of memory. The good points of this essay far outnumber its weaknesses, however, and it would certainly receive a score in the upper half of the scale, probably a six or a seven.

Student Essay 3

In Pride and Prejudice by Jane Austen, the villain in the novel is the mother of the five girls. The mother is a villain because she sees love as money, and money as love. This unloving, villainous attitude comes from the fact that she married an unwealthy man and her relationship with her husband is not very loving. She sees the absence of wealth as the reason for the absence of love. She wants her daughters to have a better life than she has had and she see's that the only way they can achieve this is by marrying wealthy men—not to mention that she also believes that she will receive some of that happiness and money too. This enhances the meaning of the work because the mother wants the wealth more than the daughters do so it would be easy for them to just go along with their mother's beliefs and marry whichever rich guy that their mother sets them up with. Luckily Elizabeth is a strong-willed individual and she knows that her mother is unfeeling and villainous because she is taking advantage of other people's money. Elizabeth is interested in real love and the only wealth she is after is wealth of their heart and mind.

The mother's villainous beliefs start to break down at the end when one of her daughters marries a man with no wealth and also when she begins to realize that although two of her other daughters are marrying wealthy men. They are marrying them for their love not for their money because they are smart, and caring enough to know that love and money are two separate things.

Student Essay 4

I think that most people would say that Heathcliff is the villain of Wuthering Heights. But he is the hero, and the reader feels a sympathy with him as he grinds the "puny" Lintons because we think that they are puny. Edgar and Isabella are uninteresting people, but they aren't villains. Hindley Earnshaw is the best choice for villain in Emily Bronte's Wuthering Heights.

His first action is to refuse to give the orphan Heathcliff a place in his bedroom and then to tease and torture him until his father's death. He then makes him a stableboy and tries to prevent his associating with Cathy. Hindley's villainy can be explained as jealousy at Heathcliffs taking his place in his father's affection, but it continues after Mr. Earnshaw's death. Hindley never stops hating Heathcliff and doing all he can to injure him.

Hindley's drinking is motivated by the death of his wife. A good sign of his villainy is his indifference and cruelty to his own son, Hareton. When Heathcliff returns, Hindley is a pitiful drunk and gambler, and Heathcliff easily outwits him. In his drunkenness, Hindley almost kills his son, and he is guilty of the attempted murder of Heathcliff, which he bungles. He dies in debt and drunk at 27, leaving his son in the hands of his enemy, Heathcliff. It is hard to find anything to say in defense of Hindley's actions. He is the best example of a villain in the novel, but the novel is not really about villains versus heroes or evil versus good.

The meaning of Wuthering Heights is not moral like it is in a Dickens novel. Catherine Earnshaw's marriage to Edgar while she loves Heathcliff is the turning point, and Heathcliff explains this meaning in their scene before Catherine's death. Hindley, like Catherine, has been guilty of social ambition, and his contempt for Heathcliff is based on his belief that Heathcliff is a "gypsy," a lower order. Catherine has avoided this mistake with Heathcliff but cannot resist the attraction of the Grange, and so she makes the fatal mistake of marrying Edgar. The novel is not about a class war. It is about following one's true nature. Whatever good was in Hindley was destroyed by the arrival of Heathcliff and by the early death of his wife. Hindley's villainy throws the actions of Heathcliff into relief, for however terrible Heathcliff's actions become, they are caused by a frustrated love and desire to right what he sees as the wrongs of his childhood. Hindley doesn't have this excuse.

Response to Student Essays 3 and 4

Essay 3 selects Mrs. Bennet as the villain of *Pride and Prejudice* and gives her preference of money to love as the cause of her villainy. Mrs. Bennet is a foolish woman, a materialist, a hypochondriac, but is she a villain? She unwittingly injures her daughters' chances for a happy marriage, and she can't tell a good man from a bad (she really does like Wickham). But if a villain is wicked, evil, or unprincipled, Mrs. Bennet doesn't qualify. One is tempted to say she is too stupid to be a villain, too dim to scheme or hatch a plot. So from the start, this essay is in trouble.

A reader of this essay would begin by deploring the choice of Mrs. Bennet but then look for redeeming features. Does the essay analyze the nature of the villainy and relate it to the meaning in the work? It is true that the novel condemns marriage solely for material motives (though Charlotte Lucas's marriage is, in its way, a success), and Mrs. Bennet is all in favor of marrying money. But the essay gets little else quite right: Mrs. Bennet doesn't marry an "unwealthy man," want a "better life" for her daughters, or expect to cash in on their wealth. The attitudes of the novel toward wealth are far more hard-headed than this essay suggests. It would probably be scored a three.

Essay 4, on the other hand, would score very high. Almost all of the essays on *Wuthering Heights* used Heathcliff as villain, and while a good case can be made for his villainy, it's not an easy essay to write. This student may have thought first about using Heathcliff, seen the difficulties, and realized that as good a case can be made for Hindley Earnshaw as the villain without the problem of his being, like Heathcliff, the hero of the novel as well. The first paragraph explains this decision, and it is an original and convincing opening.

The second and third paragraphs accurately record the evidence of Hindley's villainy. That he is an ineffectual villain does not disqualify him for the title.

The fourth paragraph rightly refuses to pin "a meaning" on *Wuthering Heights* but refers to the issue of social prestige and class distinctions and to the central idea of keeping faith with one's nature and shows how Hindley's revenge differs from Heathcliff's. Notice how this student has allowed the question to organize the essay. The first paragraph is introductory. The second and third paragraphs do the first assignment ("the nature of villainy"); the final paragraph does the second task. There is no padding, no repetition. The student never loses sight of what the question has asked.

QUESTIONS ON TWO TEXTS
AND OTHER QUESTIONS

Questions on Two Texts

Every so often, the exam includes a prose or a poetry question using two texts. The prose question used passages from Ralph Ellison and Henry James in 1980 and two versions of a paragraph from Hemingway's *A Farewell to Arms* in 1985. The poetry section has included comparisons of poems on spring by Louise Gluck and William Carlos Williams, poems by Wordworth and Frost on nature, and poems by Keats and Frost on a star. Some of these questions have been more general than the questions on a single poem, calling simply for a discussion of the similarities and differences of the two poems.

A question using two prose passages still regularly appears on the AP language exam, but in the last ten years, there has been only one, a comparison of two drafts of a passage from Hemingway's *A Farewell to Arms,* on the literature test. This question was used in 1985 at a time when the prose analysis question was the same on both the language and the literature exams. There has been no question calling for a comparison of two prose passages on the literature exam since the common question was dropped in 1986, and though it remains a possibility, the comparison of two prose passages is much more likely to appear on the language test.

Questions using two poetry texts *are* likely to continue to appear on the literature exam, and you should think about a method to use in answering them. The poems these questions use are short ones, since a student is expected to read and write about two poems in the same thirty-five or forty minutes that are usually allowed for an essay on a poem. The two works must have something in common (a response to nature, a star), but as the Frost-Keats question demonstrates, the connection may be superficial. A good comparison essay can be written using the two sonnets on the sonnet by Wordsworth and Keats discussed in the section on multiple-choice questions. The two poems are short, and the subject is the same in both. The question would read like this:

The following poems by Wordsworth and Keats are about the sonnet. Read them carefully. Then write a well-organized essay in which you discuss their similarities and differences in style and meaning.

Nuns fret not at their convent's narrow room;
And hermits are contented with their cells;
And students with their pensive citadels;
Maids at the wheel, the weaver at his loom,
(5) Sit blithe and happy; bees that soar for bloom,
High as the highest Peak of Furness-fells,
Will murmur by the hour in foxglove bells:
In truth the prison, unto which we doom
Ourselves, no prison is: and hence for me,
(10) In sundry moods, 'twas pastime to be bound
Within the Sonnet's scanty plot of ground;
Pleased if some souls (for such their needs must be)
Who have felt the weight of too much liberty,
Should find brief solace there, as I have found.

—Wordsworth—

On the Sonnet

If by dull rhymes our English must be chained,
    And, like Andromeda, the Sonnet sweet
Fettered, in spite of pained loveliness;
Let us find out, if we must be constrained,
(5)   Sandals more interwoven and complete
To fit the naked foot of poesy;
Let us inspect the lyre, and weigh the stress
Of every chord, and see what may be gained
    By ear industrious, and attention meet;
(10) Misers of sound and syllable, no less
Than Midas of his coinage, let us be
    Jealous of dead leaves in the bay-wreath crown;
So, if we may not let the Muse be free.
    She will be bound with garlands of her own.

—Keats—

Before you begin to write an answer to a comparison question like this, you should quickly list as many similarities and differences of both theme and style you can. Your essay can then be based upon a selection of the most important ones. Your notes on the poems might look something like this:

	Wordsworth	Keats
speaker	poet—first person singular ("I")	poet—first person plural ("we")
audience	unspecified general audience, readers of sonnets	other poets, writers of sonnets
structural divisions	lines 1–7, 8–9, 9–14	lines 1–6, 7–9, 10–12, 13–14
rhyme scheme	abba, abba, cddccd	abc, abd, cabcdede
subject	the sonnet	the sonnet
	the restrictions that are self-chosen are liberating	the restrictions of the sonnet should be made freer, more organic
images	sonnet = small plot of earth	poetry = woman in chains
	restriction = prison	rhyme = interwoven sandals
	nuns, hermits, students as restricted by choice	poetry personified
	bees in flowers = also chosen restraint	stale verse conventions = dead leaves
		rhyme = garlands
allusions	Furness-fells (a peak in the Lake District of England)	classical references including Andromeda, Midas, the Muse
diction	contented, happy, blithe, pastime, solace	chained, fettered, pained, constrained

Using this information, your essay would probably discuss the likenesses and important differences in the poets' views of the restrictions of the sonnet rhyme scheme. Both use the sonnet to talk about the sonnet, but Wordsworth's point is that the restrictions we choose are not really restrictions but can become a pleasure, a relief from the oppression of too much freedom. Keats, on the other hand, is impatient with unnatural restriction or dead conventions and urges a natural and organic poetry. The structural divisions and the rhyme schemes are different; both reflect the ideas about freedom and restriction the two poems express.

The images of the two poems are very different. Keats relies heavily on classical allusion, not only to persons, but to classical symbols for poetry such as the lyre, garlands, or the bay-wreath crown. Wordsworth uses five human examples of self-chosen enclosure as well as one from nature (the bee) and, unlike Keats, uses paradox. The contrast in diction reflects the difference in the two poets' attitudes toward restraints. Keats suggests its harsh side ("pained"), Wordsworth its pleasures ("blithe").

Let's look at another pair of short poems, two Renaissance lyrics by Edmund Spenser and Thomas Carew (pronounced Carey).

Write a well-organized essay in which you discuss the similarities and differences in the two following poems about spring.

> Fresh spring, the herald of love's mighty king,
> In whose cote-armor[1] richly are displayed
> All sorts of flowers the which on earth do spring
> In goodly colors gloriously arrayed,
> (5) Go to my love, where she is careless laid,
> Yet in her winter's bower not well-awake:
> Tell her the joyous time will not be stayed
> Unless she do him by the forelock take.
> Bid her therefore herself soon ready make
> (10) To wait on Love amongst his lovely crew:
> Where every one that misseth then her make[2]
> Shall be by him amerced[3] with penance due.
> Make haste therefore, sweet love, whilst it is prime,
> For none can call again the passed time.

—Edmund Spenser—

[1] garment   [2] mate   [3] punished

The Spring

Now that the winter's gone, the earth hath lost
Her snow-white robes; and now no more the frost
Candies the grass, or casts an icy cream
Upon the silver lake or crystal stream:
(5) But the warm sun thaws the benumbed earth,
And makes it tender; gives a second birth
To the dead swallow; wakes in hollow tree
The drowsy cuckoo and the bumble-bee.
Now do a choir of chirping minstrels sing,
(10) In triumph to the world, the youthful Spring:
The valleys, hills, and woods in rich array
Welcome the coming of the long'd-for May.
Now all things smile; only my love doth lower;
Nor hath the scalding noon-day sun the power
(15) To melt that marble ice, which still doth hold
Her heart congeal'd, and makes her pity cold.
The ox which lately did for shelter fly
Into the stall, doth now securely lie
In open field; and love no more is made
(20) By the fire-side, but in the cooler shade.
Amyntas now doth by his Cloris sleep
Under a sycamore, and all things keep
Time with the season: only she doth carry
June in her eyes, in her heart January.

—Thomas Carew—

The notes on these poems would be something like this:

	Spenser	Carew
speaker	the male lover	the male lover
audience	lines 1–12, spring; lines 13–14 the female beloved	no specific audience (the real, unnamed audience is the beloved)
situation	springtime	springtime
structural divisions	lines 1–8, 9–12, 13–14	lines 1–4, winter (A); lines 5–12, spring (B); lines 12–16, the lady (C); lines 17–23, spring (B); lines 23–24, the lady (C) as both winter (A) and spring (B)
rhyme	abab, bcbc, cdcd, ee	12 pentameter couplets
subject	make use of youth, spring, since time passed cannot be recalled	everyone and everything in the spring is happy and in love except the cold and beautiful lady
images	spring = herald; spring's clothes = flowers; lady as if in hibernation; time personified; love as god, Love	snow = earth's clothing; frost = sugar; ice = cream; birds = choir; ice = her heart; rich array = spring flowers; Spring, nature personified
diction	focus on time: time, not stayed, take by the forelock, soon, ready, haste, prime, passed time	focus on hot versus cold contrast: winter, frost, icy, benumbed, dead, ice, congeal'd, cold, January versus spring, warm sun, tender, birth, smile, scalding noon-day sun, June

Both poets make use of spring to argue for a warmer response from the women they love. Spenser uses the *carpe diem* line; Carew simply points out the stark contrast between the warmth of the natural and human world of lovers and the icy disdain of the lady (who incidentally is as beautiful as June). Predictably, the diction and images of Spenser support his argument and stress the rapid and inevitable passage of time, while Carew exploits the contrast of winter and spring, of hot and cold. With this sort of detailed evidence in front of you, your essay should be easy to write.

Other Questions

The wheels of the AP exam move slowly, and the chances of your finding a new kind of question on your exam are very small. In the early 1970s when the multiple-choice section had only fifteen to twenty questions, the exam had four essays, and occasionally one of the four was not a critical analysis of literature question. The 1971 exam asked for a creative essay, fable, or letter criticizing some facet of contemporary life, and the 1973 exam asked for a dialogue with two incompatible points of view. Since the multiple-choice exam increased to fifty to sixty questions in 1975, this sort of assignment has vanished.

The 1977 exam used a different kind of comparison-of-two-texts question by giving an earlier and a later draft of D. H. Lawrence's poem "Piano." Since then, the exam has stayed close to the one poem for analysis, one prose passage for analysis, and one open essay question format. There have been three uses of a complete short story as the question on prose. Joyce's "Eveline" was used in 1972, Par Lagerkvist's "Father and I," a banal existential parable, in 1975, and John Cheever's seriocomic "Reunion" in 1988. There is always the possibility that another complete short story will appear on the exam. Though the stories are longer than the usual excerpt, there has not been a problem with students' finishing the exam, though the student essays are often shorter than usual. The questions on short stories may well take the familiar form of asking for the definition of an attitude and the discussion of the techniques used to convey that view—in other words, the old paradigmatic AP exam assignment.

DEFINITIONS OF TERMS USED IN
AP LITERATURE EXAMS

TERMS USED IN ESSAY INSTRUCTIONS

The following are the most important terms used in the instructions for essay questions. All of them have been used at least once and often more frequently. You should be familiar with the meaning of these terms.

- **allusion**

  A reference in a work of literature to something outside the work, especially to a well-known historical or literary event, person, or work. Lorraine Hansberry's title *A Raisin in the Sun* is an allusion to a phrase in a poem by Langston Hughes. When T. S. Eliot writes, "To have squeezed the universe into a ball" in "The Love Song of J. Alfred Prufrock," he is alluding to the lines "Let us roll all our strength and all / Our sweetness up into one ball" in Marvell's "To His Coy Mistress." In *Hamlet,* when Horatio says, "ere the mightiest Julius fell," the allusion is to the death of Julius Caesar.

- **attitude**

  A speaker's, author's, or character's disposition toward or opinion of a subject. For example, Hamlet's attitude toward Gertrude is a mixture of affection and revulsion, changing from one to the other within a single scene. Jane Austen's attitude toward Mr. Bennet in *Pride and Prejudice* combines respect for his wit and intelligence with disapproval of his failure to take sufficient responsibility for the rearing of all of his daughters.

- **details** (also **choice of details**)

  Details are items or parts that make up a larger picture or story. Chaucer's "Prologue" to *The Canterbury Tales* is celebrated for its use of a few details to bring the characters to life. The miller, for example, is described as being brawny and big-boned, able to win wrestling contests or to break a door with his head, and having a wart on his nose on which grew a "tuft of hairs red as the bristles of a sow's ears."

• devices of sound

The techniques of deploying the sound of words, especially in poetry. Among devices of sound are rhyme, alliteration, assonance, consonance, and onomatopoeia. These are defined below under metrical terms. The devices are used for many reasons, including to create a general effect of pleasant or of discordant sound, to imitate another sound, or to reflect a meaning.

• diction

Word choice. Nearly all essay questions on a passage of prose or a poem will ask you to talk about diction or about "techniques" that include diction. Any word that is important to the meaning and the effect of a passage can be used in your essay. Often several words with a similar effect are worth discussion, such as George Eliot's use in *Adam Bede* of "sunny afternoons," "slow waggons," and "bargains" to make the leisure of bygone days appealing. These words are also *details*.

• figurative language

Writing that uses figures of speech (as opposed to literal language or that which is actual or specifically denoted) such as metaphor, simile, and irony. Figurative language uses words to mean something other than their literal meaning. "The black bat night has flown" is figurative, with the metaphor comparing night and a bat. "Night is over" says the same thing without figurative language. No real bat is or has been on the scene, but night is like a bat because it is dark.

• imagery

The images of a literary work; the sensory details of a work; the figurative language of a work. Imagery has several definitions, but the two that are paramount are the visual, auditory, or tactile images evoked by the words of a literary work or the images that figurative language evokes. When an AP question asks you to discuss the images or imagery of a work, you should look especially carefully at the sensory details and the metaphors and similes of a passage. Some diction (word choice) is also imagery, but not all diction evokes sensory responses.

- **irony**

  A figure of speech in which intent and actual meaning differ, characteristically praise for blame or blame for praise; a pattern of words that turns away from direct statement of its own obvious meaning. The term irony implies a discrepancy. In *verbal irony* (saying the opposite of what one means), the discrepancy is between statement and meaning. Sometimes, irony may simply understate, as in "Men have died from time to time . . ." When Mr. Bennet, who loathes Wickham, says he is perhaps his "favorite" son-in-law, he is using irony.

- **metaphor**

  A figurative use of language in which a comparison is expressed without the use of a comparative term like "as," "like," or "than." A simile would say, "night is like a black bat"; a metaphor would say, "the black bat night." When Romeo says, "It is the east, and Juliet is the sun," his metaphors compare her window to the east and Juliet to the sun.

- **narrative techniques**

  The methods involved in telling a story; the procedures used by a writer of stories or accounts. Narrative techniques is a general term (like "devices," or "resources of language") which asks you to discuss the procedures used in the telling of a story. Examples of the techniques you might use are point of view, manipulation of time, dialogue, or interior monologue.

- **omniscient point of view**

  The vantage point of a story in which the narrator can know, see, and report whatever he or she chooses. The narrator is free to describe the thoughts of any of the characters, to skip about in time or place, or to speak directly to the reader. Most of the novels of Austen, Dickens, or Hardy employ the omniscient point of view.

- **point of view**

  Any of several possible vantage points from which a story is told. The point of view may be omniscient, limited to that of a single character, or limited to that of several characters. And there are other possibilities. The teller may use the first person (as in *Great Expectations* or *Wuthering Heights*) or the third person (as in *The Mayor of Casterbridge* or *A Tale of Two Cities*). Faulkner's *As I Lay Dying* uses the point of view of all of the members of the Bundren family and others as well in the first person, while in *Wuthering Heights,* Mr. Lockwood tells us the story that Nelly Dean tells him, a first-person narration reported by a second first-person narrator.

- **resources of language**

  A general phrase for the linguistic devices or techniques that a writer can use. A question calling for the "resources of language" invites a student to discuss the style and rhetoric of a passage. Such topics as diction, syntax, figurative language, and imagery are all examples of resources of language.

- **rhetorical techniques**

  The devices used in effective or persuasive language. The number of rhetorical techniques, like that of the resources of language, is long and runs from apostrophe to zeugma. The more common examples include devices like contrast, repetitions, paradox, understatement, sarcasm, and rhetorical question.

- **satire**

  Writing that seeks to arouse a reader's disapproval of an object by ridicule. Satire is usually comedy that exposes errors with an eye to correct vice and folly. A classical form, satire is found in the verse of Alexander Pope or Samuel Johnson, the plays of Ben Jonson or Bernard Shaw, and the novels of Charles Dickens, Mark Twain, or Joseph Heller.

- **setting**

  The background to a story; the physical location of a play, story, or novel. The setting of a narrative will normally involve both time and place. The setting of *A Tale of Two Cities* is London and Paris at the time of the French Revolution, but the setting of *Waiting for Godot* is impossible to pin down specifically.

- **simile**

  A directly expressed comparison; a figure of speech comparing two objects, usually with "like," "as," or "than." It is easier to recognize a simile than a metaphor because the comparison is explicit: my love is like a fever; my love is deeper than a well; my love is as dead as a doornail. The plural of "simile" is "similes" *not* "similies."

- **strategy** (or **rhetorical strategy**)

  The management of language for a specific effect. The strategy or rhetorical strategy of a poem is the planned placing of elements to achieve an effect. For example, Shakespeare's sonnet 29, "When, in disgrace with fortune and men's eyes," spends the first nine lines describing the speaker's discontent, then three describing the happiness the thought of the loved-one brings, all in a single sentence. The effect of this contrast is to intensify the feelings of relief and joy in lines 10–12. The rhetorical strategy of most love poems is deployed to convince the loved-one to return the speaker's love. By appealing to the loved-one's sympathy ("If you don't return my love, my heart will break."), or by flattery ("How could I not love someone as beautiful as you?"), or by threat ("When you're old, you'll be sorry you refused me."), the lover attempts to persuade the loved-one to love in return.

- **structure**

  The arrangement of materials within a work; the relationship of the parts of a work to the whole; the logical divisions of a work. The most common principles of structure are series (A, B, C, D, E), contrast (A vs. B, C vs. D, E vs. A), and repetition (AA, BB, AB). The most common units of structure are—play: scene, act; novel: chapter; poem: line, stanza.

- **style**

  The mode of expression in language; the characteristic manner of expression of an author. Many elements contribute to style, and if a question calls for a discussion of style or of "stylistic techniques," you can discuss diction, syntax, figurative language, imagery, selection of detail, sound effects, and tone, using the ones that are appropriate. Notice that there are several phrases used in the essay questions that invite you to choose among several possible topics: "devices of style," "narrative techniques," "rhetorical techniques," "stylistic techniques," and "resources of language" are all phrases that call for a consideration of more than one technique but do not specify what techniques you must discuss. Usually one of the two essay questions on a set passage will use one of these phrases, while the other question will specify the tasks by asking for "diction, imagery, and syntax" or a similar three or four topics.

- **symbol**

  Something that is simultaneously itself and a sign of something else. Winter, darkness, and cold are real things, but in literature they are also likely to be used as symbols of death. A paper lantern and a light bulb are real things, but in *A Streetcar Named Desire,* they are also symbols of Blanche's attempt to escape from reality and reality itself. Yorick's skull is a symbol of human mortality, and Melville's white whale is certainly a symbol, but exactly what it symbolizes has yet to be agreed upon.

- **syntax**

  The structure of a sentence; the arrangement of words in a sentence. A discussion of syntax in your essay could include such considerations as the length or brevity of the sentences, the kinds of sentences (questions, exclamations, declarative sentences, rhetorical questions—or periodic or loose; simple, complex, or compound). Syntax is often an issue on the English language exam. It has also been used frequently in recent essay questions on the AP literature exams, since it is clear that many students are not prepared to write about syntax. Until this defect has been repaired, syntax questions will continue to appear regularly in both the multiple-choice and essay sections of the test.

- **theme**

  The main thought expressed by a work. Essay questions may ask for discussion of the theme or themes of a work or may use the words "meaning" or "meanings." The open question frequently asks you to relate a discussion on one subject to a "meaning of the work as a whole." When preparing the novels and plays you might use on the open question, be sure to consider what theme or themes you would write about if you are asked to talk about a "meaning of the work." The question is much harder to answer for some works than others. I'm not sure what I would say is the meaning of *Hamlet, Wuthering Heights,* or *Waiting for Godot.* But I have much less trouble defining a theme in works like *Brave New World* or *Animal Farm.*

- **tone**

  The manner in which an author expresses his or her attitude; the intonation of the voice that expresses meaning. Tone is described by adjectives, and the possibilities are nearly endless. Often a single adjective will not be enough, and tone may change from chapter to chapter or even line to line. Tone is the result of allusion, diction, figurative language, imagery, irony, symbol, syntax, and style to cite only the relevant words on this list. In the Wordsworth passage on the 1992 exam, the tone moves from quiet to apprehensive to confident to exuberant to terrified to panicked to uncertain to restive in only twenty-five lines.

Exercise on Terms Used in Essay Instructions

Read carefully the following well-known sonnet "On First Looking into Chapman's Homer" by John Keats. The title alludes to Keats's first reading of the sixteenth-century poet George Chapman's translation of Homer's *Iliad.*

> Much have I travell'd in the realms of gold,
> And many goodly states and kingdoms seen;
> Round many western islands have I been
> Which bards in fealty to Apollo hold.
> (5) Oft of one wide expanse had I been told
> That deep-brow'd Homer ruled as his demesne;
> Yet did I never breathe its pure serene
> Till I heard Chapman speak out loud and bold:
> Then felt I like some watcher of the skies
> (10) When a new planet swims into his ken;
> Or like stout Cortez when with eagle eyes
> He stared at the Pacific—and all his men
> Look'd at each other with a wild surmise—
> Silent, upon a peak in Darien.

In the following four lines, five words or phrases lettered A, B, C, D, and E have been underlined. Determine which of the following terms are appropriate to describe each word or phrase. In several cases, more than one of the terms should be cited:

> Much <u>have I travell'd</u> in <u>the realms of gold</u>
>   A   B
> And many <u>goodly states and kingdoms</u> seen;
>   C
> Round many <u>western islands</u> have I been
>   D
> Which bards in fealty to <u>Apollo</u> hold.
>   E

1. allusion	A.
2. figurative language	B.
3. imagery	C.
4. irony	D.
5. metaphor	E.
6. simile	
7. symbol	

Which of the same seven terms are illustrated by the words or phrases in this passage?

> Then felt I like some watcher of the skies
> F
> When a new planet swims into his ken;
> G
> Or like stout Cortez when with eagle eyes
> H   I
> He stared at the Pacific—and all his men
>
> Looked at each other with a wild surmise—
>
> Silent, upon a peak in Darien.
> J

1. allusion   F.
2. figurative language   G.
3. imagery   H.
4. irony   I.
5. metaphor   J.
6. simile
7. symbol

Answers

A. **"have I travell'd"**—2, 3, and 5. The poet is speaking of his readings and compares reading to traveling. This is an example of figurative language, of imagery, and of a metaphor.

B. **"the realms of gold"**—2, 3, and 5. The figure is continued: reading = traveling; the realms of gold = the works of literature the poet has read. Like A, this is a metaphor. The phrase "realms of gold" is also a metaphor for fine poetry, the value of gold equated with the worth of art.

C. **"goodly states and kingdoms"**—2, 3, and 5. The figure comparing books or poems to realms is here altered to states and kingdoms.

D. "western islands"—2, 3, and 5. The comparison now likens poems to islands; the poems have been written by bards devoted to Apollo.

E. "Apollo"—1, 7. The allusion is to the Greek god of poetry. Since we assume that Apollo represents poetry, we can also call this a symbol.

F. "like some watcher of the skies"—2, 3, 6. The figure or image here compares the poet to an astronomer. This is a simile, using "like." His discovery of Chapman's Homer is like the discovery of a new planet.

G. "swims"—2, 3, 5. The metaphor compares motion through water with the motion of a planet as seen by a telescope.

H. "stout Cortez"—1, 2, 3, 6. The allusion, though Keats confuses Cortez and Balboa, is to a Spanish explorer.

I. "eagle eyes"—2, 3, 5. The metaphor compares Cortez's eyes to those of an eagle.

J. "Silent, upon a peak in Darien"—1, 3. The allusion is to the mountain in Panama; the phrase presents an image.

The poem does not use irony.

TERMS USED IN MULTIPLE-CHOICE QUESTIONS

The following terms have been used in multiple-choice questions and answers. The more important ones are marked with an asterisk.

- **allegory**

  A story in which people, things, and events have another meaning. Examples of allegory are Bunyan's *Pilgrim's Progress,* Spenser's *Faerie Queene,* and Orwell's *Animal Farm.*

- **ambiguity**

  Multiple meanings a literary work may communicate, especially two meanings that are incompatible.

- ***apostrophe**

  Direct address, usually to someone or something that is not present. Keats's "Bright star! would I were steadfast" is an apostrophe to a star, and "To Autumn" is an apostrophe to a personified season.

- ***connotation**

  The implications of a word or phrase, as opposed to its exact meaning (denotation). Both China and Cathay denote a region in Asia, but to a modern reader, the associations of the two words are different.

- ***convention**

  A device of style or subject matter so often used that it becomes a recognized means of expression. For example, a lover observing the literary love conventions cannot eat or sleep and grows pale and lean. Romeo, at the beginning of the play is a conventional lover, while an overweight lover in Chaucer is consciously mocking the convention.

- ***denotation**

  The dictionary meaning of a word, as opposed to connotation.

- **didactic**

  Explicitly instructive. A didactic poem or novel may be good or bad. Pope's "Essay on Man" is didactic; so are the novels of Ayn Rand.

- **digression**

  The use of material unrelated to the subject of a work. The interpolated narrations in the novels of Cervantes or Fielding may be called digressions, and *Tristram Shandy* includes a digression on digressions.

- **epigram**

  A pithy saying, often using contrast. The epigram is also a verse form, usually brief and pointed.

- **euphemism**

  A figure of speech using indirection to avoid offensive bluntness, such as "deceased" for "dead" or "remains" for "corpse."

- **grotesque**

  Characterized by distortions or incongruities. The fiction of Poe or Flannery O'Connor is often described as grotesque.

- ***hyperbole**

  Deliberate exaggeration, overstatement. As a rule, hyperbole is self-conscious, without the intention of being accepted literally. "The strongest man in the world" or "a diamond as big as the Ritz" are hyperbolic.

- **jargon**

  The special language of a profession or group. The term jargon usually has pejorative associations, with the implication that jargon is evasive, tedious, and unintelligible to outsiders. The writings of the lawyer and the literary critic are both susceptible to jargon.

- ***literal**

  Not figurative; accurate to the letter; matter of fact or concrete.

- **lyrical**

  Songlike; characterized by emotion, subjectivity, and imagination.

- ***oxymoron**

  A combination of opposites; the union of contradictory terms. Romeo's line "feather of lead, bright smoke, cold fire, sick health" has four examples of the device.

- **parable**

  A story designed to suggest a principle, illustrate a moral, or answer a question. Parables are allegorical stories.

- ***paradox**

  A statement that seems to be self-contradicting but, in fact, is true. The figure in Donne's holy sonnet that concludes I never shall be "chaste except you ravish me" is a good example of the device.

- **parody**

  A composition that imitates the style of another composition normally for comic effect. Fielding's *Shamela* is a parody of Richardson's *Pamela*. A contest for parodies of Hemingway draws hundreds of entries each year.

- ***personification**

  A figurative use of language which endows the nonhuman (ideas, inanimate objects, animals, abstractions) with human characteristics. Keats personifies the nightingale, the Grecian urn, and autumn in his major poems.

- ***reliability**

  A quality of some fictional narrators whose word the reader can trust. There are both reliable and unreliable narrators, that is, tellers of a story who should or should not be trusted. Most narrators are reliable (Fitzgerald's Nick Carraway, Conrad's Marlow), but some are clearly not to be trusted (Poe's "Tell-Tale Heart," several novels by Nabokov). And there are some about whom readers have been unable to decide (James's governess in *The Turn of the Screw,* Ford's *The Good Soldier*).

- ***rhetorical question**

  A question asked for effect, not in expectation of a reply. No reply is expected because the question presupposes only one possible answer. The lover of Suckling's "Shall I wasting in despair / Die because a lady's fair?" has already decided the answer is no.

- ***soliloquy**

  A speech in which a character who is alone speaks his or her thoughts aloud. A monologue also has a single speaker, but the monologuist speaks to others who do not interrupt. Hamlet's "To be, or not to be" and "O! what a rogue and peasant slave am I" are soliloquies. Browning's "My Last Duchess" and "Fra Lippo Lippi" are monologues, but the hypocritical monk of his "Soliloquy of the Spanish Cloister" cannot reveal his thoughts to others.

- ***stereotype**

  A conventional pattern, expression, character, or idea. In literature, a stereotype could apply to the unvarying plot and characters of some works of fiction (those of Barbara Cartland, for example) or to the stock characters and plots of many of the greatest stage comedies.

- **syllogism**

  A form of reasoning in which two statements are made and a conclusion is drawn from them. A syllogism begins with a major premise ("All tragedies end unhappily.") followed by a minor premise (*"Hamlet* is a tragedy.") and a conclusion (Therefore, *"Hamlet* ends unhappily.").

- **thesis**

  The theme, meaning, or position that a writer undertakes to prove or support.

Metrical Terms

The following have been used in the questions or answers of the multiple-choice questions about the metrics of a passage. Those marked with an asterisk are the more important terms; the others appeared only as wrong answers.

- ***alliteration**

The repetition of identical or similar consonant sounds, normally at the beginning of words. "Gnus never know pneumonia" is an example of alliteration, since despite the spellings, all four words begin with the "n" sound.

- ***assonance**

The repetition of identical or similar vowel sounds. "A land laid waste with all its young men slain" repeats the same "a" sound in "laid," "waste," and "slain."

- **ballad meter**

A four-line stanza rhymed abcb with four feet in lines one and three and three feet in lines two and four.

> O mother, mother make my bed.
> O make it soft and narrow.
> Since my love died for me today,
> I'll die for him tomorrow.

- ***blank verse**

Unrhymed iambic pentameter.

> Men called him Mulciber; and how he fell
> From heaven, they fabled, thrown by angry Jove
> Sheer o'er the crystal battlements: from morn
> To noon he fell, from noon to dewy eve.

Blank verse is the meter of most of Shakespeare's plays, as well as that of Milton's *Paradise Lost.*

- **dactyl**

  A metrical foot of three syllables, an accented syllable followed by two unaccented syllables.

- ***end-stopped**

  A line with a pause at the end. Lines that end with a period, comma, colon, semicolon, exclamation point, or question mark are end-stopped lines.

- ***free verse**

  Poetry which is not written in a traditional meter but is still rhythmical. The poetry of Walt Whitman is perhaps the best-known example of free verse.

- ***heroic couplet**

  Two end-stopped iambic pentameter lines rhymed aa, bb, cc with the thought usually completed in the two-line unit.

  > When those fair suns shall set, as set they must,
  > And all those tresses shall be laid in dust,
  > This lock, the Muse shall consecrate to fame,
  > And 'midst the stars inscribe Belinda's name.

- **hexameter**

  A line containing six feet.

- ***iamb**

  A two-syllable foot with an unaccented syllable followed by an accented syllable. The iamb is the most common foot in English poetry.

- **internal rhyme**

  Rhyme that occurs within a line, rather than at the end.

  > "God save thee, ancient Mariner!
  > From the fiends, that plague thee thus!—
  > Why look'st thou so?"—With my crossbow
  > I shot the Albatross.

  Line three contains the internal rhyme of "so" and "'bow."

- **onomatopoeia**

  The use of words whose sound suggests their meaning. Examples are "buzz," "hiss," or "honk."

- ***pentameter**

  A line containing five feet. The iambic pentameter is the most common line in English verse written before 1950.

- **rhyme royal**

  A seven-line stanza of iambic pentameter rhymed ababbcc, used by Chaucer and other medieval poets.

- ***sonnet**

  Normally a fourteen-line iambic pentameter poem. The conventional Italian, or Petrachan, sonnet is rhymed abba, abba, cde, cde; the English, or Shakespearean, sonnet is rhymed abab, cdcd, efef, gg.

- ***stanza**

  Usually a repeated grouping of three or more lines with the same meter and rhyme scheme.

- **terza rima**

  A three-line stanza rhymed aba, bcb, cdc. Dante's *Divine Comedy* is written in terza rima.

- ***tetrameter**

  A line of four feet.

Grammatical Terms

- **antecedent**

  That which goes before, especially the word, phrase, or clause to which a pronoun refers. In the sentence "The witches cast their spells," the antecedent of the pronoun "their" is the noun "witches."

- **clause**

  A group of words containing a subject and its verb that may or may not be a complete sentence. In the sentence "When you are old, you will be beautiful," the first clause ("When you are old") is a dependent clause and not a complete sentence. "You will be beautiful" is an independent clause and could stand by itself.

- **ellipsis**

  The omission of a word or several words necessary for a complete construction that is still understandable. "If rainy, bring an umbrella" is clear though the words "it is" and "you" have been left out.

- **imperative**

  The mood of a verb that gives an order. "Eat your spinach" uses an imperative verb.

- **modify**

  To restrict or limit in meaning. In the phrase "large, shaggy dog," the two adjectives modify the noun; in the phrase "very shaggy dog," the adverb "very" modifies the adjective "shaggy," which modifies the noun "dog."

- **parallel structure**

  A similar grammatical structure within a sentence or within a paragraph. Winston Churchill's "We shall fight on the beaches, we shall fight on the landing grounds, we shall fight in the fields" speech or Martin Luther King's "I have a dream" speech depend chiefly on the use of parallel structure.

- **periodic sentence**

  A sentence grammatically complete only at the end. A loose sentence is grammatically complete before the period. The following are (1) periodic and (2) loose sentences.

  1. When conquering love did first my heart assail, / Unto mine aid I summoned every sense.
  2. Fair is my love, and cruel as she's fair.

Periodic sentences complete the important idea at the end, while loose sentences put the important idea first. Neither is a better sentence. Good writers use both.

- **syntax**
  The structure of a sentence. See *syntax,* page 130.

PAST AP LITERATURE ESSAY PASSAGES, OPEN QUESTIONS, AND SUGGESTED AUTHORS

The point of your AP English class is to teach you to read and write about literature well. This, not your exam score, should be your chief concern. Don't become preoccupied with what has been or what will be on the exam. Don't spend too much time writing practice exams, especially if doing so simply increases your anxiety.

Still, you must be aware of what the exam experience is like. Three hours is a long time to devote to intense concentration without a break, and many students find it is more exhausting than they had imagined. You should spend some time practicing writing using the questions from old exams. You will learn from them the level of difficulty of the texts and exactly what kind of tasks are set for you to write about. Copies of the essay questions on old exams can be ordered from the Advanced Placement Program, P.O. Box 6670, Princeton, New Jersey 08541-6670.

ESSAY PASSAGES

The following pages list the authors and the works that have been used as the basis of essay questions on past exams.

Prose Questions

1970 George Meredith: from the novel *The Ordeal of Richard Feverel*

1971 George Orwell: from the essay "Some Thoughts on the Common Toad"

1972 James Joyce: "Eveline"—complete short story from *Dubliners*

1973 Charles Dickens: from the novel *Hard Times* and E. M. Forster: from the novel *A Passage to India*

1974 Henry James: from the novel *What Maisie Knew*

1975 Pär Lagerkvist: "Father and I"—complete short story

1976 John Gardner: from the verse novel *Jason and Medeia*

1977 no prose passage question

1978 Samuel Johnson: from a review of Soame Jenyns's "A Free Enquiry into the Nature and Origin of Evil"

1979 Quentin Bell: from the biography *Virginia Woolf*

1980 Ralph Ellison: from the novel *Invisible Man* and Henry James: from an essay in *Lippincott's Magazine*

1981 George Bernard Shaw: from a letter on the death of his mother

1982 Adlai Stevenson: a letter to the Senate of the Illinois General Assembly

1983 Thomas Carlyle: from the political lectures *Past and Present*

1984 Jane Austen: from the novel *Emma*

1985 Ernest Hemingway: from the novel *A Farewell to Arms*

1986 Charles Dickens: from the novel *Dombey and Son*

1987 George Eliot: from the novel *Adam Bede*

1988 John Cheever: "Reunion"—complete short story

1989 Joseph Conrad: from the novella *Typhoon*

1990 Joan Didion: from the essay "On Self-Respect"

1991 James Boswell: from the biography *The Life of Samuel Johnson*

1992 Tillie Olsen: from the short story "I Stand Here Ironing"

Fourteen of the prose passages have been chosen from twentieth-century writers, eight from nineteenth-century writers. Three questions have used complete short stories. Half of the prose passages have come from novels and half from nonfictional sources.

Poetry Questions

In the five years missing in the following list, no essay question was based on a poetry passage. It is very unlikely that the exam will repeat the omission of a question based on a verse text. The following poems or excerpts from the following poems have appeared on the exams.

1966 Emily Dickinson: "I never lost as much but twice"

1968 Sir Edward Dyer: "The lowest trees have tops"

1969 W. B. Yeats: "The Wild Swans at Coole"

1970 Theodore Roethke: "Elegy for Jane"

1971 W. H. Auden: "The Unknown Citizen"

1974 Thomas Kinsella: from "Prologue: Downstream"

1976 Philip Larkin: "Poetry of Departures"

1977 D. H. Lawrence: "Piano"

1978 W. H. Auden: "Law Like Love"

1979 Louise Gluck: "For Jane Meyers" and William Carlos Williams: "Spring and All"

1980 Elizabeth Bishop: "One Art"

1981 Adrienne Rich: "Storm Warnings"

1982 Richard Eberhart: "The Groundhog"

1983 W. H. Auden: "As I Walked Out One Evening"

1985 William Wordsworth: "There was a boy" and Robert Frost: "The Most of It"

1986 E. K. Brathwaite: "Ogun"

1987 Sylvia Plath: "Sow"

1988 John Keats: "Bright Star" and Robert Frost: "Choose something like a star"

1989 John Updike: "The Great Scarf of Birds"

1990 William Shakespeare: "How many of my subjects . . ." from *Henry IV, Part II,* Act III

1991 Emily Dickinson: "The last Night that She lived"

1992 William Wordsworth: "One summer evening, led by her" from *The Prelude,* Book I

Since 1966, most of the poems used on the exam have been written by twentieth-century writers, though three have been chosen from the sixteenth and eighteenth centuries, and five from nineteenth-century poets. Since 1980, an increasingly large number of poems by women and by minority writers have been used.

OPEN QUESTIONS

In the past, the open question called for an essay discussing

1971 (using two works) the technical devices used to reveal the meanings of their *titles*

1972 the use of the *opening scene or chapter* to introduce significant themes of the play or novel

1973 no essay on drama or fiction

1974 the *relevance to the present* of a literary work written before 1900

1975 the use of a *stereotyped character*

1976 the moral meanings of a work in which *an individual opposed his or her society*

1977 a character's *response to the past* as a source of meaning in the work

1978 the relation of *an implausible incident or character* to the realistic aspects of the work

1979 *an ostensibly evil character* to whom the reader responds with some sympathy or understanding

1980 a character whose *private passion is in conflict with his or her moral obligations*

1981 a work in which the use of *allusion* (to myth or the Bible, for example) is significant

1982 the function in a work of *a scene of violence*

1983 a *villain,* the nature of villainy, and the relation of the character to meaning

1984 the relation of *a single memorable line of poetry or scene in a play or novel* to the whole work (an unusual and unsuccessful question)

1985 the cause of feelings of *both pleasure and disquietude* in a literary work

1986 the effect of an author's *manipulation of time* in a novel, epic, or play

1987 an author's techniques used *to change a reader's attitudes,* especially toward social ills

1988 an author's making *internal or psychological events* exciting

1989 the use of *distortion* in a literary work

1990 the significance in a work of a *parent-child conflict*

1991 the significance of *two contrasting places* in a play or novel

1992 the function of *a confidant(e)* in a play or novel

SUGGESTED AUTHORS

Based on the examinations from 1981 to 1992, the following is a list of the authors, plays, and novels that have been suggested for use on the open essay question and that students have chosen to write about. There are a handful of other titles that have appeared in the lists (Melville's novel *Redburn*, for example) that hardly anyone wrote about, and these names have been omitted. There have, of course, also been hundreds of other appropriate novels and plays that were not on the lists of suggested titles. A reading of this tabulation will give you a good idea of the range of the works that are probably the most widely taught in AP literature classes.

Chinua Achebe: *Things Fall Apart*
Aeschylus: the *Oresteia*
Aristophanes: *Lysistrata*
Jane Austen: *Pride and Prejudice*

Samuel Beckett: *Waiting for Godot*
Bertolt Brecht: *Mother Courage and Her Children*
Charlotte Brontë: *Jane Eyre*
Emily Brontë: *Wuthering Heights*

Albert Camus: *The Stranger*
Anton Chekhov: *The Cherry Orchard*
Kate Chopin: *The Awakening*
Joseph Conrad: *Heart of Darkness, Lord Jim, Victory*

Daniel Defoe: *Moll Flanders*
Charles Dickens: *David Copperfield, Great Expectations, Hard Times, A Tale of Two Cities*
Feodor Dostoevski: *Crime and Punishment*
Theodore Dreiser: *An American Tragedy, Sister Carrie*

Ralph Ellison: *Invisible Man*
Euripides: *Medea*

William Faulkner: *As I Lay Dying, Light in August, The Sound and the Fury*
Henry Fielding: *Joseph Andrews*

F. Scott Fitzgerald: *The Great Gatsby*
Gustave Flaubert: *Madame Bovary*
E. M. Forster: *A Passage to India*

William Golding: *Lord of the Flies*

Thomas Hardy: *Jude the Obscure, Tess of the D'Urbervilles*
Nathaniel Hawthorne: *The Scarlet Letter*
Joseph Heller: *Catch-22*
Lillian Hellman: *The Little Foxes*
Ernest Hemingway: *The Sun Also Rises*
Zora Neale Hurston: *Their Eyes Were Watching God*
Aldous Huxley: *Brave New World*

Henrik Ibsen: *A Doll's House, An Enemy of the People, Hedda Gabler, The Wild Duck*

Henry James: *The Turn of the Screw, Washington Square*
James Joyce: *A Portrait of the Artist as a Young Man*

Franz Kafka: *Metamorphosis, The Trial*

D. H. Lawrence: *Sons and Lovers*
Sinclair Lewis: *Main Street*

Gabriel García Márquez: *One Hundred Years of Solitude*
Herman Melville: *Billy Budd, Moby Dick*
Arthur Miller: *All My Sons, The Crucible, Death of a Salesman*
Toni Morrison: *Beloved, Song of Solomon*

Flannery O'Connor: *Wise Blood*
Eugene O'Neill: *The Hairy Ape, Long Day's Journey into Night*
George Orwell: *Animal Farm, 1984*

Alan Paton: *Cry, the Beloved Country*

Jean Rhys: *Wide Sargasso Sea*

Jean-Paul Sartre: *No Exit*

William Shakespeare: *Hamlet, Julius Caesar, King Lear, Macbeth, The Merchant of Venice, A Midsummer Night's Dream, Othello, Romeo and Juliet, Twelfth Night*

George Bernard Shaw: *Major Barbara, Man and Superman, Mrs. Warren's Profession, Pygmalion*

Mary Shelley: *Frankenstein*

Sophocles: *Antigone, Oedipus Rex*

John Steinbeck: *The Grapes of Wrath*

Tom Stoppard: *Rosencrantz and Guildenstern Are Dead*

August Strindberg: *Miss Julie*

Jonathan Swift: *Gulliver's Travels*

Leo Tolstoi: *Anna Karenina*

Mark Twain: *The Adventures of Huckleberry Finn*

Voltaire: *Candide*

Kurt Vonnegut: *Slaughterhouse Five*

Alice Walker: *The Color Purple*

Evelyn Waugh: *The Loved One*

Edith Wharton: *Ethan Frome, The House of Mirth*

Thornton Wilder: *Our Town*

Tennessee Williams: *The Glass Menagerie, A Streetcar Named Desire*

Virginia Woolf: *To the Lighthouse*

Richard Wright: *Native Son*

Once in a while, an open question allows for the choice of a poem rather than a novel or play. The following poems have been included in the list of works on the exam:

Robert Browning: "My Last Duchess"

T. S. Eliot: "The Love Song of J. Alfred Prufrock," "The Waste Land"

Homer: the *Iliad,* the *Odyssey*

Milton: *Paradise Lost*

Pope: "The Rape of the Lock"

Do not write on one of these works if the question calls for a novel or play.

Part III: Three Full-Length Practice Tests

A Note About the Essay Questions

The exam committee chooses the essay and multiple-choice questions to reflect as wide a range of English and American literature as possible. The choice of passages on the free-response section of the exam is, in part, determined by what appears in the multiple-choice section. Each exam uses passages by female and/or minority writers, and more often than not, at least one of the essay questions is about a poem or prose passage by a minority or female author. The passages on these practice exams reflect the kind of distribution you'll find in the real test. They include works by one minority and three women writers and passages from the eighteenth, nineteenth, and twentieth centuries.

If you are planning to test yourself by writing essays on the practice test topics, be sure that you do not read the discussion of the essay topics and the sample student essays (in the Answers and Explanations sections following each practice test) until after you have written your own essays for that test.

ANSWER SHEET FOR PRACTICE TEST 1
(Remove This Sheet and Use it to Mark Your Answers)

SECTION I
MULTIPLE-CHOICE QUESTIONS

1 Ⓐ Ⓑ Ⓒ Ⓓ Ⓔ	21 Ⓐ Ⓑ Ⓒ Ⓓ Ⓔ	41 Ⓐ Ⓑ Ⓒ Ⓓ Ⓔ
2 Ⓐ Ⓑ Ⓒ Ⓓ Ⓔ	22 Ⓐ Ⓑ Ⓒ Ⓓ Ⓔ	42 Ⓐ Ⓑ Ⓒ Ⓓ Ⓔ
3 Ⓐ Ⓑ Ⓒ Ⓓ Ⓔ	23 Ⓐ Ⓑ Ⓒ Ⓓ Ⓔ	43 Ⓐ Ⓑ Ⓒ Ⓓ Ⓔ
4 Ⓐ Ⓑ Ⓒ Ⓓ Ⓔ	24 Ⓐ Ⓑ Ⓒ Ⓓ Ⓔ	44 Ⓐ Ⓑ Ⓒ Ⓓ Ⓔ
5 Ⓐ Ⓑ Ⓒ Ⓓ Ⓔ	25 Ⓐ Ⓑ Ⓒ Ⓓ Ⓔ	45 Ⓐ Ⓑ Ⓒ Ⓓ Ⓔ
6 Ⓐ Ⓑ Ⓒ Ⓓ Ⓔ	26 Ⓐ Ⓑ Ⓒ Ⓓ Ⓔ	46 Ⓐ Ⓑ Ⓒ Ⓓ Ⓔ
7 Ⓐ Ⓑ Ⓒ Ⓓ Ⓔ	27 Ⓐ Ⓑ Ⓒ Ⓓ Ⓔ	47 Ⓐ Ⓑ Ⓒ Ⓓ Ⓔ
8 Ⓐ Ⓑ Ⓒ Ⓓ Ⓔ	28 Ⓐ Ⓑ Ⓒ Ⓓ Ⓔ	48 Ⓐ Ⓑ Ⓒ Ⓓ Ⓔ
9 Ⓐ Ⓑ Ⓒ Ⓓ Ⓔ	29 Ⓐ Ⓑ Ⓒ Ⓓ Ⓔ	49 Ⓐ Ⓑ Ⓒ Ⓓ Ⓔ
10 Ⓐ Ⓑ Ⓒ Ⓓ Ⓔ	30 Ⓐ Ⓑ Ⓒ Ⓓ Ⓔ	50 Ⓐ Ⓑ Ⓒ Ⓓ Ⓔ
11 Ⓐ Ⓑ Ⓒ Ⓓ Ⓔ	31 Ⓐ Ⓑ Ⓒ Ⓓ Ⓔ	51 Ⓐ Ⓑ Ⓒ Ⓓ Ⓔ
12 Ⓐ Ⓑ Ⓒ Ⓓ Ⓔ	32 Ⓐ Ⓑ Ⓒ Ⓓ Ⓔ	52 Ⓐ Ⓑ Ⓒ Ⓓ Ⓔ
13 Ⓐ Ⓑ Ⓒ Ⓓ Ⓔ	33 Ⓐ Ⓑ Ⓒ Ⓓ Ⓔ	53 Ⓐ Ⓑ Ⓒ Ⓓ Ⓔ
14 Ⓐ Ⓑ Ⓒ Ⓓ Ⓔ	34 Ⓐ Ⓑ Ⓒ Ⓓ Ⓔ	54 Ⓐ Ⓑ Ⓒ Ⓓ Ⓔ
15 Ⓐ Ⓑ Ⓒ Ⓓ Ⓔ	35 Ⓐ Ⓑ Ⓒ Ⓓ Ⓔ	
16 Ⓐ Ⓑ Ⓒ Ⓓ Ⓔ	36 Ⓐ Ⓑ Ⓒ Ⓓ Ⓔ	
17 Ⓐ Ⓑ Ⓒ Ⓓ Ⓔ	37 Ⓐ Ⓑ Ⓒ Ⓓ Ⓔ	
18 Ⓐ Ⓑ Ⓒ Ⓓ Ⓔ	38 Ⓐ Ⓑ Ⓒ Ⓓ Ⓔ	
19 Ⓐ Ⓑ Ⓒ Ⓓ Ⓔ	39 Ⓐ Ⓑ Ⓒ Ⓓ Ⓔ	
20 Ⓐ Ⓑ Ⓒ Ⓓ Ⓔ	40 Ⓐ Ⓑ Ⓒ Ⓓ Ⓔ	

CUT HERE

ANSWER SHEET FOR PRACTICE TEST 2
(Remove This Sheet and Use it to Mark Your Answers)

SECTION I
MULTIPLE-CHOICE QUESTIONS

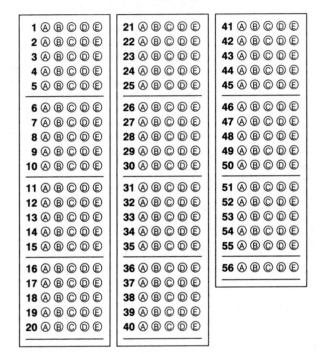

1 Ⓐ Ⓑ Ⓒ Ⓓ Ⓔ	21 Ⓐ Ⓑ Ⓒ Ⓓ Ⓔ	41 Ⓐ Ⓑ Ⓒ Ⓓ Ⓔ
2 Ⓐ Ⓑ Ⓒ Ⓓ Ⓔ	22 Ⓐ Ⓑ Ⓒ Ⓓ Ⓔ	42 Ⓐ Ⓑ Ⓒ Ⓓ Ⓔ
3 Ⓐ Ⓑ Ⓒ Ⓓ Ⓔ	23 Ⓐ Ⓑ Ⓒ Ⓓ Ⓔ	43 Ⓐ Ⓑ Ⓒ Ⓓ Ⓔ
4 Ⓐ Ⓑ Ⓒ Ⓓ Ⓔ	24 Ⓐ Ⓑ Ⓒ Ⓓ Ⓔ	44 Ⓐ Ⓑ Ⓒ Ⓓ Ⓔ
5 Ⓐ Ⓑ Ⓒ Ⓓ Ⓔ	25 Ⓐ Ⓑ Ⓒ Ⓓ Ⓔ	45 Ⓐ Ⓑ Ⓒ Ⓓ Ⓔ
6 Ⓐ Ⓑ Ⓒ Ⓓ Ⓔ	26 Ⓐ Ⓑ Ⓒ Ⓓ Ⓔ	46 Ⓐ Ⓑ Ⓒ Ⓓ Ⓔ
7 Ⓐ Ⓑ Ⓒ Ⓓ Ⓔ	27 Ⓐ Ⓑ Ⓒ Ⓓ Ⓔ	47 Ⓐ Ⓑ Ⓒ Ⓓ Ⓔ
8 Ⓐ Ⓑ Ⓒ Ⓓ Ⓔ	28 Ⓐ Ⓑ Ⓒ Ⓓ Ⓔ	48 Ⓐ Ⓑ Ⓒ Ⓓ Ⓔ
9 Ⓐ Ⓑ Ⓒ Ⓓ Ⓔ	29 Ⓐ Ⓑ Ⓒ Ⓓ Ⓔ	49 Ⓐ Ⓑ Ⓒ Ⓓ Ⓔ
10 Ⓐ Ⓑ Ⓒ Ⓓ Ⓔ	30 Ⓐ Ⓑ Ⓒ Ⓓ Ⓔ	50 Ⓐ Ⓑ Ⓒ Ⓓ Ⓔ
11 Ⓐ Ⓑ Ⓒ Ⓓ Ⓔ	31 Ⓐ Ⓑ Ⓒ Ⓓ Ⓔ	51 Ⓐ Ⓑ Ⓒ Ⓓ Ⓔ
12 Ⓐ Ⓑ Ⓒ Ⓓ Ⓔ	32 Ⓐ Ⓑ Ⓒ Ⓓ Ⓔ	52 Ⓐ Ⓑ Ⓒ Ⓓ Ⓔ
13 Ⓐ Ⓑ Ⓒ Ⓓ Ⓔ	33 Ⓐ Ⓑ Ⓒ Ⓓ Ⓔ	53 Ⓐ Ⓑ Ⓒ Ⓓ Ⓔ
14 Ⓐ Ⓑ Ⓒ Ⓓ Ⓔ	34 Ⓐ Ⓑ Ⓒ Ⓓ Ⓔ	54 Ⓐ Ⓑ Ⓒ Ⓓ Ⓔ
15 Ⓐ Ⓑ Ⓒ Ⓓ Ⓔ	35 Ⓐ Ⓑ Ⓒ Ⓓ Ⓔ	55 Ⓐ Ⓑ Ⓒ Ⓓ Ⓔ
16 Ⓐ Ⓑ Ⓒ Ⓓ Ⓔ	36 Ⓐ Ⓑ Ⓒ Ⓓ Ⓔ	56 Ⓐ Ⓑ Ⓒ Ⓓ Ⓔ
17 Ⓐ Ⓑ Ⓒ Ⓓ Ⓔ	37 Ⓐ Ⓑ Ⓒ Ⓓ Ⓔ	
18 Ⓐ Ⓑ Ⓒ Ⓓ Ⓔ	38 Ⓐ Ⓑ Ⓒ Ⓓ Ⓔ	
19 Ⓐ Ⓑ Ⓒ Ⓓ Ⓔ	39 Ⓐ Ⓑ Ⓒ Ⓓ Ⓔ	
20 Ⓐ Ⓑ Ⓒ Ⓓ Ⓔ	40 Ⓐ Ⓑ Ⓒ Ⓓ Ⓔ	

CUT HERE

159

ANSWER SHEET FOR PRACTICE TEST 3
(Remove This Sheet and Use it to Mark Your Answers)

SECTION I
MULTIPLE-CHOICE QUESTIONS

1 Ⓐ Ⓑ Ⓒ Ⓓ Ⓔ	21 Ⓐ Ⓑ Ⓒ Ⓓ Ⓔ	41 Ⓐ Ⓑ Ⓒ Ⓓ Ⓔ
2 Ⓐ Ⓑ Ⓒ Ⓓ Ⓔ	22 Ⓐ Ⓑ Ⓒ Ⓓ Ⓔ	42 Ⓐ Ⓑ Ⓒ Ⓓ Ⓔ
3 Ⓐ Ⓑ Ⓒ Ⓓ Ⓔ	23 Ⓐ Ⓑ Ⓒ Ⓓ Ⓔ	43 Ⓐ Ⓑ Ⓒ Ⓓ Ⓔ
4 Ⓐ Ⓑ Ⓒ Ⓓ Ⓔ	24 Ⓐ Ⓑ Ⓒ Ⓓ Ⓔ	44 Ⓐ Ⓑ Ⓒ Ⓓ Ⓔ
5 Ⓐ Ⓑ Ⓒ Ⓓ Ⓔ	25 Ⓐ Ⓑ Ⓒ Ⓓ Ⓔ	45 Ⓐ Ⓑ Ⓒ Ⓓ Ⓔ
6 Ⓐ Ⓑ Ⓒ Ⓓ Ⓔ	26 Ⓐ Ⓑ Ⓒ Ⓓ Ⓔ	46 Ⓐ Ⓑ Ⓒ Ⓓ Ⓔ
7 Ⓐ Ⓑ Ⓒ Ⓓ Ⓔ	27 Ⓐ Ⓑ Ⓒ Ⓓ Ⓔ	47 Ⓐ Ⓑ Ⓒ Ⓓ Ⓔ
8 Ⓐ Ⓑ Ⓒ Ⓓ Ⓔ	28 Ⓐ Ⓑ Ⓒ Ⓓ Ⓔ	48 Ⓐ Ⓑ Ⓒ Ⓓ Ⓔ
9 Ⓐ Ⓑ Ⓒ Ⓓ Ⓔ	29 Ⓐ Ⓑ Ⓒ Ⓓ Ⓔ	49 Ⓐ Ⓑ Ⓒ Ⓓ Ⓔ
10 Ⓐ Ⓑ Ⓒ Ⓓ Ⓔ	30 Ⓐ Ⓑ Ⓒ Ⓓ Ⓔ	50 Ⓐ Ⓑ Ⓒ Ⓓ Ⓔ
11 Ⓐ Ⓑ Ⓒ Ⓓ Ⓔ	31 Ⓐ Ⓑ Ⓒ Ⓓ Ⓔ	51 Ⓐ Ⓑ Ⓒ Ⓓ Ⓔ
12 Ⓐ Ⓑ Ⓒ Ⓓ Ⓔ	32 Ⓐ Ⓑ Ⓒ Ⓓ Ⓔ	52 Ⓐ Ⓑ Ⓒ Ⓓ Ⓔ
13 Ⓐ Ⓑ Ⓒ Ⓓ Ⓔ	33 Ⓐ Ⓑ Ⓒ Ⓓ Ⓔ	53 Ⓐ Ⓑ Ⓒ Ⓓ Ⓔ
14 Ⓐ Ⓑ Ⓒ Ⓓ Ⓔ	34 Ⓐ Ⓑ Ⓒ Ⓓ Ⓔ	54 Ⓐ Ⓑ Ⓒ Ⓓ Ⓔ
15 Ⓐ Ⓑ Ⓒ Ⓓ Ⓔ	35 Ⓐ Ⓑ Ⓒ Ⓓ Ⓔ	55 Ⓐ Ⓑ Ⓒ Ⓓ Ⓔ
16 Ⓐ Ⓑ Ⓒ Ⓓ Ⓔ	36 Ⓐ Ⓑ Ⓒ Ⓓ Ⓔ	
17 Ⓐ Ⓑ Ⓒ Ⓓ Ⓔ	37 Ⓐ Ⓑ Ⓒ Ⓓ Ⓔ	
18 Ⓐ Ⓑ Ⓒ Ⓓ Ⓔ	38 Ⓐ Ⓑ Ⓒ Ⓓ Ⓔ	
19 Ⓐ Ⓑ Ⓒ Ⓓ Ⓔ	39 Ⓐ Ⓑ Ⓒ Ⓓ Ⓔ	
20 Ⓐ Ⓑ Ⓒ Ⓓ Ⓔ	40 Ⓐ Ⓑ Ⓒ Ⓓ Ⓔ	

CUT HERE

161

PRACTICE TEST 1

SECTION I: MULTIPLE-CHOICE QUESTIONS

Time: 60 Minutes
54 Questions

This section contains selections from two passages of prose and two poems with questions on their content, style, and form. Read each selection carefully. Choose the best answer of the five choices.

Questions 1–13. Read the passage carefully before you begin to answer the questions.

Of Superstition

It were better to have no opinion of God at all, than such
an opinion as is unworthy of him: for the one is unbelief, the
other is contumely: and certainly superstition is the re-
proach of the Deity. Plutarch saith well to that purpose:
(5) *Surely* (saith he) *I had rather a great deal men should say there
was no such man at all as Plutarch, than that they should say
that there was one Plutarch that would eat his children as soon
as they were born;* as the poets speak of Saturn. And as the
contumely is greater towards God, so the danger is greater
(10) towards men. Atheism leaves a man to sense, to philosophy,
to natural piety, to laws, to reputation; all which may be
guides to an outward moral virtue, though religion were not,
but superstition dismounts all these, and erecteth an absolute monarchy in the minds of men. Therefore atheism did
(15) never perturb states; for it makes men wary of themselves,
as looking no further: and we see the times inclined to
atheism (as the time of Augustus Caesar) were civil times.
But superstition hath been the confusion of many states,
and bringeth in a new *primum mobile,* that ravisheth all the

163

(20) spheres of government. The master of superstition is the people; and in all superstition wise men follow fools; and arguments are fitted to practice, in a reversed order. It was gravely said by some of the prelates in the Council of Trent, where the doctrine of the Schoolmen bare great sway, *that*

(25) *the Schoolmen were like astronomers, which did feign eccentrics and epicycles, and such engines of orbs, to save the phenomena,[1] though they knew there were no such things;* and in like manner, that the Schoolmen had framed a number of subtle and intricate axioms and theorems, to save the

(30) practice of the Church. The causes of superstition are: pleasing and sensual rites and ceremonies; excess of outward and pharisaical holiness; overgreat reverence of traditions, which cannot but load the Church; the stratagems of prelates for their own ambition and lucre; the favoring too

(35) much of good intentions, which openeth the gate to conceits and novelties; the taking an aim at divine matters by human, which cannot but breed mixture of imaginations; and lastly, barbarous times, especially joined with calamities and disasters. Superstition, without a veil, is a deformed thing;

(40) for, as it addeth deformity to an ape to be so like a man, so the similitude of superstition to religion makes it the more deformed. And as wholesome meat corrupteth to little worms, so good forms and orders corrupt into a number of petty observances. There is a superstition in avoiding

(45) superstition, when men think to do best if they go furthest from the superstition formerly received: therefore care would be had that (as it fareth in ill purgings) the good be not taken away with the bad; which commonly is done, when the people is the reformer.

[1]*eccentrics . . . phenomena:* irregularities and secondary orbits (of the heavenly bodies) invented by astronomers to account for astronomical facts.

1. The passage is an example of the
   (A) short story
   (B) essay
   (C) novel
   (D) epistle
   (E) oration

2. According to the passage, the atheist is
   (A) incapable of morality
   (B) more likely to be immoral than a believer
   (C) influenced to act morally
   (D) likely to be indifferent to reputation
   (E) a danger to the harmony of the state

3. The phrase "though religion were not" (line 12) can be best understood to mean
   (A) even if religion is lacking
   (B) as religion cannot do
   (C) although religious people believe differently
   (D) in spite of religion
   (E) if religious belief were untrue

4. In line 13, the word "dismounts" is
   (A) an auxiliary verb
   (B) a plural form of a noun
   (C) a participle modifying "superstition"
   (D) a transitive verb
   (E) an intransitive verb

5. The figure of speech in lines 19–20 ("*primum mobile . . . government*") is based upon
   (A) law
   (B) political economy
   (C) astronomy
   (D) solid geometry
   (E) history

6. Which of the following is an example of what line 22 calls "arguments . . . fitted to practice, in a reversed order"?
   (A) *"astronomers, which did feign eccentrics and epicycles"* (lines 25–26)
   (B) "pleasing and sensual rites and ceremonies" (line 31)
   (C) "excess of outward and pharisaical holiness" (lines 31–32)
   (D) "the taking an aim at divine matters by human" (line 36)
   (E) "calamities and disasters" (lines 38–39)

7. Lines 25–27 compare the Schoolmen to astronomers because both
   - (A) depend upon logical arguments in their studies
   - (B) are highly educated in abstruse subjects
   - (C) are free from superstitious belief
   - (D) are uniquely committed to intellectual pursuits
   - (E) invent data to suit their conclusions

8. According to the passage, at which of the following times is superstition most likely to flourish?
   - (A) A time of prosperity
   - (B) A time of scientific discovery
   - (C) A time of political change
   - (D) A time of solar and lunar eclipse
   - (E) A time of famine and flood

9. The sentence "And as wholesome meat . . . petty observances" (lines 42–44) is an example of
   - (A) metaphor
   - (B) paradox
   - (C) understatement
   - (D) simile
   - (E) *ad hominem* argument

10. The danger described in the conclusion of the passage (lines 44–49) is that
   - (A) superstition may blind men to the truth of religion
   - (B) superstition may lead men to presume knowledge of the supernatural
   - (C) the attempt to suppress superstition may lead to injustice
   - (D) the reformation of an evil may disrupt the stability of the state
   - (E) the recurrence of superstition is most likely when people believe it has been suppressed

11. The author's condemnation of superstition is conveyed by the words of all of the following EXCEPT
    (A) "wary of themselves" (line 15)
    (B) "confusion" (line 18)
    (C) "pharisaical holiness" (line 32)
    (D) "lucre" (line 34)
    (E) "mixture of imaginations" (line 37)

12. All of the following phrases employ figurative language EXCEPT
    (A) "erecteth an absolute monarchy" (lines 13–14)
    (B) "the stratagems of prelates for their own ambition" (lines 33–34)
    (C) "which openeth the gate to conceits and novelties" (lines 35–36)
    (D) "without a veil" (line 39)
    (E) "as it fareth in ill purgings" (line 47)

13. For which of the following reasons can it be argued that the style of the passage differs from that of most modern informal prose composition?

    I. The paragraph is much longer.
    II. The syntax is more complex.
    III. The allusions are more obscure.

    (A) I only
    (B) I and II only
    (C) I and III only
    (D) II and III only
    (E) I, II, and III

Questions 14–29. Read the following poem carefully before you begin to answer the questions.

Love's Diet

To what a cumbersome unwieldiness
And burdenous corpulence my love had grown
  But that I did, to make it less
  And keep it in proportión,
(5) Give it a diet, made it feed upon
That which love worst endures, discretión.

Above one sigh a day I allowed him not,
Of which my fortune and my faults had part;
  And if sometimes by stealth he got
(10) A she sigh from my mistress' heart
And thought to feast on that, I let him see
'Twas neither very sound, nor meant to me.

If he wrung from me a tear, I brined it so
With scorn or shame that him it nourished not;
(15) If he sucked hers, I let him know
  'Twas not a tear which he had got;
His drink was counterfeit as was his meat;
For eyes which roll towards all weep not, but sweat.

Whatever he would dictate, I writ that,
(20) But burnt my letters. When she writ to me,
  And that that favor made him fat,
  I said, if any title be
Conveyed by this, ah, what doth it avail
To be the fortieth name in an entail?

(25) Thus I reclaimed my buzzard love to fly
At what, and when, and how, and where I choose;
  Now negligent of sport I lie,
  And now as other falc'ners use,
I spring a mistress, swear, write, sigh, and weep;
(30) And the game killed or lost, go talk, and sleep.

14. The extended metaphor of stanzas 1–4 compares love to
    (A) an unwilling dieter
    (B) an illness
    (C) an unruly child
    (D) a prisoner in jail
    (E) a lawyer

15. In line 2, the verb "had grown" would be written by a modern prose writer as
    (A) grew
    (B) has grown
    (C) would have grown
    (D) did grow
    (E) has been growing

16. The figure of speech used through stanzas 1–4 is an example of
    (A) simile
    (B) personification
    (C) irony
    (D) ambiguity
    (E) apostrophe

17. In the last line of the second stanza, the speaker suggests that
    (A) the lady is deeply in love
    (B) only men, not women, sigh for love
    (C) the lady does not sigh for him
    (D) the sighs of the lady are more genuine than his
    (E) true love cannot feast on sighs

18. According to the second and third stanzas, the food and drink by which love grows are
    (A) faults and fortunes
    (B) scorn and shame
    (C) the heart and the eyes
    (D) sighs and tears
    (E) stealth and counterfeiting

19. The metaphor of lines 22–24 compares winning the lady's favor with
    (A) finishing in the fortieth position in a race
    (B) being obligated to work for forty days
    (C) inheriting a fortune
    (D) waiting until middle age to be married
    (E) being placed very low on a long list

20. According to the poem, which of the following is not a potentially fattening food?
    (A) Sighs
    (B) A man's tears
    (C) A lady's tears
    (D) Discretion
    (E) Love letters

21. The word "Thus" which begins the last stanza of the poem refers to
    (A) "entail" (line 24)
    (B) lines 19 and 20
    (C) stanza 1
    (D) stanza 4
    (E) lines 1–24

22. In lines 27–28, the repeated "Now" . . . "now" would be phrased in modern English
    (A) sometimes . . . other times
    (B) now . . . then
    (C) both . . . and
    (D) if now . . . then
    (E) once . . . now

23. In the next-to-last line of the poem, the three verbs "sigh," "weep," and "write" are used to

      I. recall the events of stanzas 2, 3, and 4
     II. show how deeply the speaker now feels about love
    III. recount the expected behavior of a lover

    (A) II only
    (B) I and II only
    (C) I and III only
    (D) II and III only
    (E) I, II, and III

24. In stanza 5, all of the following words are part of the central metaphor EXCEPT
    (A) "fly" (line 25)
    (B) "negligent" (line 27)
    (C) "spring" (line 29)
    (D) "game" (line 30)
    (E) "killed" (line 30)

25. In the final stanza of the poem, the speaker
    (A) has changed and now accepts the possibility of a genuine love
    (B) is more respectful of women than he was at the beginning of the poem
    (C) has become pessimistic about the love of women
    (D) is self-congratulating, cynical, and content
    (E) is divided in his mind—wanting to believe in love but afraid of commitment

26. Which of the following best describes the logical organization of the poem?
    (A) Stanza 1—stanzas 2, 3, 4—stanza 5
    (B) Stanza 1—stanzas 2, 3—stanzas 4, 5
    (C) Stanzas 1, 2—stanza 3—stanzas 4, 5
    (D) Stanzas 1, 2, 3—stanzas 4, 5
    (E) Stanza 1—stanza 2—stanzas 3, 4, 5

27. The poem draws its imagery from all of the following EXCEPT
   (A) falconry
   (B) law
   (C) eating
   (D) drinking
   (E) music

28. Of the following words, which best suggest by their sound and length the qualities that they denote?
   (A) "cumbersome unwieldiness and burdenous corpulence" (lines 1–2)
   (B) "A she sigh" (line 10)
   (C) "that that favor made him fat" (line 21)
   (D) "the fortieth name in an entail" (line 24)
   (E) "buzzard love" (line 25)

29. The poem alludes to all of the following conventional ideas about how a lover should behave EXCEPT
   (A) the lover is unable to sleep
   (B) the lover is melancholy and often weeps
   (C) the lover sits alone thinking about the loved one
   (D) the lover is so distracted by love that his clothes are disheveled
   (E) the lover writes tender love letters to the beloved

Questions 30–42. Read the following passage carefully before you begin to answer the questions.

Falsehood is so easy, truth so difficult. The pencil is conscious of a delightful facility in drawing a griffin—the longer the claws, and the larger the wings, the better; but that marvellous facility which we mistook for genius is apt to
(5) forsake us when we want to draw a real unexaggerated lion. Examine your words well, and you will find that even when you have no motive to be false, it is a very hard thing to say the exact truth, even about your own immediate feelings— much harder than to say something fine about them which is
(10) *not* the exact truth.

It is for this rare, precious quality of truthfulness that I delight in many Dutch paintings, which lofty-minded people despise. I find a source of delicious sympathy in these faithful pictures of a monotonous homely existence, which
(15) has been the fate of so many more among my fellow-mortals than a life of pomp or of absolute indigence, of tragic suffering or of world-stirring actions. I turn, without shrinking, from cloud-borne angels, from prophets, sibyls, and heroic warriors, to an old woman bending over her flower-
(20) pot, or eating her solitary dinner, while the noonday light, softened perhaps by a screen of leaves, falls on her mob-cap, and just touches the rim of her spinning-wheel, and her stone jug, and all those cheap common things which are the precious necessaries of life to her;—or I turn to that village
(25) wedding, kept between four brown walls, where an awkward bridegroom opens the dance with a high-shouldered, broad-faced bride, while elderly and middle-aged friends look on, with very irregular noses and lips, and probably with quart-pots in their hands, but with an expression of unmis-
(30) takable contentment and good-will. "Foh!" says my idealistic friend, "what vulgar details! What good is there in taking all these pains to give an exact likeness of old women and clowns? What a low phase of life!—what clumsy, ugly people!"
(35)   But bless us, things may be lovable that are not altogether handsome, I hope? I am not at all sure that the majority of the human race have not been ugly, and even among those "lords of their kind," the British, squat figures, ill-shapen nostrils, and dingy complexions are not startling exceptions.
(40) Yet there is a great deal of family love amongst us. I have a friend or two whose class of features is such that the Apollo curl on the summit of their brows would be decidedly trying; yet to my certain knowledge tender hearts have beaten for them, and their miniatures—flattering, but still not lovely—
(45) are kissed in secret by motherly lips. I have seen many an excellent matron, who could never in her best days have been handsome, and yet she had a packet of yellow love-letters in a private drawer, and sweet children show-ered kisses on her sallow cheeks. And I believe there have
(50) been plenty of young heroes, of middle stature and feeble

beards, who have felt quite sure they could never love anything more insignificant than a Diana, and yet have found themselves in middle life happily settled with a wife who waddles. Yes! thank God; human feeling is like the
(55) mighty rivers that bless the earth: it does not wait for beauty—it flows with resistless force and brings beauty with it.

30. In the first paragraph, the author is primarily concerned with the
    (A) superiority of truth to fiction
    (B) difficulty of expressing the truth
    (C) vagaries of mythological illustration
    (D) definitions of truth and fiction
    (E) impossibility of ever reaching the truth

31. The griffin, as it is used in the first paragraph, is parallel to which of the following in the second paragraph?
    (A) "Dutch paintings" (line 12)
    (B) "lofty-minded people" (line 12)
    (C) "cloud-borne angels, . . . prophets, sibyls" (line 18)
    (D) "the rim of her spinning-wheel, and her stone jug" (lines 22–23)
    (E) "old women and clowns" (lines 32–33)

32. In the second paragraph, the author refers to "lofty-minded people" in order to
    (A) claim kinship with them
    (B) demonstrate her own humility
    (C) give the reader an ally to identify with
    (D) call their ideas into question
    (E) give an equal amount of consideration to views that differ from her own

33. In line 29, the reference to "quart-pots" in the hands of the wedding guests
    (A) suggests that women's work continued even at a wedding party
    (B) shows how overcrowded the wedding table had become
    (C) alludes to gifts of plants brought to the wedding
    (D) reveals that guests are chiefly concerned with eating
    (E) indicates that the guests are drinking ale or beer

34. Which of the following terms are used in the second paragraph to refer to those whose ideas the speaker does NOT share?

      I. "lofty-minded people" (line 12)
     II. "my fellow-mortals" (line 15)
    III. "my idealistic friend" (lines 30–31)

    (A) I only
    (B) I and II only
    (C) I and III only
    (D) II and III only
    (E) I, II, and III

35. Which of the following describes the relationship of the third paragraph to the second?

      I. The third paragraph gives additional examples of a "monotonous homely existence."
     II. The third paragraph replies to the objections raised at the end of the second paragraph.
    III. The third paragraph reaches a philosophical conclusion about the subject of the second paragraph.

    (A) I only
    (B) I and II only
    (C) I and III only
    (D) II and III only
    (E) I, II, and III

36. In the third paragraph, second sentence, "even among those 'lords of their kind,' the British, squat figures, ill-shapen nostrils, and dingy complexions are not startling exceptions" (lines 37–39) is an example of
    (A) understatement
    (B) personification
    (C) paradox
    (D) simile
    (E) syllogism

37. In the phrase "young heroes, of middle stature and feeble beards" (lines 50–51), which of the following words is used ironically?
    (A) "young"
    (B) "heroes"
    (C) "middle"
    (D) "stature"
    (E) "feeble"

38. In the third paragraph, the "friend or two" (line 41), the "excellent matron"(line 46), and the "wife" (line 53) have in common that they are
    (A) no longer beautiful
    (B) secretly in love
    (C) loved regardless of their looks
    (D) people the author has observed in real life
    (E) the objects of corrosive satire

39. In line 56, the pronoun "it" ("it flows") refers to
    (A) God
    (B) human feeling
    (C) rivers
    (D) earth
    (E) beauty

40. The passage argues that ugliness is

    I. more common than handsomeness
    II. lovable
    III. made beautiful by feeling

    (A) III only
    (B) I and II only
    (C) I and III only
    (D) II and III only
    (E) I, II, and III

41. If the author of this passage were a novelist, her novels would probably be described as
    (A) experimental
    (B) romantic
    (C) stream-of-consciousness
    (D) realistic
    (E) symbolic

42. With which of the following statements would the author of this passage be most likely to agree?
    (A) The most important quality of a painting is its accuracy in rendering life.
    (B) The novel must teach the love of virtue and the hatred of vice.
    (C) The poor are closer to reality than the rich.
    (D) The greatest of painters are the Dutch.
    (E) Human sympathy will create beauty.

Questions 43–54. Read the following poem carefully before you begin to answer the questions.

A Description of the Morning

Now hardly here and there an hackney-coach
Appearing, showed the ruddy morn's approach.
Now Betty from her master's bed had flown,
And softly stole to discompose her own;
(5) The slip-shod 'prentice from his master's door
Had pared the dirt, and sprinkled round the floor.
Now Moll had whirled her mop with dext'rous airs,
Prepared to scrub the entry and the stairs.
The youth with broomy stumps began to trace
(10) The kennel-edge, where wheels had worn the place.
The small-coal man was heard with cadence deep,
Till drowned in shriller notes of chimney-sweep:
Duns at his lordship's gate began to meet;
And brickdust Moll had screamed through half a street.
(15) The turnkey now his flock returning sees,
Duly let out a-nights to steal for fees:
The watchful bailiffs take their silent stands,
And schoolboys lag with satchels in their hands.

43. Given the title of the poem, which of the following might a reader expect but not find?
    (A) An account of the sounds of the morning
    (B) An account of the countryside at daybreak
    (C) A reference to children on the way to school
    (D) An account of the early activity indoors
    (E) A picture of urban life in the morning

44. The focus of the poem is on
    (A) working class men and women
    (B) aristocrats
    (C) children
    (D) white-collar workers
    (E) the unemployed

45. The speaker of the poem does NOT
    (A) live in the city
    (B) understand the implication of lines 3–4
    (C) approve of Moll (lines 7–8)
    (D) make overt moral judgments
    (E) perceive the intention of the bailiffs (line 17)

46. The social range of the poem encompasses all of the following
    EXCEPT the
    (A) aristocrat
    (B) servant
    (C) clergyman
    (D) apprentice
    (E) peddler

47. In line 4, Betty discomposes her bed
    (A) as part of her duties as a maidservant
    (B) in preparation for the laundry
    (C) to give the appearance she has slept in it
    (D) because the beds are made of straw
    (E) because she is unable to sleep

48. In line 13, "Duns" are
    (A) salesmen
    (B) out-of-work lawyers
    (C) fools
    (D) upper servants
    (E) bill collectors

49. In line 15, the metaphor compares the turnkey to a
    (A) shepherd
    (B) farmer
    (C) ticket-taker
    (D) cobbler
    (E) butcher

50. In line 15, the "flock" is returning to a
    (A) pub
    (B) factory
    (C) barn
    (D) slaughterhouse
    (E) prison

51. The word "Duly" in line 16 can be understood to mean

    I. fitly, appropriately
    II. punctually, on time
    III. day after day

    (A) I only
    (B) II only
    (C) III only
    (D) I and II only
    (E) II and III only

52. If successful, the "watchful bailiffs" in line 17 will provide additions to the
    (A) duns at his lordship's gate
    (B) worn kennel-edge
    (C) army and the navy
    (D) turnkey's flock
    (E) laggard schoolboys

53. The poem is an example of which of the following verse forms?
    (A) Blank verse
    (B) Couplet
    (C) Terza rima
    (D) Ballad meter
    (E) Free verse

54. Compared to most poetry, this poem is notable for infrequently using
    (A) rhyme
    (B) figurative language
    (C) realistic detail
    (D) syntax
    (E) meter

STOP. IF YOU FINISH BEFORE TIME IS CALLED, CHECK YOUR WORK ON THIS SECTION ONLY. DO NOT WORK ON SECTION II.

SECTION II: ESSAY QUESTIONS

Time: 2 Hours
3 Questions

Question 1

(Suggested time—40 minutes. This question counts one-third of the total essay section score.)

The following passage is the conclusion of Samuel Johnson's "Life of Savage," an account of the eighteenth-century writer Richard Savage, who died in great poverty in 1743.

Read the passage carefully. Write a well-organized essay in which you discuss Johnson's evaluation of Savage and the resources of language Johnson employs to communicate his opinions effectively.

> For his life, or for his writings, none who candidly consider
> his fortune will think an apology either necessary or diffi-
> cult. If he was not always sufficiently instructed in his
> subject, his knowledge was at least greater than could have
> (5) been attained by others in the same state. If his works were
> sometimes unfinished, accuracy cannot reasonably be ex-
> acted from a man oppressed with want, which he has no
> hope of relieving but by a speedy publication. The insolence
> and resentment of which he is accused, were not easily to be
> (10) avoided by a great mind, irritated by perpetual hardships,
> and constrained hourly to return the spurns of contempt,
> and repress the insolence of prosperity; and vanity surely
> may be readily pardoned in him, to whom life afforded no
> other comforts than barren praises, and the consciousness
> (15) of deserving them.
>   Those are no proper judges of his conduct who have
> slumbered away their time on the down of plenty; nor will
> any wise man presume to say, "Had I been in Savage's
> condition, I should have lived or written better than
> (20) Savage."

This relation will not be wholly without its use, if those who languish under any part of his sufferings shall be enabled to fortify their patience, by reflecting that they feel only those afflictions from which the abilities of Savage did
(25) not exempt him; or those who, in confidence of superior capacities or attainments, disregard the common maxims of life, shall be reminded that nothing will supply the want of prudence, and that negligence and irregularity, long continued, will make knowledge useless, wit ridiculous, and genius
(30) contemptible.

Question 2

(Suggested time—40 minutes. This question counts one-third of the total essay section score.)

Read the following poem carefully. Then write a cohesive essay in which you show how the language of each stanza reveals the perceptions and feelings of the speaker.

> The birds began at four o'clock,
> Their period for dawn,
> A music numerous as space
> But neighboring as noon.
>
> (5) I could not count their force,
> Their voices did expend
> As brook by brook bestows itself
> To multiply the pond.
>
> Their witnesses were not
> (10) Except occasional man,
> In homely industry arrayed
> To overtake the morn.
>
> Nor was it for applause
> (That I could ascertain)
> (15) But independent ecstasy
> Of deity and men.
>
> By six, the flood had done.
> No tumult there had been
> Of dressing, or departure,
> (20) And yet the band was gone.
>
> The sun engrossed the east,
> The day controlled the world,
> The miracle that introduced
> Forgotten, as fulfilled.

Question 3

(Suggested time—40 minutes. This question counts one-third of the total essay section score.)

An eating scene is common in drama and fiction. It may be a simple meal or a banquet, a holiday party or ordinary family dinner, but the work would not be quite the same without it.

Choose a play, epic, or novel which contains such a scene of eating, and write an essay in which you discuss what the scene reveals, how the scene is related to the meaning of the work as a whole, and by what means the author makes the scene effective.

Focus your essay on only ONE scene. Do not summarize the plot. You may write on one of the following works or any other novel, epic, or play of your choice of equivalent literary merit.

A Portrait of the Artist as a Young Man
Beowulf
Little Dorrit
Great Expectations
Jane Eyre
Wuthering Heights
The Great Gatsby
the *Iliad*
the *Odyssey*
The Tempest
Macbeth
The Mayor of Casterbridge
Pride and Prejudice
Invisible Man
The Birthday Party
The Three Sisters
Mrs. Dalloway
To the Lighthouse
Ethan Frome
A Passage to India
The Importance of Being Earnest
Our Town
Lord of the Flies
The Joy Luck Club

END OF EXAMINATION

ANSWER KEY FOR PRACTICE TEST 1

SECTION I: MULTIPLE-CHOICE QUESTIONS

First Prose Passage

1. B	6. A	11. A
2. C	7. E	12. B
3. A	8. E	13. E
4. D	9. D	
5. C	10. C	

First Poem

14. A	20. D	26. A
15. C	21. E	27. E
16. B	22. A	28. A
17. C	23. C	29. D
18. D	24. B	
19. E	25. D	

Second Prose Passage

30. B	35. E	40. E
31. C	36. A	41. D
32. D	37. B	42. E
33. E	38. C	
34. C	39. B	

Second Poem

43. B	47. C	51. D
44. A	48. E	52. D
45. D	49. A	53. B
46. C	50. E	54. B

PRACTICE TEST 1 SCORING WORKSHEET

Use the following worksheet to arrive at a probable final AP grade on Practice Test 1. While it is sometimes difficult to be objective enough to score one's own essay, you can use the sample essay answers that follow to approximate an essay score for yourself. You might also give your essays (along with the sample essays) to a friend or relative to score if you feel confident that the individual has the knowledge necessary to make such a judgment and that he or she will feel comfortable in doing so.

Section I: Multiple-Choice Questions

$$\frac{\quad\quad}{\substack{\text{right} \\ \text{answers}}} - \left(\text{¼ or .25} \times \frac{\quad\quad}{\substack{\text{wrong} \\ \text{answers}}}\right) = \frac{\quad\quad}{\substack{\text{multiple-choice} \\ \text{raw score}}}$$

$$\frac{\quad\quad}{\substack{\text{multiple-choice} \\ \text{raw score}}} \times 1.25 = \frac{\quad\quad}{\substack{\text{multiple-choice} \\ \text{converted score}}} \text{(of possible 67.5)}$$

Section II: Essay Questions

$$\frac{\quad\quad}{\substack{\text{question 1} \\ \text{raw score}}} + \frac{\quad\quad}{\substack{\text{question 2} \\ \text{raw score}}} + \frac{\quad\quad}{\substack{\text{question 3} \\ \text{raw score}}} = \frac{\quad\quad}{\substack{\text{essay} \\ \text{raw score}}}$$

$$\frac{\quad\quad}{\substack{\text{essay} \\ \text{raw score}}} \times 3.055 = \frac{\quad\quad}{\substack{\text{essay} \\ \text{converted score}}} \text{(of possible 82.5)}$$

Final Score

$$\frac{\quad\quad}{\substack{\text{multiple-choice} \\ \text{converted score}}} + \frac{\quad\quad}{\substack{\text{essay} \\ \text{converted score}}} = \frac{\quad\quad}{\substack{\text{final} \\ \text{converted score}}} \text{(of possible 150}$$

Probable Final AP Score

Final Converted Score	Probable AP Score
150–100	5
99– 86	4
85– 67	3
66– 0	1 or 2

ANSWERS AND EXPLANATIONS FOR PRACTICE TEST 1

SECTION I: MULTIPLE-CHOICE QUESTIONS

First Prose Passage

1. (B) An essay is a short composition on a single subject. This is Francis Bacon's essay "Of Superstition," written late in the sixteenth century. Most students would find this prose more difficult to read than the other texts in this multiple-choice section. If you do find a first passage hard to deal with, go on to the others and come back to the first section later. Your score is based on the total number of right answers, and you don't want to waste too much time on one passage at the expense of the rest of the exam. "Of Superstition" is nonfiction, so the two fiction forms, short story (A) and novel (C), can be eliminated. An epistle (D) is a letter, but this passage is not addressed to a specific person. An oration (E) is a formal, public speech.

2. (C) Choices (A), (B), (D), and (E) contradict the passage. Lines 10–14 argue that the atheist is less dangerous to civil order than the superstitious person, since the atheist may be guided to a natural moral virtue by philosophy and sense and by a respect for law and reputation.

3. (A) Though none of these paraphrases is ideal, the best of the five choices is (A). Remember that the instructions call only for the "best" answer of the five, not the "right," "correct," or "ideal" answer. The idiom "were not" of three hundred years ago is now expressed by "there were no." With questions like this one, you must rely on what has been said already and the immediate context of the phrase.

4. (D) Though the common modern use of the verb "to dismount" is as an intransitive verb (a verb without a direct object) as in to dismount from a horse or from gymnastics apparatus, the verb

189

here clearly has an object, "these." Be sure to look carefully at the text before answering a question like this one. The word "dismounts" could be a plural form of a noun (B) or an intransitive verb (E), and you can discover the right answer only from the context in the passage.

5. (C) The allusion is to medieval astronomy in which the outermost sphere of the universe (the *primum mobile*) was believed to control the motions of the other spheres. Even if you are unfamiliar with the notion of the *primum mobile,* the use of "spheres" should suggest astronomy. Choice (D) is nasty because "spheres" also is a term of solid geometry. The passage uses another analogy from astronomy later on.

6. (A) To answer this question, you must first understand the meaning of line 22. The phrase refers to the practice of the superstitious of inventing data to fit events that have already happened. If I spill my soup on Monday and get a parking ticket on Tuesday, I might superstitiously claim that spilling soup leads to parking tickets. The astronomers referred to in lines 25–27, who wished to confirm what they believed were the orbits of heavenly bodies, invented other motions of the bodies to explain away what did not fit their preconceived ideas.

7. (E) Bacon accuses the Schoolmen (the medieval university teachers of philosophy and theology) of being "like astronomers, which did feign . . ." That is, both invented data ("eccentrics and epicycles," "intricate axioms and theorems") to fit conclusions they had reached already. Choices (A), (B), (C), and (D) denote an approval of the astronomers and Schoolmen, just the opposite of what the essay says.

8. (E) In the list of the causes of superstition (lines 30–39), the conclusion is "barbarous times, especially joined with calamities and disasters." It is possible that a time of political change would be a time of calamity, but "famine and flood" are clearly more explicit examples of disasters.

9. (D) The sentence is a simile, a comparison with "like" or "as" expressed. The author here uses "as . . . so." The same figure as a metaphor would be "Good forms are wholesome meats corrupted." An *ad hominem* argument (E) is one that attacks an opponent rather than discussing the issues.

10. (C) The passage warns against a "superstition in avoiding superstition," that is, going too far in the *other* direction in order to avoid an error of superstition. This error may sacrifice the "good" as well as the "bad." The most plausible of the five answers is (C), which describes a good (justice) that may be lost by an overzealous suppression of the bad (superstition). Notice that the incorrect answers are not of themselves untrue. They are ideas that are plausible but simply not relevant to this question. Good wrong answers in multiple-choice exams are often sensible or even profound. Don't let the ring of moral truth distract you from exactly what the question has asked you.

11. (A) To answer a question like this, you must look at each of these phrases in context. In this case, the first option, "wary of themselves" in line 15, is used to describe an effect of atheism, which makes men "wary of themselves." A shrewd test taker would realize that this must be the right answer, since it describes the atheist, not the superstitious. To go through the passage examining options (B), (C), (D), and (E) would waste time. There are some questions where you can't avoid checking on all five answers. When you find one that you can answer without wasting time, be glad of the discovery and go on to the next question. Unfortunately, the right answer is not always the first one you come to. A mean test writer would put the correct answer here as (E).

12. (B) In this phrase, "stratagems," "prelates," and "ambition" are all used literally to refer to the deceitful practices of ambitious churchmen. Choice (E) is a simile using "as." Choices (A), (C), and (D) are metaphors, using "monarchy," "gate," and "veil" figuratively. A real monarchy cannot exist in the mind, a real gate does not lead to conceits, and superstition cannot wear a real veil.

13. (E) All three describe differences between Bacon's essay and modern informal prose. Bacon has clearly not had the advantages of modern instruction in the craft of paragraphing, since his whole essay has only one. His sentences are much longer and often more complex than is usual in modern prose. His allusions—to Plutarch, Saturn, astronomy, Roman history, medieval philosophy, for example—are likely to be unfamiliar to many modern readers.

First Poem

The poem is John Donne's "Love's Diet."

14. (A) The first four stanzas imagine a speaker and his love for a woman as two distinct people. The speaker forces the personified love to go on a diet so it will not grow out of his control. This first question of the set is an easy one, and the exam normally begins a set of questions with one of the easier questions. The conceit (an ingenious metaphor) of love as a reluctant dieter is the basis of the poem's title and the chief figure of the first four stanzas.

15. (C) Lines 1–5 could be paraphrased as follows: Unless I had put my love on a diet to decrease its size and keep it manageable, it would have grown gigantic and uncontrollable. The sentence is conditional, and the verb "had grown" is a subjunctive meaning "would have grown," though it looks like a past perfect tense of an indicative verb. The point is that the speaker saw the danger and put love on a diet before it grew too fat.

16. (B) The figure, or conceit, is a metaphor, not a simile. The comparison of a thing, quality, or idea to a human is also an example of personification. Notice that the pronouns for this love/person are "it," "he," or "him."

17. (C) To enjoy this poem, we must accept the unlikely situation of a man who does not want to be in love arguing with his personified love for a woman. The speaker hopes to disenchant love by finding fault with the lady. Here, though he admits that

lady has sighed, he argues that the sigh is unsound, impaired or invalid, and not meant for him anyway. Choice (E) contradicts the figure of this stanza; love *can* feed on sighs. The more the lovers sigh, the greater their love will grow. But the speaker argues that her sigh cannot be fattening because it is meant for someone else. The speaker's own sighs are also calorie-free because they are not for love, but sighs for his own faults and fortune.

18. (D) As stanza 2 is based on the notion of the sigh as the food of lovers, stanza 3 assumes that tears are the drink of lovers. The idea of a lover's sighing and weeping are commonplaces in love poetry, as the Romeo of Act I of *Romeo and Juliet* demonstrates. Stanza 3 argues that the salt water on the lady's face is not a tear but sweat. She has been so actively rolling her eyes at every man who passes that her eyes are sweating, not weeping.

19. (E) The metaphor compares the value of the lady's letters to being "the fortieth name in an entail." An "entail" is the sequence of heirs in a will. If the speaker were fortieth, thirty-nine others would have to die before he would inherit the estate, which is to say that her love letters are of no more value than her sighs or tears. Love will not get fat on them.

20. (D) Though the poem devalues the sighs, letters, and tears of the lady here, all of them, as well as the man's sighs, are potentially means of increasing love. Discretion, on the other hand, is the worst thing in the world for love, what it "worst endures" (line 6). The basic notion of the poem is that love is irrational, but cold, reasonable behavior can keep it in check.

21. (E) "Thus" in line 25 refers back to the first four stanzas of the poem. These stanzas describe how the speaker has prevented love from growing, how he has asserted his power by controlling love's diet. The metaphor in line 25 changes from a personified love on a restricted diet to a "buzzard love," love as a bird he has trained by these means (that is, by what lines 1–24 describe). The transition from the diet figure to the bird image will seem less abrupt if we are aware that falcons were and are

trained to hunt by strictly controlling their diet. The word "reclaimed" in line 25 is still listed in dictionaries with its obsolete meaning "to tame or subdue, as a hawk." This meaning was not obsolete when this poem was written.

22. (A) With his love wholly in his control, the speaker can do as he pleases, now (that is, sometimes) indifferent to the game of love, and now (that is, at other times) pursuing women just like other predatory men.

23. (C) The speaker does not feel deeply about love (II); it is a game to him which he can take or leave. The three verbs recall the events of stanzas 2, 3, and 4, and their use here is another structural link between the last stanza and the first part of the poem. The verbs also denote the expected behavior of a lover (III), which this man will use because he knows how the game is to be played but not because he is really in love.

24. (B) "Negligent" refers to the speaker's indifference to love. The four other words, "fly," "spring" (to cause birds to break from their cover), "game," and "killed" all allude to falconry. The verb "reclaimed" could also be added to the list of words in the stanza that refer to falconry.

25. (D) The speaker is cynical and complacent throughout the poem. The whole poem is his boast about how clever he is, how fully he has mastered his emotions. If the poem were the first act of a play, we could expect him to fall in love in act two, like Benedict in Shakespeare's *Much Ado About Nothing*.

26. (A) You should see at once that the basic organization of the poem is stanzas 1–4 (the diet) and stanza 5 (the falcon). Any organizational scheme that does not separate stanza 5 from the rest of the poem should be eliminated at once. On further consideration, we can see that stanza 1 introduces the idea of the diet and stanzas 2, 3, and 4 deal with a different component of the diet. Much the best description of the organization, then, is 1—2, 3, 4—5.

27. (E) Falconry is used in the last stanza. The entail figure in lines 22–24 is drawn from law. The images of stanzas 2 and 3 are from eating and drinking, but there are no images from music.

28. (A) Look at the size of these words, all of three or four syllables. Try to say them fast. Their sound and length reflect the size and awkwardness the words denote.

29. (D) Though it mocks many of the conventions of love poetry, this poem depends for its comic effect on the reader's recognizing how a conventional lover will behave. The central idea of a calorie-counting love in danger of gaining too much weight was probably suggested by the conventional notion of the lean and pale lover so in love that he cannot eat. Donne may have noticed that as the lover grows thinner, love grows larger. He alludes to the convention of the sleepless lover (A) in the last line. This lover has no trouble sleeping, whether or not his love-quest is successful. This lover weeps (B) and sighs but not for love. He does not sit alone (C) but socializes ("go talk," line 30). His letters, like his tears, do not increase his love (E). Choice (D) is also a conventional notion about lovers but *not* one that Donne exploits in this poem.

Second Prose Passage

The passage is from George Eliot's novel *Adam Bede.*

30. (B) The thesis of the paragraph is expressed in its first sentence: "Falsehood is so easy, truth so difficult." The idea is reasserted in the long last sentence of the paragraph. The paragraph does not claim that truth is superior to fiction (A), only that it is more difficult. Nor does it attempt to define truth and fiction (D) or to claim that truth cannot be attained (E).

31. (C) In the first paragraph, the griffin represents the fanciful, the untrue that is so much easier to draw than the reality of the lion. In the second paragraph, the angels, prophets, sibyls, and herioc warriors are parallel images of figures larger than life which the author finds less precious than the truth of Dutch

paintings (A) with their spinning wheels (D) and old women and clowns (E).

32. (D) The "lofty-minded" people of the second paragraph are those who snobbishly reject the truthful paintings that the speaker prefers. The author refers to the "lofty-minded" in order to criticize their rejection of the unglamorous truth in art. She would not claim kinship with them and is not concerned to appear to be either humble or fair.

33. (E) British English uses "pot" to refer to a vessel for holding a drink, especially beer or ale. In the paintings of village weddings such as this one, the guests would probably be drinking beer or ale from quart pots.

34. (C) The passage opposes the speaker and others who welcome the truth of the commonplace in art to those who prefer the idealized, the lofty, the beautiful. The speaker claims kinship with her "fellow mortals" who have lived homely lives. Her antagonists are the "lofty-minded" who despise the truthfulness of Dutch paintings and the "idealistic friend" whose disgust with the painting of the vulgar truth of ordinary village life is expressed at the end of the paragraph.

35. (E) Lines 40–54 ("I have a friend . . . who waddles.") give three examples of people whose existence is "homely" but who are no less cherished. It replies to the complaint at the end of the second paragraph that these clumsy, ugly people are not fit subjects for art with the argument that what is lovable is not always handsome and that more humans are plain than are beautiful. The paragraph concludes with a generalization about beauty and human feeling.

36. (A) That the "lords of their kind" should include some squat and ill-shapen men is not quite a paradox (an apparent self-contradiction), and there is no personification, simile, or syllogism in the phrase. But by using "even" and the double negative of "not startling exceptions," the author understates

what she really believes. The less-than-handsome is, in fact, not the rare exception but the rule.

37. (B) The ironic word is the one whose intended meaning is the opposite of what is stated. Here "young," "middle," "stature," and "feeble" all mean what they say. These are not "heroes," however; they are ordinary young men who do not marry goddesses but still live happily.

38. (C) The series lists three examples of people who are loved although they are not beautiful. Choice (A) is incorrect; the point is that they never were beautiful. The "friend" and "matron" have been observed, but the "wife" is not identified as someone the speaker has known or seen. They are not the objects of satire, for the speakers point is that love is more important than physical beauty.

39. (B) All three of the pronouns (it) in the sentence refer to human feeling. You could eliminate the noun "rivers" immediately because the pronoun is singular.

40. (E) The last paragraph makes all three of these points. The speaker tentatively suggests that the majority of the human race may have been ugly. There are several examples of the less-than-beautiful people who are beloved, and the passage ends with the paean to human feeling, whose irresistible flow brings beauty with it.

41. (D) As it happens, the author of this passage is a novelist, the great nineteenth-century British realist George Eliot. The passage is outspoken in its preference of "truth," the "unexaggerated," the "real," praising "faithful pictures of a monotonous homely existence." There is nothing in the passage to suggest a taste for the experimental or the romantic or the symbolic and nothing in the ordered progress of the argument to suggest an interest in a stream-of-consciousness technique.

42. (E) All of these choices present ideas that the author might endorse, but because it is explicitly stated in the last sentence of

the passage ("human feeling . . . brings beauty with it."), (E) is the best choice. The writer expresses her admiration of the realism of Dutch painting but stops short of saying this is a painting's "most important quality." Though George Eliot might agree with (B), it is certainly not in this passage, which never alludes to the novel. We cannot prove (C) or (D) wrong from the passage, but we also cannot support either convincingly. The Dutch painters are praised but not judged as "greater" or "greatest."

Second Poem

The poem is by Jonathan Swift and was written in 1709. You should see right away that this is a much shorter and much less complex poem than the Donne lyric on this exam. Most readers would agree that this is the easiest of the four passages. Try to budget your time in the multiple-choice section so that you don't have to skip an easier passage because you've spent too much time on a harder or longer one. Get a sense of the whole exam before you begin to answer the questions.

43. (B) Conditioned as most readers of poetry are by the English romantic poets or American poets of nature like Emerson or Frost, we may be surprised to find a poetic description of the morning without a single flower or birdsong. Swift's poem does give us the "ruddy morn," but its focus is entirely urban, not rural.

44. (A) The poem does allude to an aristocrat's gate, besieged by bill collectors, to reluctant schoolboys and a youth, and to the inmates of the debtors' prison, but it gives more examples of working class men and women: Betty, the apprentice, Moll, the youth, the coal seller, the chimney-sweep.

45. (D) Another unusual aspect of this poem is the author's refusal to make moral judgments. He simply describes the scene and the people with no overt evaluations.

46. (C) Though Swift was a clergyman, he has included none in this poem. We have an aristocrat ("his lordship"), a servant ("Betty"), an apprentice, and a peddler (the coal man).

47. (C) Line 3 tells that Betty has spent the night in her master's bed but left it at dawn to sneak back to "discompose her own." We are obliged to infer that Betty is disturbing her own bed to give the impression that she spent the night in her own room.

48. (E) To dun is to demand payment from a debtor. The noun refers to either an insistent request for payment of a debt or, as is the case here, a person who collects debts. The word is used today as it was in the eighteenth century.

49. (A) The turnkey is the jailer at the debtors' prison, who is compared here to a shepherd; the returning prisoners are his flock. Rather than feeding his flock, this good shepherd releases his each night so they can find the money to pay the fees that were charged for room and board at their prison.

50. (E) The "flock" of released prisoners returns at daybreak to the debtors' prison.

51. (D) Swift employs two meanings of the word "duly" here. The custom of releasing prisoners to enable them to find some money is "duly" observed, and the prison officials no doubt regard the practice as fitting. The time of the release, "a-nights," is also duly observed, that is, punctually.

52. (D) A bailiff is an officer of the court, a process-server. The watchful bailiffs here are probably on the lookout for debtors who have defaulted, and if they find their prey, the turnkey's flock will grow larger.

53. (B) Like many of the poems of the eighteenth century, this is written in couplets. Line 1 rhymes with line 2, line 3 with line 4, and so on. Nine couplets make up this eighteen-line poem.

54. (B) Normally, poetry is distinguished by its use of figurative language. This poem, however, uses hardly any (although there is the "flock" figure in line 15 and the common use of "drowned" in line 12). Rhyme, on the other hand, is used in every line. The poem is made up of a number of realistic details. The meter of the poem, a regular iambic pentameter, is used in every line. Unless one writes gibberish, it is hard not to use syntax.

SECTION II: ESSAY QUESTIONS

Question 1: Samuel Johnson

This question calls for a reading of Johnson's "evaluation of Savage" and a discussion of the "resources of language" he uses. The phrase "resources of language" allows students to decide what stylistic devices they wish to write about; the plural indicates that they must write about more than one. This is, in fact, another example of the archetypal essay question: discuss X's evaluation of Y and the stylistic devices X uses. An essay of three well-developed paragraphs that discusses Johnson's attitude in the first and deals specifically with two or more stylistic techniques in the second and third paragraphs would do the job well.

The passage is remarkable for its balance in both content and style. Johnson's sympathy with Savage does not blind him to his defects, and in almost every sentence, Johnson balances praise and blame. He sees, for example, that Savage's works are sometimes inaccurate, or uninformed, or unfinished, but he also sees that Savage's knowledge was greater than that others could have attained and that his poverty forced him to write too quickly. Similarly, though he grants that Savage may have been insolent, resentful, and vain, he understands these faults as the response of a great mind under constant and intolerable stress.

The most obvious resources of language to discuss in this passage are probably its diction and its syntax. Almost every sentence offers examples of the balance of words that praise with words that disparise. The syntax usually employs a parallel construction. To cite just one example, the conclusion of the third paragraph suggests Savage's defects by using words and phrases like "want of prudence," "negligence," and "irregularity" and his strengths by using words like "knowledge," "wit," and, most significantly, "genius." The parallel phrasing of the concluding series ("knowledge useless," "wit ridiculous," "genius contemptible") is characteristic of the entire passage, which for its first phrases ("For his life, or for his writings") also employs parallel constructions.

The following two student essays on this question will give you a better idea of the kind of answer this topic will elicit.

Student Essay 1

Samuel Johnson expressed admiration and sympathy for Richard Savage in the conclusion of his work "Life of Savage." Using his language resources effectively, Johnson manages to defend Savage from his critics, helping them to understand the hardships in life that Savage endured.

Johnson begins this passage by explaining something of Savage's background, as well as how his poverty affected his work. "If he was not always sufficiently instructed in his subject, his knowledge was at least greater than could have been attained by others in the same state. If his works were sometimes unfinished, accuracy cannot be reasonably exacted from a man oppressed by want, which he has no hope of relieving but by a speedy publication." Savage was trapped in a cycle of inability to complete works due to dire poverty, yet only could he begin to escape that poverty by sending completed works to the publisher. Johnson understood this cycle of poverty and helplessness, and wrote so that other authors and intellectuals of that time might appreciate Savage's works, as well as his misfortune.

Johnson continues on to rebut criticisms of Savage's character in a direct and solid manner. "The insolence and resentment of which he is accused, were not easily to be avoided by a great mind, irritated by perpetual hardships, and constrained hourly to return the spurns of contempt, and repress the insolence of prosperity; and vanity surely may be readily pardoned in him, to whom life afforded no other comforts than barren praises, and the consciousness of deserving them." All at once, Johnson removes questions and accusations about Savage's character with his straightforward style.

Finally, Johnson questions the validity of the critics' allegations towards Savage. "Those are no proper judges of his conduct who have slumbered away their time on the down of plenty; nor will any wise man presume to say, 'Had I been in Savage's condition, I should have lived or written better than Savage.'" In doing so, Johnson eradicates all charges against Savage simply by reminding readers and critics not to judge Savage's actions and attitudes, since those actions were a result of his singularly unfortunate experience as a poverty-stricken scholar and writer in the midst of wealthy writers.

Samuel Johnson employs direct language, thoughtful understanding, and a straightforward manner to gain understanding and acceptance for the life and works of Richard Savage in his account "Life of Savage."

Student Essay 2

Samuel Johnson admonishes those who would belittle Savage without taking into account the extreme poverty which continually wore on him. His evaluation of Savage is of a man who did the best he could with his talent, fighting adverse conditions, and emerged an inspirational figure despite the problems plaguing him. He endured. A latter day Briton might have said he "muddled through." But Johnson portrays him as doing more than muddling; despite his faults, he led a remarkable life.

Johnson has a style that is scholarly, almost erudite. He writes with elegance putting the best face on a man (Savage) who was apparently much maligned. Always Johnson uses delicacy in detailing Savage's perceived faults. Savage was not ignorant, he "was not always sufficiently instructed in his subject . . ." Accuracy at times suffered in Savage's work, but scarcely has Johnson conceded this than he adds that exacting standards cannot be set for a man "oppressed with want." His intent seems not so much to foster reader sympathy with Savage as to excuse his perceived failings, to make readers admire and respect a man who has fought hard in a cruel world.

Johnson's diction is fundamental to his evaluation. As he addresses each of Savage's flaws, he uses similar words to describe the onus of poverty and misfortune weighing on the writer. Resentment and insolence "could not be avoided" because Savage was "irritated." His hardships were not incidental, but "perpetual." He was "constrained hourly . . . life afforded no other comforts than barren praises." Johnson's evaluation, then, is irretrievably intertwined with the hardships Savage faced; Savage can ultimately be understood only in the context of his life's circumstances.

Finally Johnson turns the lens of his scrutiny on the reader. He contrasts the probable conditions of the reader's life with those of Savage to demonstrate the inability of most readers to make an empathetic criticism of the writer. Critics, Johnson alleges, have "slumbered away their time on the down of plenty." Yet they, in Savage's circumstances, could have done no better—would have probably done far worse. Johnson ends his work on a similar note: Those who are similarly disadvantaged can take heart in the successes, the brilliance of Richard Savage, who persevered and prevailed in the face of trouble and criticism; those confident and successful should extract a lesson from Johnson's portrayal, should understand that fundamental qualities of "prudence" and conscientiousness cannot be superceded by material prosperity. Without those qualities of Richard Savage, that will to do the best that he could, "knowledge [would be] useless, wit ridiculous, and genius contemptible."

The success of Johnson's persuasion arises largely from his final focus on the faults of the general public. Putting readers on the defensive by criticizing their anticipated criticism. Johnson gives them pause, effectively causing them to look at Savage in a different light than they would have had Savage's faults been illuminated but Johnson merely argued that they lacked significance.

Response to Student Essay 1

This essay is a good example of a competently written five-paragraph essay that would score no higher than a five and might well fall a point lower on the nine-point scoring scale. The writer clearly understands the meaning of the selection, though the essay overstates its effect ("Johnson eradicates all charges"). The real problem here is that almost all of the paper is either direct quotation (about one-third) or paraphrase. The quotations are well chosen, and the paraphrase is, largely, accurate, but the essay never deals with the "resources of language" half of the question. It twice calls Johnson's style "direct" and "straightforward" but makes no other comment on the language of the passage. Neither "direct" nor "straightforward" is an appropriate term to describe this prose, with its frequent double negatives, periodic sentences, and a final paragraph that comprises only one sentence eighty-seven words long.

Response to Student Essay 2

The second essay is a much better response to the question. Notice how the student quotes only words or phrases to support specific points. The third paragraph deals with Johnson's diction, and the comments on Johnson's style are accurate. The quality falls off somewhat in the fourth paragraph, which misinterprets part of Johnson's conclusion. The paper would, no doubt, be improved if the writer discussed another "resource of language." Remember that when a question calls for a discussion of "style," or "devices," or "resources" with no more specific demands, shrewd students will use in their essays such terms as "diction," "point of view," "imagery," and the like. Your reader will then be sure that you know just what "resources of language" are. This paper would receive at least a seven on the nine-point scale.

Question 2: Emily Dickinson

The question here takes a very permissive form, simply asking for a discussion of how language reveals the speaker's perceptions and feelings. The phrase "of each stanza" should tell you that you must say something about each of the six stanzas in the poem. By asking only for a discussion of "language," the question allows students to select their topics, but since the diction and imagery of the poem are so unusual and important, a successful essay would probably have to deal with both. Another topic that few would choose, but which the poem especially invites, is syntax. Just the briefest mention of the omission of words that we expect or the odd word order ("independent ecstasy of deity and men" instead of "ecstasy independent of deity and men," for example) would make a favorable impression.

In a paragraph about the first stanza of the poem, you could discuss the ambiguity and richness of the first two lines. Does "period" have only its obvious meaning of "portion of time" and refer to the four o'clock time period, or does it have its meaning as a musical term, "a group of measures that form a statement"? Is it in apposition to four o'clock or the direct object of the verb "began"? This music is described by two remarkable adjectives and two curious similes: "numerous as space" and "neighboring as noon." The first surprises because we think music exists in time not space, and though we speak of the numerous voices of a choir, we would not transfer the adjective to describe music itself.

Stanza two concludes the description of the early song of the birds. A discussion of diction might cite the word "force" (the size of their forces or the large number of birds but also the power of the song), and a discussion of images might refer to "expend," "bestow," and "multiply" as part of a financial figure. The simile of lines 5–8 that compares the songs of the birds to brooks that fill a pond will be recalled in the fifth stanza's use of "flood."

Stanzas three and four ask why the birds sing. For whose benefit? For what listeners? The speaker's feelings are especially clear in the choice of the word "ecstasy" to describe an exalted joy with no regard for deity or man. The poem reaches its climactic assertion in these lines. In stanzas five and six, it recedes.

Stanza five describes the end of the song. In line 20, "band" is probably another word with several meanings, the group and the more specific group of instrumentalists. Birdsong by Sousa. Though the sun and the day take over in stanza six, one last key word reveals the poet's feelings about the birds: "miracle."

This poem by Emily Dickinson is so rich and suggestive and the question so unspecific that the range of essays it would produce is enormous. Here are two samples.

Student Essay 1

Language is used carefully and meaningfully in each stanza of this poem, revealing the perceptions of the speaker after experiencing the chorus of birds at dawn.

In the first stanza the speaker describes the timing of the birds' songs in the early hours as "A music as numerous as space/ But neighboring as noon." Although the birds begin their chorus at four o'clock, according to the speaker it is a music as powerful and as lively as music that would be familiar during the daylight hours of civilization.

The speaker continues in the second stanza to portray the awesome power of the birds' songs, comparing the separate notes that form a song of hundreds to the insignificant brooks that flow together to become a pond. Here, the speaker is clearly impressed by the birds' strength and observes, "I could not count their force,/ Their voices did expend . . ."

In the third stanza the speaker recounts the birds' domination of those first morning hours, when cities and factories and other symbols of human civilization are unimportant, and nature reigns. Few people are fortunate enough to witness this scene of music and energy as the birds "In homely industry arrayed/ To overtake the morn." In this stanza the speaker particularly emphasizes the essential power of being as belonging solely to the birds, who are completely unaware of humanity.

Again stressing the birds' absolute autonomy from mankind, stanza four describes the song of the birds as an expression of exhilaration and freedom. "Nor was it for applause/ . . . But independent ecstasy/ Of deity and men." The speaker describes how unnecessary mankind is to the cycle of nature and the earth, proven in this wondrous song.

Stanzas five and six depict the end of this bird chorus, and the awakening of the human world as the cities and homes come back to life. The speaker realizes how rich the natural world is and how oblivious the human world is to its beauty. "The sun engrossed the east,/ The day controlled the world,/ The miracle that introduced/ forgotten, as fulfilled." In these final stanzas the speaker reveals how separate nature and humanity truly are, as the birds' concert ends and the human day begins.

The speaker of this poem uses language thoughtfully as he expresses the beauty of the birds and their song of energy, as well as their complete independence and isolation from mankind.

Student Essay 2

In this selection about the birds singing in the waning of the night, much is revealed about the poet's attitude and feelings. The reader gets the impression that the poet has great respect and love for the wonders that he wakes early to appreciate. Immediately the poet makes clear the intimate connection he feels with the birds and the awe in which he holds them. He writes, "A music numerous as space/ But neighboring as noon." He feels the music as infinite, like the dark cosmos, and yet as close and easy for him to relate to, as "neighboring," as the midday sun. Thus the poet quickly conveys much about himself and his desire to commune with the enigmas of nature, enigmas with which, numerous though they be, he feels a certain connection.

Next the poet embellishes earlier implications about their numbers, comparing them to the myriad brooks that run into a pond. Each brook is an artery to the poet, a connection to a pond that is the repository of his spirituality. Here diction is key: The brook "bestows" itself to make the pond. So the morning birds are bestowing their song; the poet regards it as a gift, perhaps a gift too often gone unnoticed and unappreciated. Indeed, in the following stanza the poet addresses the aloofness of most men, sleeping through the birds' song in contented oblivion. But what is important here is less the small numbers of those who observe, but rather the relative insignificance of the work of man juxtaposed with the more holy labor of the singing birds. The work of such early rising men is "homely," their duties not so vital as they believe them to be.

The poet notes the selfless impression imparted by the birds. He writes, "Nor was it for applause/ But independent ecstasy/ Of deity and men." Implicit in such lines is the poet's approval of the birds' independence and lack of concern for the approval of others—a vaguely nonconformist stance, almost transcendental. Obviously, the writer places great weight upon such self-confidence and lack of inhibition; again, his critique of the birds is a tacit exploration of human qualities and characteristics.

As quickly as they appear, the birds are gone, without ceremony or fanfare. The poet seems gently approving of this as well, pleased that "No tumult there had been." An apparent paradox is at play, for in the line previous, the poet refers to the morning's singing as a "flood." This flood then, since it is without tumult (and presumably spared of flotsam and fear), must be perceived by the writer as a good occurrence, requiring not an Ark, but rather an opening of the heart to receive the floodwaters. The dawn is then described in terms of a taking of power, a usurpation and nullification of the birds and their song. The sun "engrosses," the day "controls." The clearest indication yet of the poet's perception of the birds is given. Their song is nothing short of a "miracle." And yet, the writer is not saddened; though the birdsong that ushered in the day is forgotten, it has also been fulfilled. The miracle has seen fruition in the glory of a new day.

The reader has learned of the poet's reverence toward nature, his sense of childlike wonder, and his perception of things not often noticed as being miraculous. More than the birds now, one knows he who penned the poem.

Response to Student Essays 1 and 2

Though the first of these two papers avoids the occasional overwriting of the second and presents a competent reading of the poem, it lacks the specificity of the second. It paraphrases the poem adequately but does not deal fully enough with what the language actually accomplishes. The second essay gives a much more specific account of the perceptions and feelings of the poet. It also deals in detail with the effects of single words or phrases, with figures of speech, and accurately identifies those which are the most powerful in the poem. The first essay would probably be scored a six and the second an eight.

Question 3: Open Question

On the open essay question, your choice of work is crucial. Do *not* decide what novel or play you will write about before you have thought carefully about the question. Even if you like and know one work better than another, the work you prefer may not suit the question nearly so well as the other. With this question, you may well know three or four plays and books with eating scenes in them. Think about all three parts of the question before you decide which one to use. For which can you give good answers to all three tasks? You may, for example, know the dinner scene in *To the Lighthouse* and the banquet scene in *Macbeth.* On which of the two can you say more about the meaning of the scene and its relation to the meaning of the work? Can you discuss Woolf's or Shakespeare's means of making the scene effective? The easiest part of this question is the issue of what the scene reveals, but to get a top score, you would have to deal equally well with the other parts of the question.

Before you begin to write your essay, make absolutely sure you know exactly what the tasks are. In this case, after you've chosen a work with an eating scene, there are three tasks:

1. Discuss what the scene reveals.
2. Discuss how the scene is related to the meaning of the work.

3. Discuss the means by which the author makes the scene effective.

Many AP students would select Joyce's *A Portrait of the Artist as a Young Man* and write about the Christmas dinner scene in chapter one. The book is widely read in AP classes, and most students do not lose interest in it until chapter five.

A sensible organization would simply follow the order of the question. The first two tasks call for an interpretation of meaning, while the third asks for a discussion of the techniques ("means") Joyce uses in the scene. There is, of course, no single right answer to any of the essay questions, and the open question always produces the widest range of responses.

The scene presents Stephen at a time in his early childhood when his family is still prosperous. They live in a comfortable home in Bray; there are servants in the house and no lack of food and drink. Ireland at this time is still torn by the dissension that followed the death of Parnell. The young Stephen Dedalus is already puzzled by the conflict of the adults around him, in this scene notably, Mr. Casey and Mrs. Riordan (Dante), who violently attack and defend the Church's role in the downfall of Parnell. Stephen is already intensely conscious of language and wonders about the several meanings of a word like "turkey" or how the phrase "tower of ivory" can refer to a woman.

An essay dealing with the second task of this question could discuss how the Church, Irish politics, and Stephen's sensitivity to language are related to meaning in the novel. The book is centrally about Stephen's development to the brink of his career as an artist. He can continue to develop only after he has come to terms with his religious belief and with his loyalties to his family and to his homeland. This Ireland, he discovers, would ensnare him with the "nets" of nationality, language, and religion, and to become himself, to become an artist, Stephen must escape from these "nets." His assertion of independence is to deny the Church and to leave Ireland. The Christmas dinner scene presents the antagonism of two forces that would hold him captive. At the end of the book, Stephen perceives that both are dangerous to his freedom and determines to reject them.

The list of technical devices that Joyce uses to make the scene effective can be very long. The more precisely you can recall the scene you write about, the more specific and impressive your handling of this part of the question will be. You could, for example, discuss point of view in this scene. Though Joyce uses the third person, the point of view in the scene is Stephen's. Much of the scene is dialogue, the increasingly heated interchange between Simon Dedalus, Mr. Casey, and Mrs. Riordan, who defiantly defends the Church. There are also short passages of Stephen's interior monologue, and we see the action of his mind as well as the external action. The language of the passage encompasses racy, Irish vernacular, a comic story, formal description, and pious quotation from the Old and New Testaments. The effectiveness of the scene is to a large extent due to the vigor of the conflict it dramatizes. The scene begins quietly, but tempers flare and are calmed only to flare again more violently. The scene ends theatrically with Dante's enraged exit, Mr. Casey's sobbing breakdown, and Stephen's baffled contemplation of his father's tear-stained face.

The two student essays that follow answer the question using different books, the first with Joyce's *Portrait* and the second with Golding's *Lord of the Flies*.

Student Essay 1

Family meal time—whether a fancy dinner party or an everyday meal—is often included in a written work to show how the main characters communicate with each other, as well as to indicate the intricate, complicated nature of familial relationships. In James Joyce's Portrait of the Artist as a Young Man, Joyce employs the family eating scene as a means to display Stephen's family and their inter-woven relationships, as well as a symbolic tie to Ireland, her politics and history.

The Christmas dinner described by Joyce occurs when Stephen— not much more than six or seven—is home on holiday from school. The dinner begins as a happy, relaxed occasion for all the members but soon the atmosphere changes. As the conversation turns away from pleasantries and begins to include extremely different viewpoints, the meal becomes more and more uncomfortable for

Stephen. Originally a discussion on differing religious views and political radicals, the atmosphere becomes heated and soon Stephen's father and aunt are engaged in a shouting match across the table. Stephen does not understand what the conversation is about or what the reason for arguing is. While Stephen's mother tries to calm everyone down, Stephen is left wondering who Charles Parnell is and why his family is fighting about him. This is the first major introduction to Stephen's family that Joyce gives the reader, and it is indicative not only of the political atmosphere but it is also foreshadowing Stephen's future.

The basic idea of a family arguing during a holiday occasion is somewhat shocking. Stephen feels disconcerted and upset as well; and that Joyce depicts a family who cannot discuss different viewpoints without screaming at each other indicates how opinionated and proud they are. On a elementary level, this eating scene demonstrates the Dedalus family's inability to communicate as thinking, rational adults. It shows the reader the lack of affection and respect the family members have for each other. This is an unfortunate situation which contrasts sharply with the theme of holiday joy and caring.

That the family is arguing about religion and political figures, two volatile subjects, reinforces the theme of Irish history and politics. Charles Parnell is mentioned often throughout the book, a symbol of Ireland's explosive political atmosphere. This argument is the beginning of several similar arguments that Stephen will observe and participate in, in school and in his home. This idea of political unrest and debate that shakes the nation of Ireland is a persistent theme that Joyce employs.

This dinner scene is also a method of foreshadowing. At the dinner table Stephen feels confused and no one will explain the argument to him. This major theme of isolation is expanded upon during Christmas dinner. Stephen feels upset and alienated, and it is possible for the reader to begin to see a rift between the generations present at the table. This rift continues as Stephen grows older and further away from his parents emotionally. At this meal Stephen is unable to relate to the family's discussion, a pattern that continues later in his life as he is unable to relate to his parents and siblings. At this meal Joyce begins the alienation of Stephen, a motif that continues during his school years, and perhaps the most impressive theme of the novel.

James Joyce uses a family holiday meal to create the beginnings of several themes that reappear throughout the book. Foreshadowing, symbolism, and the idea of isolation are apparent in this commotion, which Joyce utilizes effectively to tie this scene to the work as a whole.

Student Essay 2

Eating ranks among the most primal and sensual activities of mankind. No drive is more primitive or essential, more able to push men to fight or kill. William Golding addresses that primitive nature with the barbaric feast scene in Lord of the Flies. The meal becomes part of a primeval ritual that begins in defiance and ends in violent death. The feast represents the point of no return for the boys on the isle, the moment when most of them descend into irredeemable savagery. Golding metaphorically represents the depths to which the boys have sunk and the power of their instinctual drives in the eating scene.

The castaways have yet to recognize the true identity of the beast they fear. Ignorant of their own innate evil, they hunt and kill, perpetually on the lookout for some horrid demon. Wild boars become ritualistic targets, and they roast the pigs on spits over the fire, crazy with crude salivary lust. When messianic Simon enters the circle of the boys' feverish tribal dance he is devoured as well. The Christ-figure, who has seen the truth about the boys' rejection of reason and civilization, indeed seen the face of evil incarnate as characterized by the Lord of the Flies, is not literally eaten, but the result is similar. Like the roasting pigs on the spit, the wild boys pounce upon him and tear him apart. Their hunger, the hunger of fear and desperation in the face of a shadowy figure they fail to recognize, is the same fear with which they devour the meal.

The boys have failed to acknowledge their savior, sealing their own doom in the process. By joining Jack's lawless tribe and rejecting Ralph and Piggy, the boys have reverted to the darker side of human nature. The feast, as well as being the dramatic high point of the novel (and arguably its climax), is a visceral scene of ravenous impulses central to the theme. Nowhere is the boys' reversion to beastliness more evident than in the feast scene, as they pounce upon the meat and upon their comrade.

Golding makes use of readers' senses to describe the scene, evoking archetypal images of fire and storm, chanting and thunder. The feast is melodramatic, not just because of the power-struggle between Ralph and Jack, but because of the setting. The boys dance around an enormous fire on the beach, even as the clouds gather and thunder crashes in the night sky. The storm builds, the suspense mounts, and the boys descend into amorality. When Simon appears from the brush, he is a pitiful figure, strong of character but weak of body. The boys attack, and the results are chilling. As the corpse drifts out to sea, the martyr is food for the fish; another corrupt feast ensues.

The eating scene is indispensable to <u>Lord of the Flies,</u> and through the feast Golding addresses some of his most significant and topical ideas. Both aesthetically and symbolically, the ritual proves crucial to the novel.

Response to Student Essays 1 and 2

There are several problems with the Joyce paper. The first is its inaccurate recollection of the book. Mr. Casey is not a relative. Dante is not Stephen's aunt and not a relative of the Dedalus family, so the argument that the scene demonstrates the family's lack of affection and respect is simply untrue. At this point in the book, the Dedalus family is affectionate. The essay does too little with the role religion is to play in the novel. Its chief defect is its failure to deal with the third task (the "means" by which the author makes the scene effective).

The essay on the Golding novel, on the other hand, is much more convincing. It deals fully and clearly with all three parts of the question, and though it is much shorter than the Joyce essay, it tells us much more about the meaning of the novel and the techniques by which Golding makes this scene so powerful. Inaccurate and incomplete, the Joyce essay would probably be scored a five, while the Golding paper would receive a seven or eight.

PRACTICE TEST 2

SECTION I: MULTIPLE-CHOICE QUESTIONS

Time: 60 Minutes
56 Questions

This section contains selections from two passages of prose and two poems with questions on their content, style, and form. Read each selection carefully. Choose the best answer of the five choices.

Questions 1–16. Read the poem carefully before you begin to answer the questions.

> When men shall find thy flower, thy glory pass,
> And thou, with careful brow sitting alone,
> Receivèd hast this message from thy glass,
> That tells thee truth, and says that all is gone,
> (5) Fresh shalt thou see in me the wounds thou madest,
> Though spent thy flame, in me the heat remaining,
> I that have loved thee thus before thou fadest;
> My faith shall wax, when thou art in thy waning.
> The world shall find this miracle in me,
> (10) That fire can burn when all the matter's spent;
> Then what my faith hath been thyself shall see,
> And that thou wast unkind thou mayst repent.
> Thou mayst repent that thou hast scorned my tears,
> When winter snows upon thy golden hairs.

1. The speaker and the person addressed in the poem are probably
   (A) an old man speaking to an old woman
   (B) an old woman speaking to another old woman
   (C) a young man speaking to an old woman
   (D) a young man speaking to a young woman
   (E) a young man speaking to himself

215

2. Setting aside considerations of rhythm and rhyme, a modern writer would probably replace the verb form "pass" in line 1 with
   (A) passing
   (B) is passing
   (C) to pass
   (D) will have passed
   (E) to have passed

3. The word "glass" in line 3 means
   (A) tumbler
   (B) mirror
   (C) crystal ball
   (D) decanter
   (E) window

4. The "miracle" referred to in line 9 is
   (A) his continuing love
   (B) his suffering
   (C) her beauty
   (D) her remaining beautiful in old age
   (E) her returning his love

5. In line 10, "all the matter's spent" can be best rephrased as
   (A) all cares are over
   (B) all my reasons for living have vanished
   (C) all the fuel is gone
   (D) all difficulties have been ended
   (E) the subject has been closed completely

6. In line 14, "winter" is a symbol of
   (A) love rejected
   (B) isolation
   (C) old age
   (D) indifference
   (E) death

7. Which of the following are arguments of the poem?

    I. When you are old, you will be sorry you ignored my love.

   II. Poetry will preserve your beauty despite the passage of time.

  III. No matter how you look, I will still love you.

(A) II only
(B) I and II only
(C) I and III only
(D) II and III only
(E) I, II, and III

8. On which of the following constructions, does the poem implicitly or explicitly most rely?
(A) Both . . . and
(B) When . . . then
(C) If . . . then
(D) If . . . but
(E) Since . . . therefore

9. One meaning of the word "glory" is a halo; if this meaning is intended in line 1, the image recurs in
(A) line 2
(B) line 5
(C) line 9
(D) line 11
(E) line 14

10. The poem deliberately repeats all of the following words and phrases EXCEPT
(A) "spent"
(B) "in me"
(C) "fire"
(D) "repent"
(E) "faith"

11. All of the following words and phrases are used to represent the beauty of the woman EXCEPT
    (A) "flower" (line 1)
    (B) "glory" (line 1)
    (C) "thy flame" (line 6)
    (D) "miracle" (line 9)
    (E) "golden hairs" (line 14)

12. All of the following are used to represent the continuing love of the speaker EXCEPT
    (A) "truth" (line 4)
    (B) "wounds" (line 5)
    (C) "heat" (line 6)
    (D) "faith" (line 8)
    (E) "miracle" (line 9)

13. The rhetorical purpose of the speaker of the poem is to
    (A) convince the lady to return his love now
    (B) inform the lady about what the future will bring
    (C) warn the lady of the consequences of vanity
    (D) convince himself to give up a useless pursuit
    (E) convince the lady of the superiority of poetry to passion

14. Which of the following contrasts does the poem employ?
    I.   Youth vs. age
    II. Growth vs. decline
    III. Permanence vs. transience
    IV. Truth vs. lie

    (A) I and III only
    (B) I, III, and IV only
    (C) II, III, and IV only
    (D) I, II, and III only
    (E) I, II, III, and IV

15. The poem employs religious diction in all of the following words
    EXCEPT
    (A) "faith" (line 8)
    (B) "miracle" (line 9)
    (C) "faith" (line 11)
    (D) "repent" (line 12)
    (E) "scorned" (line 13)

16. The form of this poem is a
    (A) Shakespearean sonnet
    (B) Petrarchan sonnet
    (C) romantic ode
    (D) ballad
    (E) villanelle

Questions 17–28. Read the following passage carefully before you
begin to answer the questions.

     Dombey sat in the corner of the darkened room in the
great arm-chair by the bedside, and Son lay tucked up warm
in a little basket bedstead, carefully disposed on a low settee
immediately in front of the fire and close to it, as if his
(5) constitution were analogous to that of a muffin, and it was
essential to toast him brown while he was very new.
     Dombey was about eight-and-forty years of age. Son
about eight-and-forty minutes. Dombey was rather bald,
rather red, and though a handsome well-made man, too
(10) stern and pompous in appearance to be prepossessing. Son
was very bald, and very red, and though (of course) an
undeniably fine infant, somewhat crushed and spotty in his
general effect, as yet. On the brow of Dombey, Time and his
brother Care had set some marks, as on a tree that was to
(15) come down in good time—remorseless twins they are for
striding through their human forests, notching as they
go—while the countenance of Son was crossed and re-
crossed with a thousand little creases, which the same
deceitful Time would take delight in smoothing out and

(20) wearing away with the flat part of his scythe, as a preparation of the surface for his deeper operations.

Dombey, exulting in the long-looked-for event, jingled
and jingled the heavy gold watch-chain that depended from
below his trim blue coat, whereof the buttons sparkled
(25) phosphorescently in the feeble rays of the distant fire. Son,
with his little fists curled up and clenched, seemed, in his
feeble way, to be squaring at existence for having come upon
him so unexpectedly.

"The house will once again, Mrs. Dombey," said Mr.
(30) Dombey, "be not only in name but in fact Dombey and Son;
Dom-bey and Son!"

The words had such a softening influence that he ap-
pended a term of endearment to Mrs. Dombey's name
(though not without some hesitation, as being a man but
(35) little used to that form of address) and said, "Mrs. Dombey,
my—my dear."

A transient flush of faint surprise overspread the sick
lady's face as she raised her eyes towards him.

"He will be christened Paul, my—Mrs. Dombey—of
(40) course."

She feebly echoed, "Of course," or rather expressed it by
the motion of her lips, and closed her eyes again.

"His father's name, Mrs. Dombey, and his grandfather's!
I wish his grandfather were alive this day!" And again he
(45) said "Dom-bey and Son," in exactly the same tone as before.

Those three words conveyed the one idea of Mr. Dombey's
life. The earth was made for Dombey and Son to trade in,
and the sun and moon were made to give them light. Rivers
and seas were formed to float their ships; rainbows gave
(50) them promise of fair weather; winds blew for or against
their enterprises; stars and planets circled in their orbits to
preserve inviolate a system of which they were the centre.
Common abbreviations took new meaning in his eyes, and
had sole reference to them: A.D. had no concern with anno
(55) Domini, but stood for anno Dombei—and Son.

17. The passage is probably taken from
    (A) a journal
    (B) an epistolary novel
    (C) a Victorian novel
    (D) a stream-of-consciousness novel
    (E) an essay

18. In lines 13–17 of the second paragraph, which of the following
    are compared?
    I. Time is compared to a forester.
    II. The brow is compared to a tree.
    III. The lines on a face are compared to marks on a tree to be
         felled.

    (A) II only
    (B) I and II only
    (C) I and III only
    (D) II and III only
    (E) I, II, and III

19. In line 29, the "house" is
    (A) Parliament
    (B) a business firm
    (C) a place of residence
    (D) a family
    (E) a social unit

20. Dombey and Son is evidently a
    (A) trading company
    (B) law firm
    (C) retailer of domestic goods
    (D) religious denomination
    (E) ship-building company

21. In the lines dealing with Mrs. Dombey, she is characterized as all of the following EXCEPT
    (A) passive
    (B) accustomed to her husband's stern demeanor
    (C) frail
    (D) loving
    (E) reticent

22. In lines 37–38, Mrs. Dombey is surprised because
    (A) she has not yet recovered from her labor
    (B) Mr. Dombey has spoken affectionately
    (C) she has misunderstood Mr. Dombey's words
    (D) Mr. Dombey has called her "Mrs. Dombey"
    (E) Mr. Dombey is delighted that the child is a son rather than a daughter

23. The central concern of Mr. Dombey's life is his
    (A) wife
    (B) child
    (C) riches
    (D) company
    (E) sense of well-being

24. In lines 51–52 ("stars and planets . . . centre"), the antecedent of the pronoun "they" is
    (A) "stars"
    (B) "planets"
    (C) both "stars" and "planets"
    (D) "orbits"
    (E) "Dombey and Son"

25. The point of view expressed in the last paragraph of the passage is that of
    (A) the narrator of the passage
    (B) the author of the passage
    (C) Dombey
    (D) Mrs. Dombey
    (E) Dombey and Son

26. The last paragraph of the passage uses all of following EX-
CEPT
    (A) repartee
    (B) repetition
    (C) blasphemous comparison
    (D) parallel construction
    (E) overstatement

27. Given the remarks on Time in the second paragraph and Mr.
Dombey's obsession, we may infer that young Paul Dombey will
    (A) become a successful man of business
    (B) alienate his wife
    (C) not become rich
    (D) die young
    (E) refuse to carry on the business

28. The use of irony in the passage is most apparent in the
    (A) first paragraph
    (B) second paragraph
    (C) third paragraph
    (D) dialogue between Mr. and Mrs. Dombey
    (E) final paragraph

Questions 29–42. Read the following poem carefully before you
begin to answer the questions.

Ode on the Death of a Favorite Cat

Drowned in a Tub of Goldfishes

1

'Twas on a lofty vase's side,
Where China's gayest art had dyed
    The azure flowers that blow;
Demurest of the tabby kind,
(5) The pensive Selima reclined,
    Gazed on the lake below.

2

Her conscious tail her joy declared;
The fair round face, the snowy beard,
    The velvet of her paws,
(10) Her coat, that with the tortoise vies,
Her ears of jet, and emerald eyes,
    She saw; and purred applause.

3

Still had she gazed; but 'midst the tide
Two angel forms were seen to glide,
(15)   The genii of the stream:
Their scaly armor's Tyrian hue
Through richest purple to the view
    Betrayed a golden gleam.

4

The hapless nymph with wonder saw;
(20) A whisker first and then a claw,
    With many an ardent wish,
She stretched in vain to reach the prize.
What female heart can gold despise?
    What cat's averse to fish?

5

(25) Presumptuous maid! with looks intent
Again she stretched, again she bent,
    Nor knew the gulf between.
(Malignant Fate sat by and smiled)
The slippery verge her feet beguiled,
(30)   She tumbled headlong in.

6

Eight times emerging from the flood
She mewed to every watery god,
    Some speedy aid to send.
No dolphin came, no nereid stirred:
(35) Nor cruel Tom, nor Susan heard.
    A favorite has no friend!

7

From hence, ye beauties, undeceived,
Know, one false step is ne'er retrieved,
   And be with caution bold.
(40) Not all that tempts your wandering eyes
And heedless hearts is lawful prize;
   Nor all that glisters gold.

29. Lines 1–3 describe
   (A) a garden
   (B) an embroidered dress
   (C) a cat
   (D) a china bowl
   (E) an oriental painting

30. The subject(s) of the sentence in lines 8–12 ("The fair . . . saw")
   is (are)
   (A) "face"
   (B) "coat"
   (C) "jet"
   (D) "face," "beard," "velvet," "coat," "ears," "eyes"
   (E) "she"

31. In line 10, Selima's coat is said to vie "with the tortoise"
   because
   (A) it is silky
   (B) it is parti-colored
   (C) the cat is lazy and slow moving
   (D) the cat is attracted to water
   (E) it is tinged with green

32. In the second stanza, Selima is purring applause
   (A) because of the natural contentment of a cat at rest
   (B) for her own reflection
   (C) at the sight of the fishbowl
   (D) at the sight of the fish
   (E) at the sight of her tail

33. In line 13, "Still had she gazed" can be best paraphrased as
    (A) Quietly she stared
    (B) She looked without stirring
    (C) She would yet be watching
    (D) Nevertheless, she looked intently
    (E) Constantly she stared

34. In the third stanza, the poem employs elevated diction in all of
    the following EXCEPT
    (A) "tide" (line 13)
    (B) "glide" (line 14)
    (C) "genii" (line 15)
    (D) "armor's" (line 16)
    (E) "Tyrian hue" (line 16)

35. The "hapless nymph" in stanza 4 is
    (A) Selima
    (B) the genii of stanza 3
    (C) the goldfish
    (D) the nereid of stanza 6
    (E) Susan

36. In line 20, "claw" is the
    (A) object of "saw"
    (B) subject of its clause
    (C) object of a preposition
    (D) object of "stretched"
    (E) object of "reach"

37. Line 34 alludes to the dolphin and nereid because they
    (A) rescue drowning men in myth
    (B) are decorations on the fish tub
    (C) identify Tom and Susan
    (D) are inhabitants of water
    (E) are examples of watery gods

38. In stanza 6, the implication of the aphorism "A favorite has no friend" is

    I. the servants resent the pampered cat
   II. other cats in the house refuse to help Selima out of envy
  III. those who have been most fortunate have the most to lose

  (A) I only
  (B) III only
  (C) I and III only
  (D) II and III only
  (E) I, II, and III

39. The metaphor developed through stanzas 1–6 compares
  (A) the fate of a cat and the fate of beautiful women
  (B) a cat and a goldfish
  (C) a cat and an epic hero
  (D) a cat and an epic heroine
  (E) goldfish and epic heroes

40. The conclusions drawn in the final stanza are primarily intended to
  (A) morally instruct the reader
  (B) prevent a reader from suffering a fate like Selima's
  (C) amuse the reader
  (D) warn against the lure of specious wealth
  (E) warn against pride

41. The style of the poem as a whole may be best described as
  (A) informal
  (B) mock-heroic
  (C) understated
  (D) ironic
  (E) impressionistic

42. In which of the following meters is the poem written?

    I. Iambic trimeter
    II. Iambic tetrameter
    III. Iambic pentameter

  (A) III only
  (B) I and II only
  (C) I and III only
  (D) II and III only
  (E) I, II, and III

Questions 43–56. Read the following passage carefully before you begin to answer the questions.

    I mention the spawning of the toads because it is one of the phenomena of spring which most deeply appeal to me, and because the toad, unlike the skylark and the primrose, has never had much of a boost from the poets. But I am
(5) aware that many people do not like reptiles or amphibians, and I am not suggesting that in order to enjoy the spring you have to take an interest in toads. There are also the crocus, the missel thrush, the cuckoo, and the blackthorn, etc. The point is that the pleasures of spring are available to
(10) everybody, and cost nothing. Even in the most sordid street the coming of spring will register itself by some sign or other, if it is only a brighter blue between the chimney pots or the vivid green of an elder sprouting on a blitzed site. Indeed it is remarkable how Nature goes on existing
(15) unofficially, as it were, in the very heart of London. I have seen a kestrel flying over the Deptford gasworks, and I have heard a first-rate performance by a black-bird in the Euston Road. There must be some hundreds of thousands, if not millions, of birds living inside the four-mile radius, and it is
(20) rather a pleasing thought that none of them pays a half-penny of rent.

    As for spring, not even the narrow and gloomy streets round the Bank of England are quite able to exclude it. It comes seeping in everywhere, like one of those new poison

(25) gases which pass through all filters. The spring is commonly
referred to as "a miracle," and during the past five or six
years this worn-out figure of speech has taken on a new
lease of life. After the sort of winters we have had to endure
recently, the spring does seem miraculous, because it has
(30) become gradually harder and harder to believe that it is
actually going to happen. Every February since 1940 I have
found myself thinking that this time winter is going to be
permanent. But Persephone, like the toads, always rises
from the dead at about the same moment. Suddenly towards
(35) the end of March, the miracle happens and the decaying
slum in which I live is transfigured. Down in the square the
sooty privets have turned bright green, the leaves are
thickening on the chestnut trees, the daffodils are out, the
wallflowers are budding, the policeman's tunic looks posi-
(40) tively a pleasant shade of blue, the fishmonger greets his
customers with a smile, and even the sparrows are quite a
different color, having felt the balminess of the air and
nerved themselves to take a bath, their first since last
September.

43. From details in the passage, we can infer that it was written
   (A) sometime in the mid-nineteenth century
   (B) during World War I
   (C) in the spring of 1925
   (D) in 1945 or 1946
   (E) sometime in the 1970s

44. In the opening sentence of the passage, the author refers to the
"spawning of the toads" for which of the following reasons?

   I. He is interested in and informed about natural history.
   II. He wishes to be different from other writers.
   III. The reference will surprise his readers.

   (A) I only
   (B) I and II only
   (C) I and III only
   (D) II and III only
   (E) I, II, and III

45. The diction of a phrase like "the toad . . . has never had much of a boost from the poets" can be best described as
    (A) formal
    (B) interpretive
    (C) colloquial
    (D) jargon-ridden
    (E) reproachful

46. The author refers to the "crocus, the missel thrush, the cuckoo, and the blackthorn" (lines 7–8)
    (A) as examples of birds and plants that are especially beautiful
    (B) as examples of birds and plants that are not usually associated with early spring
    (C) to demonstrate the range of his knowledge of the natural world
    (D) as examples of the birds and plants he prefers to toads
    (E) as examples of the birds and plants conventionally associated with spring

47. In a more conventionally written passage of expository prose, the sentence in lines 9–10—"the pleasures of spring are available to everybody, and cost nothing"—would probably be
    (A) edited out of the passage
    (B) placed first as a topic sentence
    (C) changed from a loose to a periodic sentence
    (D) changed from a periodic to a loose sentence
    (E) divided into two complete simple sentences

48. All of the following are figurative EXCEPT
    (A) "boost from the poets" (line 4)
    (B) "many people do not like reptiles or amphibians" (line 5)
    (C) "a first-rate performance by a black-bird" (line 17)
    (D) "new lease of life" (lines 27–28)
    (E) "like the toads" (line 33)

49. The author juxtaposes the natural world and the urban scene in all of the following phrases EXCEPT
    (A) "brighter blue between the chimney pots" (line 12)
    (B) "elder sprouting on a blitzed site" (line 13)
    (C) "kestrel flying over the Deptford gasworks" (line 16)
    (D) "a black-bird in the Euston Road" (lines 17–18)
    (E) "leaves are thickening on the chestnut trees" (lines 37–38)

50. If nature exists in London "unofficially" (line 15), official London is best represented by
    (A) "millions, of birds living inside the four-mile radius" (line 19)
    (B) "the narrow and gloomy streets round the Bank of England" (lines 22–23)
    (C) "one of those new poison gases which pass through all filters" (lines 24–25)
    (D) "winter" (line 32)
    (E) "positively a pleasant shade of blue" on "the policeman's tunic" (lines 39–40)

51. In the sentence "this worn-out figure of speech has taken on a new lease of life" (lines 27–28), the author employs
    (A) a worn-out figure of speech
    (B) a simile based on real estate
    (C) a common error in syntax
    (D) a symbol
    (E) poetic license

52. The most unconventional figure of speech used to describe spring in the passage is probably
    (A) "it" (line 23)
    (B) "one of those new poison gases" (lines 24–25)
    (C) "miracle" (line 26)
    (D) "Persephone . . . rises from the dead" (lines 33–34)
    (E) "miracle" (line 35)

53. In the second paragraph, the idea of spring as a miracle is

    I. advanced tentatively at first, then boldly
   II. initially qualified by the use of "commonly referred to" and "does seem"
  III. intensified by the bleakness of the winter

  (A) III only
  (B) I and II only
  (C) I and III only
  (D) II and III only
  (E) I, II, and III

54. In the last sentence of the passage (lines 36–44), the optimism of the description is undermined by which of the following words or phrases?
  (A) "different"
  (B) "balminess"
  (C) "air"
  (D) "nerved"
  (E) "bath"

55. From the passage, we can infer that the author is
  (A) eager to earn money
  (B) poor
  (C) unrealistic
  (D) sympathetic to the capitalist system
  (E) conservative

56. All of the following adjectives could properly be used to describe the style and effect of this passage EXCEPT
  (A) pedantic
  (B) comic
  (C) optimistic
  (D) realistic
  (E) spontaneous

STOP. IF YOU FINISH BEFORE TIME IS CALLED, CHECK YOUR WORK ON THIS SECTION ONLY. DO NOT WORK ON SECTION II.

SECTION II: ESSAY QUESTIONS

Time: 2 Hours
3 Questions

Question 1

(Suggested time—40 minutes. This question counts one-third of the total essay section score.)

Read the following passage carefully. Write an essay in which you discuss how the choice of detail, diction, and syntax are used to reveal the speaker's attitude to Sir Walter Elliot.

Sir Walter Elliot, of Kellynch Hall, in Somersetshire, was a man who, for his own amusement, never took up any book but the Baronetage; there he found occupation for an idle hour, and consolation in a distressed one; there his faculties
(5) were roused into admiration and respect by contemplating the limited remnant of the earliest patents; there any unwelcome sensations arising from domestic affairs changed naturally into pity and contempt as he turned over the almost endless creations of the last century; and there, if
(10) every other leaf were powerless, he could read his own history with an interest that never failed. This was the page at which the favourite volume was always opened:—

"Elliot of Kellynch Hall"

"Walter Elliot, born March 1, 1760, married July 15, 1784,
(15) Elizabeth, daughter of James Stevenson, Esq., of South Park, in the City of Gloucester; by which lady (who died 1800) he has issue, Elizabeth, born June 1, 1785; Anne, born August 9, 1787; a stillborn son, November 5, 1789; Mary born November 20, 1791."

(20)   Precisely such had the paragraph originally stood from the printer's hands; but Sir Walter had improved it by adding, for the information of himself and his family, these words, after the date of Mary's birth:—"Married December 16, 1810, Charles, son and heir of Charles Musgrove, Esq.,

(25) of Uppercross, in the county of Somerset," and by inserting
most accurately the day of the month on which he had lost
his wife.

Then followed the history and rise of the ancient and
respectable family in the usual terms; how it had been first
(30) settled in Cheshire, how mentioned in Dugdale, serving the
office of high sheriff, representing a borough in three
successive parliaments, exertions of loyalty, and dignity of
baronet, in the first year of Charles II with all the Marys and
Elizabeths they had married; forming altogether two hand-
(35) some quarto pages, and concluding with the arms and
motto:—"Principal seat, Kellynch Hall, in the country of
Somerset," and Sir Walter's handwriting again in this
finale:—

"Heir presumptive, William Walter Elliot, Esq.,
(40)   great-grandson of the second Sir Walter."

Vanity was the beginning and end of Sir Walter Elliot's
character: vanity of person and of situation. He had been
remarkably handsome in his youth, and at fifty-four was still
a very fine man. Few women could think more of their
(45) personal appearance than he did, nor could the valet of any
new-made lord be more delighted with the place he held in
society. He considered the blessing of beauty as inferior only
to the blessing of a baronetcy; and the Sir Walter Elliot, who
united these gifts, was the constant object of his warmest
(50) respect and devotion.

Question 2

(Suggested time—40 minutes. This question counts one-third of the total essay section score.)

Read the following poem by the Jamaican-born writer Claude McKay carefully. Then write an essay in which you discuss the ways in which the author's style (diction, imagery, selection of detail) reveals his feeling about what he recalls and cannot remember about his youth.

Flame-Heart

So much have I forgotten in ten years,
    So much in ten brief years! I have forgot
What time the purple apples come to juice,
    And what month brings the shy forget-me-not.
(5) I have forgot the special, startling season
    Of the pimento's flowering and fruiting;
What time of year the ground doves brown the fields
    And fill the noonday with their curious fluting.
I have forgotten much, but still remember
(10) The poinsettia's red, blood-red in warm December.

I still recall the honey-fever grass,
    But cannot recollect the high days when
We rooted them out of the ping-wing path
    To stop the mad bees in the rabbit pen.
(15) I often try to think in what sweet month
    The languid painted ladies used to dapple
The yellow by-road mazing from the main,
    Sweet with the golden threads of the rose-apple.
I have forgotten—strange—but quite remember
(20) The poinsettia's red, blood-red in warm December.

What weeks, what months, what time of the mild year
    We cheated school to have our fling at tops?
What days our wine-thrilled bodies pulsed with joy
    Feasting upon blackberries in the copse?
(25) Oh, some I know! I have embalmed the days,
    Even the sacred moments when we played,
All innocent of passion, uncorrupt,
    At noon and evening in the flame-heart's shade.
We were so happy, happy, I remember,
(30) Beneath the poinsettia's red in warm December.

Question 3

(Suggested time—40 minutes. This question counts one-third of the total essay section score.)

Many plays and novels that focus upon the courtship or marriage of a man and a woman include a second pair who help to define the central figures. Write a well-organized essay in which you discuss how the secondary man and woman illuminate the central characters of the work.

You may write on one of the following works or any other play or novel of your choice of equivalent literary merit.

The Merchant of Venice
Twelfth Night
She Stoops to Conquer
The Way of the World
Hedda Gabler
Mrs. Warren's Profession
Man and Superman
The Three Sisters
The Importance of Being Earnest
The Little Foxes
A Doll's House
Macbeth
Who's Afraid of Virginia Woolf?
Pride and Prejudice
Emma
Wuthering Heights
Jane Eyre
Adam Bede
Middlemarch
Hard Times
Great Expectations
The Return of the Native
The Mayor of Casterbridge
The House of Mirth
The Great Gatsby

END OF EXAMINATION

ANSWER KEY FOR PRACTICE TEST 2

SECTION I: MULTIPLE-CHOICE QUESTIONS

First Poem

1. D	7. C	12. A
2. E	8. B	13. A
3. B	9. E	14. D
4. A	10. C	15. E
5. C	11. D	16. A
6. C		

First Prose Passage

17. C	21. D	25. C
18. E	22. B	26. A
19. B	23. D	27. D
20. A	24. E	28. E

Second Poem

29. D	34. B	39. D
30. E	35. A	40. C
31. B	36. D	41. B
32. B	37. A	42. B
33. C	38. A	

Second Prose Passage

43. D	48. B	53. E
44. D	49. E	54. D
45. C	50. B	55. B
46. E	51. A	56. A
47. B	52. B	

PRACTICE TEST 2 SCORING WORKSHEET

Use the following worksheet to arrive at a probable final AP grade on Practice Test 2. While it is sometimes difficult to be objective enough to score one's own essay, you can use the sample essay answers that follow to approximate an essay score for yourself. You might also give your essays (along with the sample essays) to a friend or relative to score if you feel confident that the individual has the knowledge necessary to make such a judgment and that he or she will feel comfortable in doing so.

Section I: Multiple-Choice Questions

$$\frac{\quad}{\substack{\text{right} \\ \text{answers}}} - (\text{¼ or } .25 \times \frac{\quad}{\substack{\text{wrong} \\ \text{answers}}}) = \frac{\quad}{\substack{\text{multiple-choice} \\ \text{raw score}}}$$

$$\frac{\quad}{\substack{\text{multiple-choice} \\ \text{raw score}}} \times 1.20 = \frac{\quad}{\substack{\text{multiple-choice} \\ \text{converted score}}} \text{ (of possible 67.5)}$$

Section II: Essay Questions

$$\frac{\quad}{\substack{\text{question 1} \\ \text{raw score}}} + \frac{\quad}{\substack{\text{question 2} \\ \text{raw score}}} + \frac{\quad}{\substack{\text{question 3} \\ \text{raw score}}} = \frac{\quad}{\substack{\text{essay} \\ \text{raw score}}}$$

$$\frac{\quad}{\substack{\text{essay} \\ \text{raw score}}} \times 3.055 = \frac{\quad}{\substack{\text{essay} \\ \text{converted score}}} \text{ (of possible 82.5)}$$

Final Score

$$\frac{\quad}{\substack{\text{multiple-choice} \\ \text{converted score}}} + \frac{\quad}{\substack{\text{essay} \\ \text{converted score}}} = \frac{\quad}{\substack{\text{final} \\ \text{converted score}}} \text{ (of possible 150)}$$

Probable Final AP Score

Final Converted Score	Probable AP Score
150–100	5
99– 86	4
85– 67	3
66– 0	1 or 2

ANSWERS AND EXPLANATIONS FOR PRACTICE TEST 2

SECTION I: MULTIPLE-CHOICE QUESTIONS

First Poem

Unlike the two other practice exams, this one begins with a relatively easy passage, especially for students with some experience of Renaissance poetry. The poem is short and carefully patterned, so once you've seen its point, most of the details will fall into place. This is a text you'll certainly want to work with right away, leaving the more difficult prose and the other poem to be handled in order.

1. (D) The poem, part of a sequence of sonnets by Samuel Daniel, was written in the late sixteenth century. The speaker is probably a young man and the person addressed a young woman. The poem looks ahead to a future when both of them are old. At the time of the poem, the lady is still beautiful (line 7) and her hair is still golden (line 14).

2. (E) The poet is imagining a future when the woman's beauty will have faded. The expected form of the verb is "to have passed." The rest of the verbs in the sentence are unremarkable. The poem uses "pass" because it is part of a sequence of sonnets where the last line of one poem is, in part, repeated by the first line of the following poem, and the poem before this has ended with "her flower, her glory, pass." Though you are not expected to know this fact, you should see that the verb form is odd in its context.

3. (B) Though in other contexts "glass" might mean "tumbler" or even "barometer," here, as is often the case in Renaissance poetry, it means "mirror" or "looking glass." Her mirror will in time reveal the fact that her beauty has faded.

4. (A) The "miracle" here is his continuing to love her despite her cruel treatment of him and despite the fact that she has grown old and is no longer beautiful.

5. (C) Line 10 explains by metaphor what the miracle is. The fire can continue to burn although there is no fuel to feed it. That is, his love will be just as ardent although the beauty that inspired his love has gone.

6. (C) Though "winter" might be a symbol of any of these choices in other works, the details here point to "old age." Throughout the poem, the speaker has looked to a future when the lady is old and no longer beautiful. Here he speaks of winter's snowing upon her golden hairs, the turning of the blond hair to white in old age.

7. (C) Although the idea of the poem's preserving the beauty of the lady despite time's passing is a common notion in the sonnets of this period, in Spenser's and Shakespeare's, for example, the concept does not appear here. Lines 12–13 warn that she may be sorry she spurned his love, while lines 5–11 assert that he will love her despite the loss of her beauty.

8. (B) Like many lyrics of the period, this poem uses the "when . . . then" construction. The "when" is explicit in line 1 and introduces the clause of lines 1–4. The "then" is implicit as the beginning of the completion of this sentence (lines 5–8). In lines 13–14, the order is reversed, the "then" implied in line 13 and the "when" explicit in line 14.

9. (E) If the "glory" of line 1 is an image of the lady's hair that once surrounded her head like the golden halos in pictures of the saints, the figure is recalled in the last line of the poem. The "glory" that has passed away in line 1 becomes the "golden hairs" that have turned white in line 14.

10. (C) The word "fire" is used only once. The number of repetitions is an indication of how carefully crafted this poem is.

The repetitions are "spent" (lines 6 and 10), "in me" (lines 5, 6, and 9), "repent" (lines 12 and 13), and "faith" (lines 8 and 11).

11. (D) The woman's beauty is represented by the metaphors of "flower," "glory," and "flame" and by "golden hairs." The miracle is performed by the man, not the lady.

12. (A) The "truth" of line 4 is the loss of beauty in old age. The lover's "wounds" are his continued suffering for love of the lady, the "heat" is the ardency of his love, the "faith" is his always-growing devotion to her, and the "miracle" is the continuation of his love into her old age.

13. (A) The rhetorical purpose is the real reason for the poem, the argument that the speaker most wants to express. Probably ninety-five percent of all the world's love poetry has the same intention: to convince the beloved to return the love of the speaker. Though choices (C), (D), and (E) appear at times in love poetry, they are not issues in this sonnet. The poem does warn the lady of what the future will bring (B), but that is not its rhetorical purpose. The poet is arguing that if the lady returns his love now, she can avoid the regret and guilt that he predicts she will feel when she is old.

14. (D) The poem contrasts the woman's and the lover's present (youth) with the future (old age). It contrasts the growth of his love ("wax," line 8) with her decline into age ("waning," line 8) and the permanence of his love in the face of human mutability. The poem uses the word "truth" in line 4 but does not oppose truth to lie.

15. (E) The word "scorned" here has no religious overtone. It denotes the lady's indifference to the lover's suffering. There are religious associations, however, with the words "faith," "miracle," and "repent."

16. (A) The poem is a Shakespearean, or English, sonnet. It is written in iambic pentameter and rhymed abab, cdcd, efef, gg.

First Prose Passage

17. (C) Since the passage presents a narrative about related characters, we can infer that it is not from a journal, a day-to-day personal record, or from an essay, a nonfictional personal account of a single subject. We must choose among three forms of the novel. It is not epistolary (in letters), and it is not a stream-of-consciousness technique (presented through the thoughts of one of the characters). The only choice remaining is Victorian novel. You don't have to be able to distinguish a Victorian novel from a novel of another period to answer this question, since the other four options can be eliminated. The AP exam won't ask you questions about dates that can't be inferred from the passage or the answer choices. This passage is from *Dombey and Son,* written by Charles Dickens in 1848.

18. (E) All three figures are used. Time is compared to a forester "striding through . . . forests" and notching the trees to be felled. Time's marks have been set on Dombey's brow, and these notches signify a tree "to come down in good time."

19. (B) The "house" is the firm of Dombey and Son. The last paragraph speaks of Dombey and Son's trading ventures, ships, and enterprises.

20. (A) The details of the last paragraph indicate that the company is engaged in international trade.

21. (D) In the few sentences that deal with Mrs. Dombey, she is characterized as passive, frail, and reticent. She is surprised by her husband's unaccustomed tenderness. Whether or not she is loving is unsaid.

22. (B) She is startled because her husband, who usually addresses her as Mrs. Dombey, has used the words "my dear." By producing a son, she has greatly pleased him. He almost uses the affectionate phrase a second time (line 39) but thinks better of it. Mr. Dombey, clearly, is a very cold fish.

23. (D) As lines 46–47 state, the "one idea" of Mr. Dombey is the firm Dombey and Son. His first words in this passage are about the business, and he repeats its name like an incantation.

24. (E) The last paragraph elaborates on the importance of Dombey and Son to Mr. Dombey. The "them" in line 50 and the "their" in line 51 also refer to Dombey and Son in line 47.

25. (C) The point of view is that of Mr. Dombey. It is only he who believes his company is the center of the universe. The author of the passage (Dickens) and the narrator (an invention of the author) do not share Mr. Dombey's view that, for example, A.D. stands for "anno Dombei—and Son."

26. (A) Repartee is witty and surprising dialogue, not a talent of Mr. Dombey's and not in evidence in this paragraph. The replacement of "Domini" by "Dombei" is a striking example of blasphemous comparison and overstatement. The repetition of words like "was made," "were made," "were formed," or the pronouns "them" and "their" and the series of passive clauses in lines 47–49 are examples of parallel construction.

27. (D) This question calls for an inference, that is, something not explicit in the passage. The question points us to the paragraph on Time, and that paragraph speaks of preparation for death. Nothing in that paragraph has any relation to Paul's business abilities or marital situation, so the best inference is that he will die young. *Dombey and Son* is, in fact, a novel about Dombey and daughter.

28. (E) The author does not, like Mr. Dombey, believe in the all-importance of Dombey and Son. All of the assertions here are the opposite of what the writer really thinks. Nowhere else in the passage is the irony so clear.

Second Poem

The poem is by Thomas Gray.

29. (D) The lines describe a china bowl filled with water in which goldfish are swimming. It is probably blue and white porcelain.

30. (E) The word order in this stanza is inverted. The series of nouns in lines 8–11 are all the direct objects of the verb "saw" (line 12). The subject of the sentence is "she" (line 12), that is, the cat, Selima. The cat is looking at her reflection in the water of the goldfish tub.

31. (B) In this context, the word "tortoise" refers to tortoise shell, the hard, variegated material used to make combs or eyeglass frames. Tortoise shell, in its mottled yellow and brown colors, is like a tabby cat.

32. (B) Since the poem denotes the purring as "applause" (line 12), the cat is celebrating her own appearance, which is reflected in the water of the bowl.

33. (C) To answer this question, you must look at the whole sentence, which goes on to say, "but . . . two . . . forms were seen to glide." This construction with the conjunction "but" makes it clear that "had stared" is a subjunctive verb, not an indicative past perfect tense. In this context, "still" has the meaning of "yet," "even now."

34. (B) The use of the verb "glide" to describe the motion of goldfish is not unusual. To describe motion of the water of a goldfish bowl, even a very large one, as "tide" is elevated diction. So is to speak of goldfish as "genii" or their scales as a "scaly armor" or their color as a "Tyrian hue." This inflated diction to describe ordinary things exemplifies the poem's mock-heroic language.

35. (A) The hapless (unlucky) nymph is the cat, Selima, who is about to drown.

36. (D) There is a semicolon after "saw" in line 19. That sentence is complete. In lines 20–22, the subject and verb of the sentence are "She stretched," and the objects of the verb are "whisker" and "claw."

37. (A) If they are decorations (B), the verbs "came" and "stirred" make no sense. Tom and Susan are servants in the house (C). Nereids are watery gods, but dolphins are not (E). They are inhabitants of water (D), but that does not explain the line. In classical myth, dolphins or nereids may be the rescuers of drowning men, as in the myth of Arion. Notice that this question could be answered by the process of elimination and by common sense. It is easier, of course, for the student with some familiarity with Greek myth. Because no mythical rescuers come to her aid, Selima will drown.

38. (A) Selima gets no supernatural or human help from Tom or Susan. The use of the adjective "cruel" for Tom followed by the remark about a "favorite" suggests that the servants resent the cat.

39. (D) The metaphor of the six stanzas compares the cat with an epic heroine. She is demure, pensive, fair, with eyes of emerald, a hapless nymph, a presumptuous maid who meets her fate when the gods fail to intervene to save her. The goldfish may be like epic heroes, since they do wear armor, but the metaphor is not developed through stanzas 1–6.

40. (C) The improving advice of the last stanza cannot be taken seriously, though the death of the cat is ingeniously turned into a lesson for beautiful women. Nonetheless, the primary intention of stanza 7 is not moral instruction. This is a comic poem, well aware of the incongruity of this high moral tone set against the accidental death of a cat. The poem takes the death of the cat too seriously to be serious.

41. (B) The terms "informal," "understated," and "impressionistic" are not at all suitable. Though there is irony in the poem, mock-heroic is the better choice. The mock-heroic style uses an

elevated language to treat a trivial subject in an apparently serious manner.

42. (B) Although iambic pentameter is the most common meter in English poetry, this poem uses only iambic trimeter and tetrameter. In each stanza, lines 1, 2, 4, and 5 are iambic tetrameter (four feet), while lines 3 and 6 are iambic trimeter (three feet).

Second Prose Passage

43. (D) The passage was written by George Orwell. It was first published in April, 1946. We can infer from the passage that it must have been written near the end of or shortly after World War II. The first paragraph refers to a "blitzed site." The second paragraph refers specifically to every "February since 1940" and "the past five or six years."

44. (D) His uncertainty about whether toads are reptiles or amphibians does not suggest that the speaker is especially interested in or well informed about natural history. It is much more likely that he chooses to favor the toad for an effect of originality and surprise. If he had said that his favorite sign of spring was the robin, many readers would not go on. The toad is the first of several surprises in this passage.

45. (C) This phrase, and indeed the whole passage, is colloquial. Many dictionaries still list "boost" as colloquial, and the idea of poets as boosters is another of the passage's small surprises. Formal (A) is exactly the wrong word to describe Orwell's prose in this passage. Nor is it interpretive (B), reproachful (E), or jargon-ridden (too dependent on a specialized vocabulary and idiom).

46. (E) These plants and birds are those that *have* had a boost from the poets as signs of spring—for example, by Shakespeare (the cuckoo), Rossetti (the blackthorn), and Hopkins (the thrush). The casual "etc." at the end of the list indicates Orwell's lack of enthusiasm for these conventional signs of spring.

47. (B) In the formula essay, this sentence would probably begin the paragraph—the topic sentence. By not using it first, Orwell can get away with this less-than-original assertion without losing his reader. Imagine how different this paragraph would be if this sentence came first instead of the sentence about the spawning of toads. Next time someone tells you to begin all paragraphs with a topic sentence, show him or her this passage.

48. (B) The line "many people do not like reptiles or amphibians" is literal. It means exactly what it says. Choices (A), (C), and (D) are all metaphors. The metaphors are in the words "boost," "performance," and "lease." "Like the toads" is a simile.

49. (E) One of the techniques Orwell uses several times to present the coming of spring to London is to place a detail from the urban scene next to something from the natural world. Each of the first four options here use part of nature (blue sky, elder in leaf, flying kestrel, blackbird) next to part of the cityscape (chimney pots, blitzed site, Deptford gasworks, Euston Road). Choice (E) describes a natural scene but has no detail of the city.

50. (B) Like a scene from Dickens, the passage suggests that the city has its own life and is at odds with nature, which pays no rent. The narrow and gloomy streets near the Bank of England, the commercial heart of the city, are presented as trying their best but failing to keep spring out.

51. (A) One of the jokes of the passage is Orwell's using the cliché ("new lease of life") in a sentence that speaks of another cliché ("miracle") as a "worn-out figure of speech." The allusion may be to real estate (B), but the phrase is a metaphor, not a simile. It is not an error in syntax, a symbol, or an example of poetic license.

52. (B) This is certainly the most unexpected comparison for spring I have read; spring is like a poison gas. The Persephone and the miracle figures are old hat. In line 23, "it" is simply a pronoun, not a figure of speech.

53. (E) The paragraph begins by putting quotation marks around "a miracle" and calling the term a worn-out figure of speech for spring. Others, the author suggests, might use this word, but not me. Because the winters have been so terrible, spring does "seem miraculous." Notice the hedge is still there in "seem." Finally, several lines later, all hesitation disappears, and "the miracle happens."

54. (D) Though the air is "warm," that the sparrows must "nerve" themselves to take a bath serves to control the optimism of the passage. The image of the bird with six months of accumulated London grime is characteristic of the unique approach to spring of this passage.

55. (B) A few details suggest that the author is unsympathetic to capitalism (D). No details support choices (A), (C), or (E). We can infer his poverty from the description of his home as a "decaying slum."

56. (A) The passage is never pedantic. It is, at times, comic, optimistic, realistic, and spontaneous.

SECTION II: ESSAY QUESTIONS

Question 1: Jane Austen

Unlike the question on the passage by Dr. Johnson in the first practice test, this one lists three specific techniques to be discussed: choice of detail, diction, and syntax. Since it would be hard to misread the author's contemptuous attitude to Sir Walter, the scores on this question would be determined chiefly by the answers on technique. Most students will be able to deal with diction well; more will have some trouble in handling choice of detail; a huge number will leave out any discussion of syntax. Others will use the word but never talk about it. The few who know what the word means and find something to say about it will score very well.

If you wrote your own essay for this question, compare it to the two student essays that follow. If you did not write an answer for this particular question, you should still read the passage carefully and plan how you would answer the question. In either case, ask yourself the following questions: What are the strengths and weaknesses of the first essay? Of the second? Which of the two is better? Was yours or would yours have been better than these?

Student Essay 1

Sir Walter Elliot appears to be a man profoundly impressed with himself. The author describes a man who is his own biggest fan, a pompous blueblood enthralled with his lineage, wholly self-centered and reverent toward himself. Elliot is not openly criticized in the passage: rather, the author "plays it straight," allowing readers to form their own impressions based on the depiction of the baron. This method is far more effective than a lecture from the author describing in general terms Elliot's arrogance and self-absorption. Readers will put together the details of her description, come to their own conclusions, and inevitably be far more satisfied with the results.

Narcissism is delineated by the author through careful diction. Sir Walter looks at the Baronetage's writings from the past with "pity and contempt." He is a man concerned primarily with "his own amusement." Rather than reading, as some do, to learn or enrich himself, Sir Walter reads so that he may revel in a character he deems already perfect. No possibility of the need for enrichment exists in Elliot's self-conception; reading the Baronetage is the amusement of an idle hour, and the impression that results is that of an idle man. The author's most impacting phrase comes not when it is plainly stated that Elliot is vain in both character and situation. The final sentence, drenched in irony, presents the definitive portrait of Elliot in the reader's mind: "Sir Walter Elliot . . . was the constant object of his warmest respect and devotion." While referring to Elliot as someone capable of warmth and caring, the author subtextually belies the apparent meaning of the sentence. Of course Elliot is brimming with good feeling—but for himself.

The author also has a skillful command of detail, using specifics to further flesh out Elliot's character. Most grieving husbands or proud parents would be forgiven for amending a volume in which they appeared, so that it included the significant episodes of their lives. Indeed, this would even be admirable were it done for posterity, for the information of future generations and the historical record. Yet one gets the impression that Elliot is little concerned with such matters, that his revision of the history is intended for the present, exclusively for the sake of his own enjoyment. The joy comes to Elliot not in seeing the record set down accurately, but in the revision itself, the act of embellishing his own life even as the baron's impression of himself is repeatedly embellished by his own ever-expanding respect for his good looks and noble bearing. The image of Elliot, needing to have the last word over the printer, sitting in his study improving the volume, seems the best indication of the author's attitude toward Elliot.

Elliot's final amendment to the book is telling as well. He takes great pride in setting down the name of his future heir. This indicates the paramount importance and pride with which he regards his own position; he feels he will be giving over something truly great.

Through such effective details and diction, the author makes clear the nature of Sir Walter's character. The author's scornful attitude will surely be shared by the reader who meets with the vanity and snobbishness of Sir Walter Elliot.

Student Essay 2

Diction, syntax, and choice of detail are often important keys to understanding an author's attitude prevalent in his written works. In this excerpt, these elements of style demonstrate the author's writing style and amused tone to the reader.

The passage opens with a description of Sir Walter Elliot and his favorite form of amusement: reading the Baronetage. The author explains that this book serves not only as an enjoyable pastime for Elliot, but also as a comfort when life seems disagreeable to him. ". . . there he found occupation for an idle hour, and consolation in a distressed one; there his faculties were roused into admiration and respect . . ." The tone in the first paragraph of the passage is quite straightforward, and because of the author's objectivity and absolute wording, little is revealed about the writer's attitude.

The author continues to describe Elliot's extreme interest in the page that contained his personal family genealogy, and for the first time in this passage the reader is able to understand Elliot's self-absorbed nature better. "Precisely such had the paragraph [of his family's genealogy] originally stood from the printer's hands; but Sir Walter had improved it by adding, for the information of himself and his family, these words . . ." This detail, chosen by the author, shows the reader Elliot's meticulous and almost obsessive nature about preserving his personal history. The author continues to describe the pages of Elliot family history and Elliot's absurd pride in perfectly recording the family's reputation for "serving the office of high sheriff, representing a borough in three successive parliaments, exertions of loyalty, and dignity of baronet . . . forming altogether two handsome quarto pages, and concluding with the arms and motto . . ." Here the author uses a satirical tone to express the silliness of Elliot's actions. Words such as "handsome pages," "loyalty," and "dignity" all communicate the writer's true feelings of amusement as he chooses to use irony to describe the Elliot family's feats, reinforcing the satirical tone. The author also continually refers to Elliot as "Sir Walter," a pretentious title and humorous use of satire. The last detail also contributes to the prevailing attitude of absurdity when the author notes that "Sir Walter's handwriting again in . . . finale . . ." edited the original document to correctly include his heir.

The final paragraph directly expresses the author's feelings as he clearly writes, "Vanity was the beginning and end of Sir Walter Elliot's character: vanity of person and of situation." Although the writer makes his opinion of Elliot obvious, he is not judgmental or condescending. The tone in the final paragraph is simple and direct, yet truthful. It is with amusement that the writer concludes, "He considered the blessing of beauty as inferior only to the blessing of a baronetcy; and the Sir Walter Elliot, who united these gifts, was the constant object of his warmest respect and devotion."

The author of this passage employs word choice, irony, and objective detail to express his attitude of gentle humor towards his subject, Sir Walter Elliot.

Comments on Question 1

The passage is the opening of Jane Austen's novel *Persuasion,* describing Sir Walter Elliot. Sir Walter is a baronet, the lowest of the British hereditary ranks (the ascending order is baronet, baron, viscount, earl, marquis, duke—if you should ever need to know), and the Baronetage, his favorite book, lists all of the families who hold the title of baronet. If the pretesting of this question disclosed that many students were unable to determine what the Baronetage is from the passage, the word would be explained in a footnote. A modern equivalent to Sir Walter would be a successful man whose only recreational reading was his own biographical entry in *Who's Who in America.*

Response to Student Essay 1

The first student essay begins strongly but goes on to say that the passage does not "openly" criticize Sir Walter. The passage begins somewhat obliquely, but when it says, "Vanity was the beginning and end of sir Walter Elliot's character," it is as direct as it could possibly be; this frontal assault continues when Sir Walter is said to be more pleased with his looks than almost any woman and as proud of his station as the valet of a man who has just been given a title. Inconsistently, the second paragraph of the essay says, "it is plainly stated that Elliot is vain in both character and situation." The treatment of detail in the third paragraph is plausible. Nothing is said about syntax. This essay would be scored in the middle of the scale, at five or possibly six.

Response to Student Essay 2

The second essay is also inaccurate and incomplete. Can anyone reading Jane Austen's first paragraph be in doubt about her attitude to Sir Walter? The paragraph tells us that the Baronetcy is the *only* book he reads "for his own amusement," that he is contemptuous of those whose titles are not as old as his own, and that no matter how often he does so, nothing can give him pleasure equal to that of reading about himself.

The third paragraph has several errors. Jane Austen's paragraph that begins "Then followed the history" is indirectly repeating the words of the Baronetage, not what Sir Walter records. The references to Sir Walter as "Sir" are not "pretentious" or "satiric." "Sir" is simply the proper form of address for a baronet and is no more satirical than speaking of Sir Lawrence Olivier or Lord Nelson. On the real exam, an error like the former, which is caused by careless reading of the passage, would be held against a paper, but an error like the second, due to the student's not knowing the protocol of British titles, would probably have little effect on the score of the essay.

Notice that though this essay's first words are "Diction, syntax, and choice of detail," the last sentence speaks of "word choice, irony, and objective detail." Somehow, syntax has disappeared. The inaccuracy and omissions of this paper would drop its score to the lower half of the scale at four.

Restudy the Jane Austen passage, taking notes only on its syntax. Put your notes together into a paragraph. Add this paragraph to the best things in the two student essays here, and you should have a good answer to this question.

Question 2: Claude McKay

A small sampling of student responses to the first and second practice tests suggests that the McKay poem is the easiest of the four questions on required texts. In the first test, the Emily Dickinson poem gave more trouble than the passage from Dr.

Johnson. In this exam, the Jane Austen passage appears to be more difficult than the poem.

The question on McKay's "Flame-Heart," unlike the question on Emily Dickinson's poem, specifies a discussion of diction, imagery, and selection of detail. The three are interrelated, and an observant reader will notice that almost all the details of the poem come from the natural world: flowers, fruits, grasses, shrubs, birds, bees. Only a few details are man-made (by-road, school, tops).

In the process of telling what has been forgotten, the poem also tells us what has been remembered. In stanza one, for example, if the speaker has forgotten what time the purple apples come to juice, he has not forgotten the purple apples, or the pimento's flowering, or the sight and sound of the ground doves. The poem is not about the loss of memory, but the loss of childhood. The child here was close to nature, surrounded by colors and richly fruitful plants. The time was "sweet," and life was "so happy" because the speaker was still innocent of passion. The adult, the poem implies, is no longer innocent, uncorrupt. The blood-red flame-heart, which sounds to us like a symbol of passion, was then just another splash of color in the warm December landscape.

The following student essay, an eight on the nine-point scale, exemplifies the good answers that this question should elicit.

Student Essay

Among the most poignant subjects of poetry has been that misty past of memory, as poets strive to comprehend and tenaciously cling to the past, to childhood innocence. In "Flame-Heart," Claude McKay addresses such memories, attempting to explain his youth in terms of memories still with him. He mourns the things he has forgotten, but takes note of the details he remembers. Despite ambivalence expressed in the first two stanzas, the poem is ultimately a celebration of youth, revealing McKay's positive and affectionate feelings toward the past.

McKay claims to have forgotten much in the past decade. But it becomes clear that the things he has forgotten are ancillary details, matters of time and season rather than impressions of vibrant natural beauty. The poet conveys to readers the degree that he loved his youth by the way he associates it with flowers and other manifestations of natural beauty; he may regret what he has forgotten, but loves the details he does remember, of "purple apples come to juice . . . pimento's flowering and fruiting . . . honey fever grass . . . languid painted ladies dappl[ing]." Because he has forgotten the season of such beauties, because he lacks the context of their occurrence, McKay's memories are bittersweet. That he remembers specifics other than these perhaps indicates a difficulty in putting his past in perspective and understanding or accepting its place in the chronology of his life.

McKay's diction is as important as his imagery in gaining clues to his attitude toward the past. The terms in which he describes the natural wonders of his half-remembered childhood are terms of innocence and youth; because he has difficulty remembering when these memories imbedded themselves in his psyche, the implication is that he has lost his connection to such qualities. He has changed beyond recognition and is haunted by the ghosts of what he once was. The forget-me-nots are "shy," the ground doves' song is one of "curious fluting," the painted ladies dapple "languidly," and the "rose-apple" is "sweet with . . . golden threads." That is, all that McKay is struggling to place, to secure in the solid soil of time and place, is tied closely to qualities of innocence and wonder. Indeed, in the third stanza, McKay writes of playing "All innocent of passion, uncorrupt."

The piece's most striking image is the repetitive motif of the poinsettias. McKay ends the first two stanzas of the lament with the qualification that he does remember "The poinsettia's red, blood-red in warm December." At once an unsettling, surreal image, its repetition sets the work's mood. In his frustrated remembrance, McKay compares the holiday flower's color to blood, and notes that the Decembers of his childhood were warm; in conjunction with "blood-red," the resulting image is disturbing.

The past is mournfully dead to McKay because of his aging. He leaves clues to the reason for his sorrow when he writes that he has "embalmed" his days of innocence. McKay's sadness stands in stark relief next to the joy of his childhood amidst the glory of nature. The one thing he does remember is that he used to be happy. When he was happy, he did not see the world in such a fatalistic light; the poinsettias were not "blood-red," nor does he describe them so in the last stanza. Remembering his former happiness amidst the dour mood of the present, McKay concludes: "We were so happy, happy, I remember,/ Beneath the poinsettia's red in warm December."

"Flame-Heart" ends then on a note of hope, as McKay finally immerses himself in childhood happiness despite the loss of details. In a sense reconciling himself to their loss, he acknowledges that the times were good. His feelings of longing toward the past are thereby at least partially assuaged.

Question 3: Open Question

There are so many possible approaches to an open question like this that it is hard to know where to begin. There is only one task: to discuss how a secondary couple illuminates the central figures in a play or novel that focuses on courtship or marriage. Most of Shakespeare's comedies contain second and even third couples (Jessica and Lorenzo in *The Merchant of Venice,* Olivia and Sebastian or Toby and Maria in *Twelfth Night,* Celia and Oliver in *As You Like It,* any three of the four couples in *A Midsummer Night's Dream*). If you argue that *Othello* is about marriage, even Iago and Emilia would fit this question.

The nineteenth-century British and American novel from Scott to Hardy or Cooper to James provides many examples of a defining secondary pair. Many of these novels have a fair and a dark heroine, a fair hero and a dark villain, with the blond woman (inevitably presented as beautiful, conventional, chaste, and passive) married in the final chapters to an equally conventional, chaste, and handsome hero. The darker couple, on the other hand, are vital, passionate beings. Figures like Emily Brontë's Edgar and Isabella Linton or George Eliot's Adam Bede and Dinah Morris are set against Heathcliff and Catherine Linton, Arthur Donnithorne and Hetty Sorrel. The genre reaches its Hollywood apotheosis with Melanie and Ashley and Rhett and Scarlett in Margaret Mitchell's *Gone with the Wind.*

This excellent student essay, an eight on the nine-point scale, on *Pride and Prejudice* will give you an idea of what might be done with this question. The writer makes her points clearly and concisely, and unlike many AP students, resists the temptation to retell the plot. The essay shows how Jane and Bingley throw light on Elizabeth and Darcy and on the meaning of the title of the novel.

Student Essay

Courtship and marriage are often primary focuses in written works. In Jane Austen's Pride and Prejudice, Jane Bennet and Mr. Bingley are helpful in defining Elizabeth Bennet and Mr. Darcy.

For all her beauty, wit, and intelligence, Elizabeth's greatest fault is her nature to judge people too quickly. Her initial prejudice towards Darcy and her pride in her ability to judge people prevent her from knowing his true nature. Similarly, Darcy's pride and his inability to overcome his prejudice against some of the connections of Jane and Elizabeth deter his pursuit of Elizabeth. Jane and Bingley, on the other hand, have no pride and prejudice. They fall in love almost at first sight. Being without pride, they are also passive, and Bingley lets Darcy draw him away from Jane. Darcy, misled by Jane's placid behavior, genuinely believes she does not love Bingley, and Bingley accepts Darcy's view. If Darcy is too proud, Bingley is too modest to trust his own judgment. If Elizabth is too quick to find faults, Jane is too nice and can see only the best in people. For this reason, she fails to understand Caroline Bingley or to judge Darcy as harshly as Elizabeth does. Darcy and Elizabeth show the danger of too much pride and prejudice; Jane and Bingley show the danger of too little.

The two couples also illuminate each other's strong points. Darcy is interfering but also motivated by genuine concern for Bingley's well-being. Elizabeth's dislike of Darcy is partly caused by her love for Jane. When Elizabeth realizes how proud and prejudiced she has been, she realizes more than ever before Jane's true strength and value. The wit of Elizabeth is set off by the kinder but far less interesting character of Jane, just as Darcy's greater depth, intelligence, and complexity is set off by contrast with the genial but bland Bingley.

Because of the roles that Jane and Bingley play, the characters of Elizabeth and Darcy are brought more clearly into focus. Jane Austen uses this secondary couple to clarify Elizabeth and Darcy's relationship, giving meaning to the title Pride and Prejudice.

PRACTICE TEST 3

SECTION I: MULTIPLE-CHOICE QUESTIONS

Time: 60 Minutes
55 Questions

This section contains selections from two passages of prose and two poems with questions on their content, style, and form. Read each selection carefully. Choose the best answer of the five choices.

Questions 1–12. Read the following passage carefully before you begin to answer the questions.

Meditation

We say that the world is made of sea and land, as though
they were equal; but we know that there is more sea in the
western than in the eastern hemisphere. We say that the
firmament is full of stars, as though it were equally full; but
(5) we know that there are more stars under the northern than
under the southern pole. We say the elements of man are
misery and happiness, as though he had an equal proportion
of both, and the days of man vicissitudinary, as though he
had as many good days as ill, and that he lived under a
(10) perpetual equinoctial, night and day equal, good and ill
fortune in the same measure. But it is far from that; he
drinks misery, and he tastes happiness; he mows misery, and
he gleans happiness; he journeys in misery, he does but walk
in happiness; and, which is worst, his misery is positive and
(15) dogmatical, his happiness is but disputable and problemati-
cal. All men call misery misery, but happiness changes the
name by the taste of man. In this accident that befalls me,
now that this sickness declares itself by spots to be a
malignant and pestilential disease, if there be a comfort in
(20) the declaration that thereby the physicians see more clearly
what to do, there may be as much discomfort in this, that the

malignity may be so great as that all that they can do shall do nothing; that an enemy declares himself then when he is able to subsist and to pursue and to achieve his ends is no (25) great comfort. In intestine conspiracies, voluntary confessions do more good than confessions upon the rack; in these infections, when nature herself confesses and cries out by these outward declarations which she is able to put forth of herself, they minister comfort; but when all is by the (30) strength of cordials, it is but a confession upon the rack, by which, though we come to know the malice of that man, yet we do not know whether there be not as much malice in his heart then as before his confession; we are sure of his treason, but not of his repentance; sure of him, but not of his (35) accomplices. It is a faint comfort to know the worst when the worst is remediless, and a weaker than that to know much ill and not to know that that is the worst. A woman is comforted with the birth of her son, her body is eased of a burden; but if she could prophetically read his history, how (40) ill a man, perchance how ill a son he would prove, she should receive a greater burden into her mind. Scarce any purchase that is not clogged with secret encumbrances; scarce any happiness that hath not in it so much of the nature of false and base money as that the allay is more than (45) the metal. Nay, is it not so (at least much towards it) even in the exercise of virtues? I must be poor and want before I can exercise the virtue of gratitude; miserable and in torment before I can exercise the virtue of patience. How deep do we dig and for how coarse gold! And what other touchstone (50) have we of our gold but comparison, whether we be as happy as others, or as ourselves at other times? O poor step toward being well, when these spots do only tell us that we are worse than we were sure of before!

1. The speaker of the passage is
    (A) an Old Testament prophet
    (B) a sick person
    (C) a physician
    (D) a man who has died and is recalling his last days
    (E) a geographer

2. The comparisons in the first 11 lines of the passage are to illustrate the fact that
   - (A) the western oceans are larger than the eastern
   - (B) life contains both happiness and sorrow
   - (C) good fortune and bad fortune cannot be measured
   - (D) the sorrow in life outweighs the happiness
   - (E) neither misery nor joy is lasting in men's lives

3. As it is used in line 15, "dogmatical" means
   - (A) arrogantly asserted
   - (B) authoritatively affirmed
   - (C) asserted without any reference to evidence
   - (D) suggested, formulated
   - (E) ungrammatically stated

4. The argument in lines 17–23 is that because the disease has now been identified
   - I. it may be so serious that the doctors can be of no use
   - II. it can be more easily treated
   - III. the physicians recognizing its contagion may refuse to treat the disease

   - (A) I only
   - (B) II only
   - (C) I and II only
   - (D) I and III only
   - (E) I, II, and III

5. In line 25, the word "intestine" is used to
   - (A) modify "voluntary confessions"
   - (B) refer to a part of the body
   - (C) mean murderous or fatal
   - (D) mean forceful or violent
   - (E) mean domestic or internal

6. The metaphor in lines 23–25
   (A) argues that an unseen enemy is more dangerous than an open one
   (B) compares a disease and physicians to an invader and a town under siege
   (C) argues that the enemy has been discovered too late to be defeated
   (D) argues that the temporary defeat of an enemy is no consolation
   (E) compares the enemy to an army with the advantage

7. We can infer that the latest symptoms of the speaker's disease have appeared
   (A) without raising his physicians' increased concern
   (B) without having been noticed by the physicians
   (C) without increasing the concern of the speaker
   (D) because they have been induced by medicines
   (E) in the natural course of his illness

8. In line 36, "that" refers to
   (A) "repentance" (line 34)
   (B) "faint comfort" (line 35)
   (C) "to know the worst" (line 35)
   (D) "remediless" (line 36)
   (E) "that that" (line 37)

9. In lines 43–45, the comparison of happiness to coinage in which the "allay is more than the metal" is parallel to the comparison of
   (A) the sea and land as equal (lines 1–2)
   (B) drinking misery and tasting happiness (lines 11–12)
   (C) the taste of man (line 17)
   (D) the voluntary confessions and confessions under torture (lines 25–26)
   (E) the woman in childbirth (lines 37–41)

10. The "coarse gold" of line 49 is
    (A) riches
    (B) virtue
    (C) patience
    (D) misery
    (E) happiness

11. The style of the paragraph is most notably characterized by its use of
    (A) extended metaphors
    (B) carefully reasoned syllogism
    (C) reasoning from the specific to the general
    (D) ironic understatements
    (E) citation of intellectual authorities

12. The tone of the passage may be best described as
    (A) ambiguous
    (B) skeptical
    (C) pessimistic
    (D) servile
    (E) anxious

Questions 13–27. Read the following poem carefully before you begin to answer the questions.

Another Letter to Her Husband, Absent upon Public Employment

As loving hind that (hartless) wants her deer,
Scuds through the woods and fern with hark'ning ear,
Perplext, in every bush and nook doth pry,
Her dearest deer, might answer ear or eye;
(5) So doth my anxious soul, which now doth miss
A dearer dear (far dearer heart) than this,
Still wait with doubts, and hopes, and failing eye,
His voice to hear or person to descry.
Or as the pensive dove doth all alone

(10) (On withered bough) most uncouthly bemoan
      The absence of her love and loving mate,
      Whose loss hath made her so unfortunate,
      Ev'n thus do I, with many a deep sad groan,
      Bewail my turtle true, who now is gone,
(15) His presence and his safe return still woos,
      With thousand doleful sighs and mournful coos.
      Or as the loving mullet, that true fish,
      Her fellow lost, nor joy nor life do wish,
      But launches on that shore, there for to die,
(20) Where she her captive husband doth espy.
      Mine being gone, I lead a joyless life,
      I have a loving peer, yet seem no wife;
      But worst of all, to him can't steer my course,
      I here, he there, alas, both kept by force.
(25) Return my dear, my joy, my only love,
      Unto thy hind, thy mullet, and thy dove,
      Who neither joys in pasture, house, nor streams,
      The substance gone, O me, these are but dreams.
      Together at one tree, oh let us browse,
(30) And like two turtles roost within one house
      And like the mullets in one river glide,
      Let's still remain but one, till death divide.
            Thy loving love and dearest dear,
            At home, abroad, and everywhere.

13. Which of the following best identifies the genre of this poem?
    (A) Verse meditation
    (B) Verse epistle
    (C) Elegy
    (D) Love lyric
    (E) Verse essay

14. In line 6, the parenthetical phrase "far dearer heart" is

    I. more logically printed without the parentheses
   II. in apposition to "dearer dear"
   III. an apostrophe to the absent husband

    (A) I only
    (B) I and II only
    (C) I and III only
    (D) II and III only
    (E) I, II, and III

15. On what figure of speech do lines 1–8 chiefly rely?
    (A) Simile
    (B) Metaphor
    (C) Metonymy
    (D) Synecdoche
    (E) Allegory

16. In line 19, "launches" is best defined as
    (A) boats
    (B) sets afloat
    (C) puts to sea
    (D) sets in operation
    (E) throws herself

17. The images of the deer, the dove, and the mullet (lines 1–20) are alluded to later in the poem in all of the following words or phrases EXCEPT
    (A) "pasture" (line 27)
    (B) "house" (line 27)
    (C) "browse" (line 29)
    (D) "glide" (line 31)
    (E) "abroad" (line 34)

18. Of the following definitions of "substance," which is the primary meaning in line 28?
    (A) Wealth, resources
    (B) That which exists independently
    (C) Essence, reality
    (D) Material, physical matter
    (E) Passport, true meaning

19. In line 28, the phrase "these are but dreams" can be best paraphrased as
    (A) my dreams are of your return
    (B) I dream of you so long as you are gone
    (C) these dreams are mine
    (D) these dreams have no reality
    (E) on the other hand, dreams are more real

20. Of the following, which is the best synonym for "house" in line 30?
    (A) Dovecote
    (B) Manor
    (C) Hiding place
    (D) Dwelling place
    (E) Shelter

21. Grammatically, the sentence in the last two lines of the poem (lines 33–34) differs from the rest of the poem because it has no
    (A) subject
    (B) verb
    (C) prepositions
    (D) pronouns
    (E) adjectives

22. The last two lines of the poem are used to
    (A) recapitulate the argument of the poem
    (B) reassert the optimism of the speaker
    (C) serve as a signature to a letter
    (D) express what the speaker most wishes for
    (E) reassert the universality of the mutual love of husband and wife

23. All of the following words refer to the dove figure of speech
    EXCEPT
    (A) "mate" (line 11)
    (B) "turtle" (line 14)
    (C) "coos" (line 16)
    (D) "peer" (line 22)
    (E) "house" (line 27)

24. On which of the following structural devices does the poem
    chiefly depend?
    (A) A series of parallel analogies
    (B) A series of contrasts
    (C) An alternation of the specific and the general
    (D) A logically developed argument
    (E) A series of literal assertions about the same subject

25. With which of the following words does the poem exploit a
    double meaning?
    (A) "hind" (line 1)
    (B) "deer" (line 1)
    (C) "bough" (line 10)
    (D) "turtle" (line 14)
    (E) "coos" (line 16)

26. Which of the following best describes the logical structural
    divisions of the poem?
    (A) Lines 1–4; lines 5–8; lines 9–12; lines 13–16; lines 17–20;
        lines 21–24; lines 25–26; lines 27–28; lines 29–31; lines
        32–34
    (B) Lines 1–10; lines 11–16; lines 17–28; lines 29–34
    (C) Lines 1–8; lines 9–16; lines 17–20; lines 21–24; lines 25–28;
        lines 29–32; lines 33–34
    (D) Lines 1–16; lines 17–22, lines 23–34
    (E) Lines 1–16; lines 17–24; lines 25–30; lines 31–34

27. To a modern reader, which of the following is NOT an off-rhyme?
    (A) "eye"/"descry" (lines 7–8)
    (B) "mate"/"unfortunate" (lines 11–12)
    (C) "groan"/"gone" (lines 13–14)
    (D) "browse"/"house" (lines 29–30)
    (E) "deer"/"everywhere" (lines 33–34)

Questions 28–40. Read the following passage carefully before you begin to answer the questions.

(from *Joan of Arc*)

What is to be thought of *her?* What is to be thought of the poor shepherd girl from the hills and forests of Lorraine, that—like the Hebrew shepherd boy from the hills and forests of Judea—rose suddenly out of the quiet, out of the

(5) safety, out of the religious inspiration, rooted in deep pastoral solitudes, to a station in the van of armies, and to the more perilous station at the right hand of kings? The Hebrew boy inaugurated his patriotic mission by an *act,* by a victorious *act,* such as no man could deny. But so did the girl

(10) of Lorraine, if we read her story as it was read by those who saw her nearest. Adverse armies bore witness to the boy as no pretender; but so they did to the gentle girl. Judged by the voices of all who saw them *from a station of good-will,* both were found true and loyal to any promises involved in

(15) their first acts. Enemies it was that made the difference between their subsequent fortunes. The boy rose to a splendor and a noonday prosperity, both personal and public, that rang through the records of his people, and became a byword among his posterity for a thousand years,

(20) until the sceptre was departing from Judah. The poor, forsaken girl, on the contrary, drank not herself from that cup of rest which she had secured for France. She never sang together with the songs that rose in her native Domrémy as echoes to the departing steps of invaders. She

(25) mingled not in the festal dances at Vaucouleurs which celebrated in rapture the redemption of France. No! for her

voice was then silent; no! for her feet were dust. Pure, innocent, noble-hearted girl! whom, from earliest youth, ever I believed in as full of truth and self-sacrifice, this was
(30) amongst the strongest pledges for *thy* truth, that never once—no, not for a moment of weakness—didst thou revel in the vision of coronets and honor from man. Coronets for thee! Oh no! Honors, if they come when all is over, are for those that share thy blood. Daughter of Domrémy, when the
(35) gratitude of thy king shall awaken, thou wilt be sleeping the sleep of the dead. Call her, King of France, but she will not hear thee. Cite her by the apparitors to come and receive a role of honor, but she will be found *en contumace*. When the thunders of universal France, as even yet may happen, shall
(40) proclaim the grandeur of the poor shepherd girl that gave up all for her country, thy ear, young shepherd girl, will have been deaf for five centuries. To suffer and to do, that was thy portion in this life; that was thy destiny; and not for a moment was it hidden from thyself. Life, thou saidst, is
(45) short; and the sleep which is the grave is long; let me use that life, so transitory, for the glory of those heavenly dreams destined to comfort the sleep which is so long! This pure creature—pure from every suspicion of even a visionary self-interest, even as she was pure in senses more
(50) obvious—never once did this holy child, as regarded herself, relax from her belief in the darkness that was travelling to meet her. She might not prefigure the very manner of her death; she saw not in vision, perhaps, the aerial altitude of the fiery scaffold, the spectators without end on every road
(55) pouring into Rouen as to a coronation, the surging smoke, the volleying flames, the hostile faces all around, the pitying eye that lurked but here and there, until nature and imperishable truth broke loose from artificial restraints;— these might not be apparent through the mists of the
(60) hurrying future. But the voice that called her to death, *that* she heard forever.

28. The Hebrew shepherd boy, lines 1–15, is
    (A) Jesus
    (B) Solomon
    (C) Moses
    (D) David
    (E) Isaac

29. For which of the following reasons were the Hebrew shepherd boy and the French shepherd girl alike?

    I. They were religiously inspired.
    II. Their motives were patriotic.
    III. They initially won victories.
    IV. The armies they opposed testified to their greatness.

    (A) II and IV only
    (B) I, II, and III only
    (C) I, III, and IV only
    (D) II, III, and IV only
    (E) I, II, III, and IV only

30. The first 26 lines of the passage are organized by a use of
    (A) comparison and contrast
    (B) arguing the general from the specific
    (C) repeated rhetorical questions
    (D) recurrent appeals to authority
    (E) syllogistic logic

31. The series of three sentences from line 20 to line 26 ("The poor ... of France") have which of the following in common?

    I. They describe Joan's inability to participate in the victory she had won.
    II. They are all expressed through negatives.
    III. They describe figurative rather than literal events.

    (A) II only
    (B) III only
    (C) I and II only
    (D) II and III only
    (E) I, II, and III

32. The passage attributes Joan's tragedy to
    (A) her innocence
    (B) her enemies
    (C) envy of her success
    (D) adverse armies
    (E) the King of France

33. Phrases like "if we read her story as it was read by those who
    saw her nearest" (lines 10–11) or "the voices of all who saw
    them *from a station of good will*" (line 13) suggest that
    (A) there can be no doubt about Joan's greatness
    (B) there have been hostile interpretations of Joan's story
    (C) the author has consulted all the relevant historical sources
    (D) we can trust only the testimony of eyewitnesses
    (E) the truth should be sought in both written and eyewitness
        reports

34. In line 32, the word "coronets" is most precisely defined as
    (A) trumpets
    (B) praises
    (C) flowers
    (D) medals
    (E) crowns

35. From details of this passage, we can infer that Joan dies
    (A) by fire
    (B) by hanging
    (C) in battle
    (D) by gunfire
    (E) at the hands of the king

36. In lines 52–61, the account of Joan's death is presented as
    (A) her prophetic vision of the future
    (B) the report of an eyewitness
    (C) what Joan may not have foreseen
    (D) an instance of state suppression of religion
    (E) an illustration in a medieval manuscript

37. Although the passage contains only one paragraph, it could most easily be broken into two paragraphs after
    (A) "Judah" (line 20)
    (B) "dust" (line 27)
    (C) "no!" (line 33)
    (D) "thee" (line 37)
    (E) "her" (line 52)

38. The passage employs all of the following EXCEPT
    (A) apostrophe
    (B) exclamation
    (C) direct quotation
    (D) extended definition
    (E) parallel syntax

39. At one time or more, the passage uses direct address to which of the following?
    I.   A general reader
    II. Joan of Arc
    III. The King of France
    IV. The enemies of Joan of Arc

    (A) I only
    (B) II and IV only
    (C) I, II, and III only
    (D) II, III, and IV only
    (E) I, II, III, and IV

40. The speaker's attitude toward Joan of Arc is one of
    (A) awed veneration
    (B) rational approval
    (C) guarded criticism
    (D) bemused uncertainty
    (E) vexed incredulity

Questions 41–55. Read the following poem carefully before you begin to answer the questions.

S.I.W.

> I will to the King,
> And offer him consolation in his trouble,
> For that man there has set his teeth to die,
> And being one that hates obedience,
> Discipline, and orderliness of life,
> I cannot mourn him.
>
> W. B. Yeats

I. THE PROLOGUE

Patting good-bye, doubtless they told the lad
He'd always show the Hun a brave man's face;
Father would sooner him dead than in disgrace,—
Was proud to see him going, aye, and glad.
(5) Perhaps his mother whimpered how she'd fret
Until he got a nice safe wound to nurse.
Sisters would wish girls too could shoot, charge, curse;
Brothers—would send his favourite cigarette.
Each week, month after month, they wrote the same,
(10) Thinking him sheltered in some Y.M. Hut,
Because he said so, writing on his butt
Where once an hour a bullet missed its aim
And misses teased the hunger of his brain.
His eyes grew old with wincing, and his hand
(15) Reckless with ague. Courage leaked, as sand
From the best sand-bags after years of rain.
But never leave, wound, fever, trench-foot, shock,
Untrapped the wretch. And death seemed still withheld
For torture of lying machinally shelled,
(20) At the pleasure of this world's Powers who'd run amok.

He'd seen men shoot their hands, on night patrol.
Their people never knew. Yet they were vile.
"Death sooner than dishonour, that's the style!"
So Father said.

II. THE ACTION

(25)   One dawn, our wire patrol
        Carried him. This time, Death had not missed.

        We could do nothing but wipe his bleeding cough.
        Could it be accident?—Rifles go off . . .
        Not sniped? No. (Later they found the English ball.)

III. THE POEM

(30) It was the reasoned crisis of his soul
        Against more days of inescapable thrall,
        Against infrangibly wired and blind trench wall
        Curtained with fire, roofed in with creeping fire,
        Slow grazing fire, that would not burn him whole
(35) But kept him for death's promises and scoff,
        And life's half-promising, and both their riling.

IV. THE EPILOGUE

        With him they buried the muzzle his teeth had kissed,
        And truthfully wrote the Mother, "Tim died smiling."

41. The title of the poem is an army abbreviation for self-inflicted
    wound used by the British as, say, K.P. or G.I. are used by the
    American army; that such an abbreviation exists suggests that

    I. it is common for soldiers to wound or kill themselves
   II. the army is reluctant to face the fact that soldiers may kill
       themselves
  III. the army does not wish the civilian population to know
       about suicides at the front

    (A) I only
    (B) II only
    (C) III only
    (D) II and III only
    (E) I, II, and III

42. The poem takes place during
    (A) the Civil War
    (B) World War I
    (C) World War II
    (D) the Vietnam War
    (E) any fictitious British war

43. The chief speaker of the poem is
    (A) an omniscient unnamed narrator
    (B) the dead soldier's parents
    (C) another soldier
    (D) Tim
    (E) the dead soldier's commanding officer

44. The diction of the phrase "nice safe wound" in line 6 represents
    that of the
    (A) commanding officer
    (B) dead soldier
    (C) narrator of the poem
    (D) soldier's father
    (E) soldier's mother

45. In line 17, "leave, wound, fever, trench-foot, shock" are

    I. reasons for leaving the trenches
    II. the common dangers of life in the trenches
    III. potential causes of death in the trenches

    (A) I only
    (B) II only
    (C) I and II only
    (D) II and III only
    (E) I, II, and III

46. Line 20 metrically is different from the rest of the prologue
    because
    (A) its rhythm is trochaic
    (B) it has more syllables
    (C) it has no alliteration
    (D) it has no rhyming line
    (E) it uses feminine rhyme

47. In line 29, "ball" is a
    (A) sphere
    (B) root
    (C) dance
    (D) bullet
    (E) uniform

48. The effect of part III is to

    I. obliquely call into question the soldier's decision to kill
       himself
    II. dramatize the inescapable horrors of trench warfare
    III. justify the soldier's choice of suicide

    (A) I only
    (B) II only
    (C) I and II only
    (D) I and III only
    (E) II and III only

49. The "muzzle" of line 37 is
    (A) the butt or handle of a gun
    (B) the front of the barrel of a gun
    (C) a medal
    (D) a blindfold
    (E) a mouthpiece

50. The poet uses the word "truthfully" in the last line of the poem because
   (A) it will console the family of the dead soldier
   (B) "smiling" refers to the happiness of the soldier whose war is over
   (C) he realizes that "Tim died smiling" is not the truth
   (D) "Tim died smiling" is the literal truth
   (E) the poem has been too pessimistic to this point

51. The poem directly presents the words or thoughts of which of the following?

   I. Tim
   II. The narrator
   III. Members of the patrol

   (A) II only
   (B) I and II only
   (C) I and III only
   (D) II and III only
   (E) I, II, and III

52. With which of the following does the poem implicitly or explicitly find fault?

   I. The world's Powers
   II. Tim's family
   III. The wire patrol

   (A) I only
   (B) I and II only
   (C) I and III only
   (D) II and III only
   (E) I, II, and III

53. All of the following words or phrases are ironic EXCEPT
   (A) "always" (line 2)
   (B) "sooner him dead than in disgrace" (line 3)
   (C) "nice safe wound" (line 6)
   (D) "Courage leaked, as sand" (line 15)
   (E) "Yet they were vile" (line 22)

54. The only feminine rhyme in the poem occurs in
    (A) the second and third lines of the Yeats quotation
    (B) line 20
    (C) lines 26 and 27
    (D) line 35
    (E) lines 36 and 38

55. The crucial action of the poem takes place
    (A) in The Prologue (I)
    (B) between The Prologue (I) and The Action (II)
    (C) in The Action (II)
    (D) in The Poem (III)
    (E) between The Poem (III) and The Epilogue (IV)

STOP. IF YOU FINISH BEFORE TIME IS CALLED, CHECK YOUR WORK ON THIS SECTION ONLY. DO NOT WORK ON SECTION II.

SECTION II: ESSAY QUESTIONS

Time: 2 Hours
3 Questions

Question 1

(Suggested time—40 minutes. This question counts one-third of the total essay section score.)

Read the following poem carefully. Then write an essay in which you discuss how the use of language in the poem determines the reader's response to the speaker and his situation.

The Farmer's Bride

       Three Summers since I chose a maid,
       Too young maybe—but more's to do
       At harvest-time than bide and woo.
           When us was wed she turned afraid

(5)   Of love and me and all things human;
       Like the shut of a winter's day
       Her smile went out, and 'twadn't a woman—
           More like a little frightened fay.
           One night, in the Fall, she runned away.

(10)   'Out 'mong the sheep, her be,' they said,
       'Should properly have been abed;
       But sure enough she wadn't there
       Lying awake with her wide brown stare.
  So over seven-acre field and up-along across the down

(15)   We chased her, flying like a hare
       Before our lanterns. To Church-Town
           All in a shiver and a scare
       We caught her, fetched her home at last
           And turned the key upon her, fast.

(20)   She does the work about the house
              As well as most, but like a mouse:
                   Happy enough to chat and play
                   With birds and rabbits and such as they,
                   So long as men-folk keep away.

(25)   'Not near, not near!' her eyes beseech
              When one of us comes within reach.
                   The women say that beasts in stall
                   Look round like children at her call.
                   I've hardly heard her speak at all.

(30)   Shy as a leveret, swift as he,
              Straight and slight as a young larch tree,
              Sweet as the first wild violets, she,
              To her wild self. But what to me?

              The short days shorten and the oaks are brown,
(35)   The blue smoke rises to the low grey sky,
              One leaf in the still air falls slowly down,
                   A magpie's spotted feathers lie
              On the black earth spread white with rime,
              The berries redden up to Christmas-time.
(40)   What's Christmas-time without there be
                   Some other in the house than we!

                   She sleeps up in the attic there
                   Alone, poor maid, 'Tis but a stair
              Betwixt us. Oh! my God! the down,
(45)   The soft young down of her, the brown,
              The brown of her—her eyes, her hair, her hair!

                                        —Charlotte Mew

Question 2

(Suggested time—40 minutes. This question counts one-third of the total essay score.)

Read carefully the following passage from Thackeray's *Vanity Fair*. Write an essay that defines the targets of Thackeray's criticism and how the choice of details, the diction, and the syntax convey the satire.

> Miss Crawley was, in consequence, an object of great respect when she came to Queen's Crawley, for she had a balance at her banker's which would have made her beloved anywhere.
> (5)   What a dignity it gives an old lady, that balance at the banker's! How tenderly we look at her faults, if she is a relative (and may every reader have a score of such), what a kind, good-natured old creature we find her! How the junior partner of Hobbs & Dobbs leads her smiling to the carriage
> (10) with the lozenge upon it, and the fat wheezy coachman! How, when she comes to pay us a visit, we generally find an opportunity to let our friends know her station in the world! We say (and with perfect truth) I wish I had Miss MacWhirter's signature to a cheque for five thousand pounds. She
> (15) wouldn't miss it, says your wife. She is my aunt, say you, in an easy careless way, when your friend asks if Miss Mac-Whirter is any relative? Your wife is perpetually sending her little testimonies of affection, your little girls work endless worsted baskets, cushions, and footstools for her. What a
> (20) good fire there is in her room when she comes to pay you a visit, although your wife laces her stays without one! The house during her stay assumes a festive, neat, warm, jovial, snug appearance not visible at other seasons. You yourself, dear sir, forget to go to sleep after dinner, and find yourself
> (25) all of a sudden (though you invariably lose) very fond of a rubber. What good dinners you have—game every day, Malmsey-Madeira, and no end of fish from London. Even the servants in the kitchen share in the general prosperity; and, somehow, during the stay of Miss MacWhirter's fat

(30) coachman, the beer is grown much stronger, and the
      consumption of tea and sugar in the nursery (where her
      maid takes her meals) is not regarded in the least. Is it so, or
      is it not so? I appeal to the middle classes. Ah, gracious
      powers! I wish you would send me an old aunt—a maiden
(35) aunt—an aunt with a lozenge on her carriage, and a front of
      light coffee-coloured hair—how my children should work
      work-bags for her, and my Julia and I would make her
      comfortable! Sweet, sweet vision! Foolish, foolish dream!

Question 3

(Suggested time—40 minutes. This question counts one-third of the total essay section score.)

Injustice, either social or personal, is a common theme in literature. Choose a novel or a play in which injustice is important. Write an essay in which you define clearly the nature of the injustice and discuss the techniques the author employs to elicit sympathy for its victim or victims.

You may use one of the following works or another work of equivalent literary merit.

Othello
King Lear
A Doll's House
All My Sons
A Streetcar Named Desire
Antigone
Justice
Billy Budd
Tess of the D'Urbervilles
Jude the Obscure
Cry, the Beloved Country
Beloved
An American Tragedy
The Jungle
Invisible Man
A Passage to India
Native Son
The Grapes of Wrath
The Color Purple
Animal Farm
1984
Crime and Punishment
Catch-22
Oliver Twist

END OF EXAMINATION

ANSWER KEY FOR PRACTICE TEST 3

SECTION I: MULTIPLE-CHOICE QUESTIONS

First Prose Passage

1. B	5. E	9. B
2. D	6. C	10. E
3. B	7. D	11. A
4. C	8. C	12. C

First Poem

13. B	18. C	23. D
14. D	19. D	24. A
15. A	20. A	25. B
16. E	21. B	26. C
17. E	22. C	27. A

Second Prose Passage

28. D	33. B	37. B
29. E	34. E	38. D
30. A	35. A	39. C
31. C	36. C	40. A
32. B		

Second Poem

41. A	46. B	51. E
42. B	47. D	52. B
43. C	48. E	53. D
44. E	49. B	54. E
45. A	50. D	55. B

PRACTICE TEST 3 SCORING WORKSHEET

Use the following worksheet to arrive at a probable final AP grade on Practice Test 3. While it is sometimes difficult to be objective enough to score one's own essay, you can use the sample essay answers that follow to approximate an essay score for yourself. You might also give your essays (along with the sample essays) to a friend or relative to score if you feel confident that the individual has the knowledge necessary to make such a judgment and that he or she will feel comfortable in doing so.

Section I: Multiple-Choice Questions

$$\frac{}{\substack{\text{right} \\ \text{answers}}} - (\frac{1}{4} \text{ or } .25 \times \frac{}{\substack{\text{wrong} \\ \text{answers}}}) = \frac{}{\substack{\text{multiple-choice} \\ \text{raw score}}}$$

$$\frac{}{\substack{\text{multiple-choice} \\ \text{raw score}}} \times 1.23 = \frac{}{\substack{\text{multiple-choice} \\ \text{converted score}}} \text{ (of possible 67.5)}$$

Section II: Essay Questions

$$\frac{}{\substack{\text{question 1} \\ \text{raw score}}} + \frac{}{\substack{\text{question 2} \\ \text{raw score}}} + \frac{}{\substack{\text{question 3} \\ \text{raw score}}} = \frac{}{\substack{\text{essay} \\ \text{raw score}}}$$

$$\frac{}{\substack{\text{essay} \\ \text{raw score}}} \times 3.055 = \frac{}{\substack{\text{essay} \\ \text{converted score}}} \text{ (of possible 82.5)}$$

Final Score

$$\frac{}{\substack{\text{multiple-choice} \\ \text{converted score}}} + \frac{}{\substack{\text{essay} \\ \text{converted score}}} = \frac{}{\substack{\text{final} \\ \text{converted score}}} \text{ (of possible 150)}$$

Probable Final AP Score

Final Converted Score	Probable AP Score
150–100	5
99– 86	4
85– 67	3
84– 0	1 or 2

ANSWERS AND EXPLANATIONS FOR PRACTICE TEST 3

SECTION I: MULTIPLE-CHOICE QUESTIONS

First Prose Passage

Like the Bacon essay in the first practice exam, this "Meditation" by John Donne is challenging prose. It was written early in the seventeenth century.

1. (B) As a rule, the first question of each set of multiple-choice questions is an easy one. Here the speaker does not identify himself until lines 17–19, where he speaks of his "malignant and pestilential disease" and uses the pronoun "me."

2. (D) To answer this question, you must read not only the first 11 lines, but 5 more lines before the real point is made. Each of the first three sentences begins with "We say"; they go on to speak of the sea in the two hemispheres, the stars under the northern and southern poles, and the sorrow and joy in human life. In line 11, Donne contradicts our suggesting that the seas, stars, or joys and sorrows are equally divided. There is far more misery than happiness. The passage does make the points of choices (A) and (B), but they are not the thesis that the 11 lines are used to demonstrate.

3. (B) It is often the case when a multiple-choice question asks you to define a reasonably familiar word that the common modern meaning is not the right answer. The AP exam is not likely to test vocabulary as the SAT does. You must look very carefully at the context of the word in the passage. We all know that the word "dogmatic" means "arrogantly asserted," and a student who answers this question without checking the passage would choose (A). But it is used in this passage in a different sense, and the clue we are given is the linking of "dogmatical" with "positive." Here the meaning is "authoritatively affirmed." In theology, "dogma" is an authoritatively affirmed doctrine.

4. (C) The lines say nothing about the physicians' fear of contagion. The depressing consequence of the identification is that the disease may be so far advanced that the doctors can do nothing to help (lines 21–23); the small consolation is that they now know better how to deal with the disease (lines 20–21).

5. (E) This is another instance where you should not assume that you know a word until you check the context. As a noun for an organ of the body, "intestine" is an easy word. Here it is used as an adjective modifying "conspiracies" and meaning "internal" or "domestic."

6. (C) The metaphor is comparing the identified disease to the enemy who reveals himself ("declares himself") after he is strong enough to survive and to win ("achieve his ends"). To know of this enemy whom it is too late to defeat, the passage argues, is "faint comfort."

7. (D) The passage gives us no information about the physicians' response to the symptoms, and it is clear that the speaker's concern has increased; we can eliminate choices (A), (B), and (C). We must sort out more figures of speech to answer this question. Donne likens the new symptoms to two kinds of confession, that which is freely given and that obtained by torture. The freely given confession is like the natural development of a disease in which new symptoms appear (lines 26–29). The appearance of new symptoms induced by administering medicines ("the strength of cordials") is like the confession obtained by torture and is of less comfort to the sufferer.

8. (C) The sentence may be paraphrased as follows: It is a small consolation to know the worst when that worst is something that cannot be remedied; it is even less comforting than knowing the worst to know something very bad and not know that the worst has been reached.

9. (B) The allay, or alloy, of a counterfeit coin is the base metal (for example, iron) as opposed to the genuine (for example, gold). According to the figure, the alloy (misery) is larger than

the genuine (happiness). In lines 11–12, the figure of drinking misery (swallowing it) as opposed to just tasting happiness makes the same, depressing point.

10. (E) The gold that requires such an effort to find is a metaphor for happiness. Lines 49–51 expand the figure using the word "happy."

11. (A) Take away the metaphors and there would be hardly anything left on the page. What makes this passage so difficult and so interesting is its figurative language. None of the other options is so notable as the use of metaphor, though (C) is at least a remote possibility, since the author uses his own disease to make a case for the preponderance of misery over happiness in human life.

12. (C) By far the best choice here is "pessimistic." The next best are "anxious" and "skeptical," but they are not strong enough. Neither "ambiguous" nor "servile" is at all appropriate.

First Poem

This poem by American poet Anne Bradstreet was probably written in the second half of the seventeenth century.

13. (B) Though the poem expresses the speaker's love for her husband, it is not a lyric, normally a songlike expression of feeling. It is a verse epistle, that is, a letter in verse addressed by the wife to her husband, who is away.

14. (D) The phrase is grammatically parenthetical, and the line without parentheses would be very obscure. The more likely use of the phrase is in apposition to "dearer dear." The phrase says she misses a dearer dear and heart. It is also possible that the phrase is an interjected direct address (apostrophe) to her absent husband.

15. (A) The extended figure compares the female deer seeking her mate (hart) to the wife who misses her husband. The figure is a

simile, not a metaphor, since it uses "As" in line 1 and "So" in line 5.

16. (E) The verb "launch" can be transitive or instransitive. There is no object here, so the best choice of definitions is "throws herself," describing the unlikely event of a mullet that beaches herself to join her mate. This use of the verb is still common, as in the sentence "He launched into an attack on the media."

17. (E) In line 27, the "pasture," "house," and "streams" are, respectively, where the deer, dove, and mullet live. In line 29, the verb "browse" refers to the deer, while "glide" in line 31 refers to the fish. In line 34, "abroad" refers to Bradstreet, not the animals.

18. (C) Be sure to consult the text in questions about the meaning of a word. Here the line says that without the substance, alas, everything is unreal or just a dream. In this context, "reality" or "essence" is the best choice.

19. (D) The "but" here means "only" or "merely." The best of the five answers is (D). The dreams are the shadow, the insubstantial, the unreal.

20. (A) Since this is a "house" for doves ("turtles" are turtledoves, not the reptiles), the best choice is dovecote.

21. (B) The last two lines of the poem have no verb. The subjects of the phrase are "love" and "dear." "At" is a preposition, "Thy" a pronoun, and "loving" and "dearest" adjectives.

22. (C) The explanation for the missing verb in the last lines is that they are the complimentary close and signature of the letter—two lines of verse instead of "Very truly yours, Anne Bradstreet."

23. (D) The noun "peer" as it is used here has no reference to the turtledove figure. The four other words are all part of the bird imagery of the poem.

24. (A) Lines 1–8 develop an analogy of the wife and the hind. Lines 9–16 develop a similar comparison of the wife and the turtledove. Lines 17–24 make a third comparison using the mullet. The animals used in these similes are reintroduced in the metaphors of lines 25–28 and 29–32. Choices (B), (C), (D), and (E) are potentially useful structural devices, but none of them is important in this poem.

25. (B) The poem plays on the words "dear" and "deer" as well as on the words "hart" and "heart." Both of these wordplays are very common in English love poetry of the Renaissance.

26. (C) The fastest way to solve a question of this sort, which may be very time consuming, is to identify at once a structural unit that you are very sure about. It is clear that the first coherent part of this poem must be the eight lines of the first sentence that make up the deer-wife simile. Look now at the answers and eliminate any option that does not begin with lines 1–8 as the first unit. In this case, we can isolate (C) right away. Now check the rest of answer (C). Lines 9–16 is fine, the next simile. Lines 17–20 and 21–24 could have made up one unit, but both are complete sentences, and the division is plausible. The rest of the answer also makes good sense. If there had been two answers with lines 1–8 first, you would have to continue to work through both until you found an error. Your savings in time would still have been great. An easy system to use is to determine with certainty what the first unit and what the last unit are. If you can do this, you will probably have eliminated the four wrong answers right away. In this poem, for example, the last unit must be the signature lines, 33 and 34. Only one of the five answers has 33–34 as its last section, reconfirming (C) as the correct choice.

27. (A) An off-rhyme, or slant-rhyme, is an approximate rhyme where the vowels do not in fact have the same sound. The vowel sound of "eye" and "descry" or "eye" and "cry" is the same, so it is not an off-rhyme. But in the other four pairs, the two vowel sounds differ; all of them are off-rhymes.

Second Prose Passage

The passage is from the nineteenth century, Thomas de Quincy on Joan of Arc.

28. **(D)** Though the passage never identifies the Hebrew shepherd by name, the author assumes his readers know enough of the Old Testament to recognize David. We are told of his religious inspiration, his leading armies, his initial victorious action (the defeat of Goliath), and his success and fame in the kingdom of Judah. The exams do not attempt to test your knowledge of history or religion, but they are written with the understanding that AP students will be familiar with the major themes of Greek and Roman myth and of the Judaic and Christian religious traditions. The exams will never ask you about a minor Old Testament prophet or the Egyptian myths of Anubis, but one or two of the multiple-choice questions may require a familiarity with Zeus or Sampson or Mars.

29. **(E)** The passage cites all four of these likenesses: both rose "out of . . . religious inspiration" (lines 4–5); their missions are "patriotic" (line 8), inaugurated by a victorious "act" (line 9); both are praised by "adverse armies" (line 11).

30. **(A)** The passage begins with a comparison of the great achievements of both David and Joan (lines 1–15). In lines 16–26, DeQuincy describes the triumphs of David and the contrasting fate of the martyred Joan. The passage does begin with two questions, but repeated rhetorical questions are not the organizing principle of the passage. None of the other devices is used here.

31. **(C)** All three sentences describe Joan's inability to participate in the victory. All three sentences are cast as negatives: "drank not," "never sang," and "mingled not." The lines are both literal and figurative. The "cup of rest" is figurative, but the songs may be literal, and the dances surely are real.

32. (B) In lines 15–16, the author blames enemies for the difference between David's success and Joan's tragedy. It might be argued that all of the five options are reasonable answers, but the question calls for the answer attributed by the passage.

33. (B) Both of these phrases suggest that DeQuincy's awestruck view of Joan is not the only one possible. The implication of the phrase "those who saw her nearest" is that those whose view of Joan questions her heroism are those who were not nearest—not close enough to know the truth. Similarly, "all who saw . . . *from a station of good will*" implies that those men in the adverse armies who judged Joan harshly were not to be believed because they were men of ill-will. The defensiveness of the phrases attests to an alternate interpretation.

34. (E) A coronet is a small crown worn by princes or others of high rank. Though an ornamental band of flowers or jewels is also called a coronet, the first meaning is used here to symbolize rank and to accord with the word "honors."

35. (A) Joan was burned at Rouen in 1431. The passage alludes to the "fiery scaffold," the "surging smoke," and the "volleying flames."

36. (C) Oddly, the whole scene is presented as a vision of the future which Joan may not have foreseen. The verbs controlling the body of the sentence are "she might not prefigure" and "she saw not in vision, perhaps." The sentence illustrates the rhetorical device by which an author can get something said by appearing not to say it. The political candidate who says, "I will not allude to the fact that my opponent spent two years in prison for mail fraud" understands the technique.

37. (B) The logical division in the paragraph is after "no! for her feet were dust." At this point, the contrast between the prosperous David and the forsaken Joan has been completed. In the following sentence, the author switches from the use of the third person ("she") to address Joan directly, using the second person ("thou" and "thy"). The subject is no longer the

similarity or difference of Joan and David but the nature of Joan's difference from her countrymen. Choice (A) is unlikely, since it falls in the middle of the comparison of Joan and David. Choice (C) interrupts a consideration of the worldly honors that Joan rejected. Choice (D) interrupts a series of parallel imperatives ("Call her . . . Cite her . . ."), and (E) interrupts two closely related sentences.

38. (D) The passage does not employ extended definition, but the other devices are used several times. Apostrophe (words addressed to a person or thing) is directed to the reader, Joan, and the King of France. There are nearly as many exclamation points in this passage as there are periods. Joan's words are quoted in lines 44–47. The first of many examples of parallel syntax is the second sentence, which repeats the first six words of the first sentence exactly.

39. (C) The passage alludes to enemies of Joan but does not address them directly. The opening lines address the reader, lines 27–36 address Joan, and lines 36–38 address the King of France.

40. (A) Nothing in the headlong prose of this passage suggests anything like the controlled approval or guarded disapproval suggested by (B), (C), (D), and (E). The only possible choice here is (A).

Second Poem

The poem is by Wilfred Owen, a World War I poet who was killed shortly before the war ended in 1918.

41. (A) If the event happens often enough for the army to have a familiar abbreviation for it, it cannot be very rare. The very existence of the abbreviation is a grim reminder of how common the event is. The soldier in the poem thinks about other men who have wounded themselves to escape the trenches (line 21) but at first rejects the idea. Although the second and third statements in this question may be true, the

abbreviation does not suggest either, for the meaning of the letters is not secret.

42. (B) A number of the details of the poem make it clear that the war is World War I. These include the terms "the Hun" for the German enemy, "sand-bags," "trench-foot," shell "shock," "wire patrol," and "trench wall" and the reference to "this world's Powers."

43. (C) The speaker, we learn in II, is a member of the patrol ("our wire patrol") that finds Tim's body. The details of The Prologue are what he infers but does not certainly know. He uses "doubtless" in line 1 and "Perhaps" in line 5 to reveal that this is his version of events. This soldier's insight reconstructs the mental anguish of III. The narrator is not named, but since he is not quite omniscient, (C) is a better choice than (A).

44. (E) No one directly connected with war would use the word "nice" to describe a wound. The not-so-subtle satire here is directed at the whimpering and fretful mother who would nurse a nice wound.

45. (A) The wounds, fevers, and maladies like trench-foot or shell shock are dangers of life in the trenches, and wounds and fevers might be life threatening. Leave is neither dangerous nor potentially fatal. Like the others, it is a way of escaping from the trenches.

46. (B) The line is probably scanned as follows:

u   u   / | u   u   / | /   / | u   / |u   /
At the pleasure of this world's Powers who'd run amok.

"Powers" is probably a monosyllable here, and the line is a pentameter, with two three-syllable feet. The basic meter of the stanza is iambic pentameter, but there are many substitutions and many lines with nine or eleven syllables. Line 20 is not trochaic (A). Many lines in The Prologue have no alliteration, but line 20 has two words with initial "p" sounds. Line 20 rhymes with line 17 ("shock"/"amok")(D). This is a masculine rhyme (E).

47. (D) Lines 27 and 28 present fragments of the wire patrol soldiers' words. Was it an accident? Maybe he was killed by a sniper's bullet? The parentheses make the suicide clear. It was an English not a German bullet.

48. (E) Part III presents the dead soldier's decision to take his own life as a "reasoned crisis." With nothing but a continuation of the agony to look forward to and no hope of death to end his suffering, he makes his choice. The effect of the stanza is to dramatize the horrors of war and to show the justice or reason of the soldier's choice. The poem does not question his decision.

49. (B) The muzzle is the front of the barrel of the gun.

50. (D) The point of the grim last line is its physical specificity. To place the muzzle of the gun against his teeth, the soldier would have to twist his lips into a last smile.

51. (E) Tim's words or thoughts are directly presented in lines 22–24. Most of the poem is spoken by the narrator. Lines 27–28 present the words of members of the patrol.

52. (B) The narrator, who is a member of the wire patrol, is an understanding and sympathetic commentator of whom the author wholly approves. The poem does criticize the unthinking chauvinism of Tim's family and the world's Powers, who are responsible for the war.

53. (D) The events of the poem reveal the irony in claiming eternal valor for the dead soldier. The father's preference of death before dishonor (for someone else) is realized in a way he could not have forseen. The real wound here is neither "safe" nor "nice." Tim's condemnation of others who wound themselves is premature. The phrase "Courage leaked as sand" is figurative, but it is not ironic.

54. (E) A feminine rhyme is a rhyme on the next-to-last syllable followed by an unstressed last syllable that is identical: "go" and "flow" is a masculine rhyme, "going" and "flowing," feminine. The only feminine rhyme in the poem is lines 36 and 38, "riling" and "smiling."

55. (B) Tim's suicide takes place after The Prologue and before The Action.

SECTION II: ESSAY QUESTIONS

Question 1: Charlotte Mew

The question which asks how the "use of language" determines the reader's response to the speaker and his or her situation opens the door for an essay on aspects of the poem chosen by the student. Almost everyone will write on diction, and most will write on imagery as well. Other possible topics in this essay include the use of the first person, the use of dialect, and the use of repetition.

"The Farmer's Bride" is a narrative poem about two characters. The pathos of the young bride, shy, silent, and terrified by the approach of any male, needs no comment. The question calls for our response to the husband and speaker of the poem. By using some words and constructions of a rural dialect, the poet creates a simple farmer articulate enough to suggest the full anguish of his unhappy marriage.

The first three lines are, perhaps, the least sympathetic to the speaker. Granting the possibility that his bride was "too young, perhaps," he defends their marriage as necessary for a farmer too busy to woo at length or wait around at harvest time. The rest of the poem presents the farmer's pained coping with an intolerable situation; his recaptured wife sleeps alone in the attic. His desire for her has not abated, yet he refers to her as "poor maid."

Most of the comparisons of the poem are similes, likening the bride to animals or plants. She is compared to a hare, a mouse, a leveret, a larch, and the first wild violets. Most of these figures suggest her skittishness, her fragility, her inhuman quality, "like a frightened fay." The husband is intensely aware of her beauty ("Sweet as the first wild violets"), which he cannot come near ("But what to me?"). His desperate frustration is poignantly dramatized by the repetitions of the last two lines. The reader's sympathies are equally divided between both of these innocent victims, whose tragedy is played out against the slow-changing background of the cycle of the seasons.

Student Essay

The same character can be interpreted by the reader in drastically different terms, depending upon the clues left for the reader by the author. Many of the heroes of our literature are actually anti-heroes, rogues who are nevertheless possessed of a certain rakish charm. Such a character might likely be presented as a despicable reprobate by one author, a charismatic and entirely sympathetic devil by another. Subtle clues left by the author must be the guides careful readers heed to discover the true nature of a character who may seem culpable to objective analysis.

Charlotte Mew presents such a character in the farmer, narrator, and protagonist of her poem "The Farmer's Bride." A man who repeatedly thinks of his wife as an animal and a possession, who locks her in her room after she runs away unhappy, and fails to treat her as an equal, the farmer nevertheless becomes a profoundly sympathetic character. While it is important to keep in mind the mores and marital customs of the day, Mew makes the farmer likable without resorting to reminding readers that things are relative, that men often treated their wives in such a way in days past, and therefore the farmer was not an aberration in his own times. Mew accomplishes this by taking readers inside the farmer's mind, revealing that he is a complex human being.

The poem's language provides great insight into the farmer's character and makes the reader feel sorry for the beleaguered husband. The farmer's folksy tone and broken English elicit immediate reader sympathy for the rube. The rustic has no understanding of his wife as a human being, treating her as something of a curiosity. Mew writes, "Like the shut of a winter's day/ Her smile went out, and 'twadn't a woman—/ More like a little frightened fay./ One night, in the Fall, she runned away." She is like a fairy; she does not leave him, but rather runs away like an animal or supernatural sprite. The reader comes to realize that the farmer has no idea of his own possible inadequacies. He cannot conceive of any reason she might leave him personally, aside from that she "turned afraid" of "all things human." The farmer can only explain her disappearance as an enigma.

During the chase, she is again described by the farmer as something not human. She is found among the sheep (and he will later note that she seems most at home among the barn animals, when men are not around). When caught, the stray creature is "All in a shiver and a scare," like an animal in the headlights. She does her housework "like a mouse." While readers still identify with the narrator of the poem, Mew makes them aware of the wife's situation as well, feeling sorry for the vulnerable woman completely misunderstood by her well-meaning husband.

Mew's diction later implies that while the farmer may treat his captured wife unkindly, caging her like an animal, he is not himself unkind. She does not condemn, nor will the reader, because the poet's words make it clear that the farmer knows no better. While this may not be sufficient for absolution, it at least makes the reader look with soft eyes on the man's plight. Mew writes, "We caught her, fetched her home at last/ And turned the key upon her, fast." The farmer has no cognizance that anything he is doing may be morally questionable. He "fetches" her rather than "grabbing" her or "snatching" her; "fetches" is a wholly innocuous word, and the farmer sees his actions as totally innocuous.

He is utterly perplexed as to the source of the barrier between him and his wife, who has "turned afraid." Still, the reader cannot help but feel sorry for a man who is so unhappy, so unable to communicate with someone he genuinely loves. The farmer pines away at poem's close: "'Tis but a stair/ Betwixt us. Oh! my God! the down,/ The soft young down of her, the brown,/ The brown of her—her eyes, her hair, her hair!"

Pathos and pity rule the day. The reader ends up pitying the wife, trapped, incomplete, and the husband, lonely and longing, questioning. Mew's diction has been effective, and the reader is bound to respond to "The Farmer's Wife" with true feeling for both characters and leave it, perhaps, with a great understanding of the conflict between the sexes and the condition of humanity.

Response to the Student Essay

This student essay on Charlotte Mew's poem is instructive for its strengths and its limitations. It answers the question well, defining clearly the reader's response to the farmer and discussing how the diction and imagery function in the poem. The paper would certainly be scored in the upper half of the scale, probably at seven of a possible nine points. Papers with higher scores would focus more rigorously on the language of the poem and deal more fully with some of the subjects like tone, point of view, or dialect, which this essay merely mentions. The writing here is uneven. The essay would be better without the first paragraph. It is not necessary to begin your papers with uplifting generalizations about literature or life. Be careful about your tone. An essay that condescends to the "mores and marital customs" of an earlier period as less enlightened than our own should not refer to a west of England dialect as "broken" or to a farmer as a "rube."

Question 2: William Makepeace Thackeray

The following essay on the passage from *Vanity Fair* is typical of the student responses to this question.

Student Essay

In Thackeray's *Vanity Fair,* diction, syntax, and choice of detail are all used to convey a feeling of satire as Thackeray defines the targets of his criticism as the middle class relations of rich older ladies.

The first important detail that Thackeray gives the reader is a hint as to the nature of the passage as he notes, ". . . for she had a balance at her banker's which could have made her beloved anywhere." The author continues by describing "What a dignity it gives an old lady, that balance at the banker's! How tenderly we look at her faults, if she is a relative . . . what a kind, good-natured old creature we find her!" Immediately the reader sees what sort of relationship exists between old, rich women and their younger nieces and nephews who are burdened by the cost of owning homes and raising children. From this initial detail of the old lady's wealth, a satirical tone is apparent, and Thackeray is no doubt criticizing the greedy, younger relations who are hoping for an inheritance. This tone is also exemplified by the author's use of "we" instead of "they." This use of the first person makes Thackeray appear to be supporting the avaricious relatives in their efforts, which makes his true disgust of their actions more forceful. The author's friendly tone and warm understanding only emphasize his true feelings, making the use of satire effective.

Again, both satire and disgust are brought forth in an artful manner as Thackeray describes how the children make ". . . endless worsted baskets, cushions, and footstools for her." These self-serving notions are confirmed as the speaker openly states his desire for his aunt's ". . . signature to a cheque for five thousand pounds." Thackeray also includes descriptions of how rich and expensive the meals are when this aunt visits, how the house "assumes a festive, neat, warm, jovial, snug appearance . . ." All these efforts are in an attempt to become unforgettable to this rich aunt as it comes time to draw up a will, and Thackeray compels readers to admit to this truth as he writes simply, "I appeal to the middle classes." It is not until the end of the passage that he contradicts himself, revealing his sincere feelings, as he writes, "Sweet, sweet vision! Foolish, foolish dream!"

Thackeray's diction and choice of detail define the targets of his criticism, emphasizing his true feelings as he writes satirically about the nature of relationships between different family members.

Response to the Student Essay

This paper would be scored no higher than a six. The essay quotes from the question in its first sentence ("diction, syntax, and choice of detail") but never deals with the syntax. The final sentence speaks only of "diction and choice of detail." Most students will have no trouble dealing with these two topics. The better papers notice that the details describing the family's kowtowing to the rich relation include not just the husband, wife, and children; accomodations are made to impress even her fat coachman and her maid. That the family should court Miss MacWhirter by spending unusual amounts of money to insure her comfort is apt. Since money is the root of their values, what could be more natural?

Thackeray's satire is contained in a single long paragaraph with a wide range of sentence forms. He begins with five exclamations introduced by "what" or "how," but no answer is needed to these questions. He moves then to dialogue, quoting the imagined words of the imagined audience, husband and wife. More exclamations introduced by "what" alternate with loose sentences. A direct question is put to the reader: "Is it so, or is it not?" Then, an appeal to the middle class. Then, a prayer to the "gracious powers." Then, three final exclamations. The paragraph has very long (up to forty-eight words) and very short (three words) sentences. Four times Thackeray interrupts himself with parentheses. The effect is to create a genial, intimate tone, a suggestion that this very carefully composed prose is spontaneous. Thackeray makes readers his accomplices and, by confessing his own venality, lures them, as it were, to confess their own.

Is the final "Foolish, foolish dream!" a rejection of the idea of courting a rich relation, a dropping of the mask to reveal the moralist? Or is it just a realistic comment on the extreme unlikelihood of the gracious powers' sending a rich aunt—something the speaker still longs for but which he is forced to admit is only a wish that can never come true?

Question 3: Open Question

The danger of an essay on a topic like this is that students will spend all of the essay defining the injustices by retelling the plot of the play or novel and neglect the second part of the question. This is a question where it is necessary to deal with the plot of the work you select, and so long as you keep in mind that what you say about the plot is to define the nature of a personal or social injustice, you should deal with the events of the work. But don't spend too much time on this easier task at the expense of the second requirement, discussing the techniques the author uses to make us sympathetic to the victims.

The two student essays that follow both handle the question well, and both make good points about the plays as a whole. Though the essay on *Lear* has some minor writing flaws and breaks off before its last paragraph is complete, it sees the connection between Lear's and the Duke of Gloucester's personal injustices and the larger issues of social injustice in the play. Both of these papers would receive high scores, sevens certainly and maybe eights.

Student Essay 1

The greatest tragedy is that of good intentions gone awry, the tragedy that leaves one to question what might have been. When sympathetic, basically decent people are driven by their characters toward a horrid outcome, when who is at fault for the tragic result becomes ambiguous—this is the greatest of tragedy. Sophocles' play Antigone tells such a story. Antigone is full of injustice, but Sophocles leaves no clear answers, and viewers (or readers) are left only with a sorrowful feeling toward both Antigone and Creon.

Central to the play is the enduring question of conflict between terrestrial and spiritual laws. Antigone wishes to bury her brother Polynices, but the king of Thebes dictates that only Eteocles, Polynices' brother and enemy in the attack on Thebes, be buried. Antigone falls victim to the apparent injustice of being unable to bury both of her brothers because of Creon's austere insistence that Polynices be left outside the city to rot. In the face of such moral injustice, Antigone feels a spiritual imperative to give Polynices a decent burial; she places the law of the gods as she understands it superior to Creon's dictate of Theban law.

Creon does not appear a complete villain, however. By burying her brother against Creon's orders, Antigone has defied the king and violated the law of the land, usurping his authority and thus, he feels, endangering the security of the entire kingdom. Creon's tragic flaw is his immutability, and he makes a victim of himself through his own stubbornness.

Sophocles lets his audience sympathize with both Antigone and Creon so that they might fully understands the intractable nature of the problem. In a world governed by law rather than anarchy, that law must be respected and upheld, despite differing personal opinions or reactions to it; if the law is wrong, then the law must be changed. Antigone clearly violates this tenet of orderly government. In contrast, Creon brings about perhaps the graver injustice of violating the precepts of the gods. Antigone feels the pain of Creon's spiritual injustice. Creon places the letter of the law and the form of procedure above essential truth and decency and this leads to Antigone's torment and his own downfall.

Sophocles guides readers to immediate sympathy with Antigone. She is a rebel, defying government and king, but Sophocles makes it eminently clear that Antigone is driven by moral impetus. She does what she does, making herself a victim of Creon's wrath, because she has no other choice but to obey her conscience. Creon, a wise and good-hearted ruler, is also sympathetic to audiences because of the same sense of inevitability about what he does. Each is driven by their own central qualities, their sense of duty, of right and wrong.

Through their dialogue and their lamentations (such as Antigone's initial discussion with Ismene about her intention to disobey the law), Sophocles serves to make the reader identify with the wrenching internal conflicts of the drama's participants. Indeed, more than anything else, *Antigone* is the story of conflicted souls in torment. This makes the injustices felt on both sides of the argument all the more acute.

Student Essay 2

Injustice, both social and personal, is a prevalent theme throughout literature. This is especially true of William Shakespeare's play *King Lear*. The private injustices that Lear and Duke Gloucester suffer lead to their understanding of the larger injustices in the world at large in which they hold privileged positions. The play presents a series of unjust actions beginning in the first scene when Lear resigns his kingship, an irresponsible action that is unjust to his subjects. The contest to decide which daughter gets the biggest share of the kingdom is unjust to all of his daughters and especially to Cordelia, who gets nothing because she tells the truth. Lear's banishing Kent is another injustice in this scene because, like Cordelia, Kent tells the truth.

Goneril and Reagan next act unjustly when they refuse to allow Lear to keep his knights. Lear rushes out into the storm, where he feels sympathy for Tom and his fool and realizes that as king he failed to care enough for the poor wretches of his kingdom. He says if the world's goods were divided more equally the heavens would be "more just." In the other plot, Gloucester unjustly condemns Edgar without even hearing his defense and in turn is unjustly betrayed by his bastard son and by Reagan and her husband. In his blind condition, Gloucester also sees the wider injustices of the world due to excess.

The actions of the play make us feel sorry for Lear and Gloucester. Just seeing these events, like Lear's going mad and suffering through the storm and Gloucester having his eyes gouged out, is horrifying. That both of them endure this suffering and use it to understand other people's suffering also makes us more sympathetic. Our sympathy is increased to a climax when Lear comes in carrying Cordelia's dead body.

Another reason we are sympathetic is that Lear speaks in such powerful poetry.

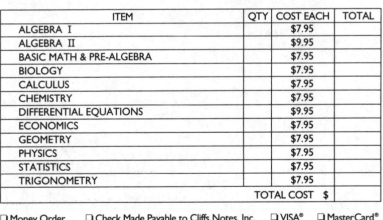